FEDERAL INCOME TAXATION OF PARTNERS AND PARTNERSHIPS

IN A NUTSHELL

Second Edition

By

KAREN C. BURKE
Professor of Law
University of Minnesota

WEST
GROUP

ST. PAUL, MINN.
1999

Nutshell Series, In a Nutshell, the Nutshell Logo and the West Group symbol are registered trademarks used herein under license.

COPYRIGHT © 1992 WEST PUBLISHING CO.
COPYRIGHT © 1999 By WEST GROUP
                        610 Opperman Drive
                        P.O. Box 64526
                        St. Paul, MN 55164–0526
                        1–800–328–9352

TEXT IS PRINTED ON 10% POST
CONSUMER RECYCLED PAPER

2nd Reprint — 2003

PREFACE TO
THE SECOND EDITION

Federal income taxation of partners and partnerships is a dynamic and fascinating field. The mechanical rules have become increasingly complex in recent years, partly as a result of Congress' tinkering with the statute, but mostly in response to the sophisticated implementing regulations promulgated by the Treasury Department. This complexity, while sometimes daunting, should not be allowed to obscure the internal logic and consistency of the underlying concepts.

This book is intended to introduce lawyers and students to the basic structure of partnership taxation. It is designed for use as a supplement to traditional courses and teaching materials, and its goal is to provide sufficient background and explanatory discussion to enable the reader to grasp the principles of partnership taxation in a problem-oriented course. Numerous concrete examples illustrate the treatment of specific transactions, emphasizing the economic arrangement and its consequences. In the author's experience, this approach proves helpful not only for students in a regular law school course but also for students in graduate tax or accounting programs. Frequent references to the statute and regulations highlight the importance of having those sources available and reading them along with this book. Students interested in pursuing matters further will find more exhaustive discussions in the leading treatises on partnership taxation. The condensed presentation in this book covers topics of primary interest to students and reflects developments through December 31, 1998, including proposed regulations on optional basis adjustments.

This book is organized along the same lines as many courses and teaching materials. Chapter 1 introduces partnership capital accounts and important concepts such as inside and outside basis; it also discusses elective entity classification and anti-abuse rules. Chapter 2 focuses on partnership formation, including contributions of encumbered property and admission of service partners. Chapter 3 deals with the passthrough of income or loss. Chapters 4 through 6 provide a systematic introduction to the detailed regulations under §§ 704 and 752 governing partnership allocations, the treatment of contributed property, and sharing of recourse and nonrecourse liabilities. Chapters 7 through 10 discuss other discrete topics, including partner-partnership transactions, sales and exchanges of partnership interests, distributions, and death of a partner.

KAREN C. BURKE

Newton, Massachusetts
January, 1999

OUTLINE

V

OUTLINE

*

TABLE OF CASES

References are to Pages

XVII

TABLE OF INTERNAL REVENUE CODE SECTIONS

UNITED STATES

UNITED STATES CODE ANNOTATED
26 U.S.C.A.—Internal Revenue Code

UNITED STATES CODE ANNOTATED
26 U.S.C.A.—Internal Revenue Code

UNITED STATES CODE ANNOTATED
26 U.S.C.A.—Internal Revenue Code

TABLE OF INTERNAL REVENUE CODE SECTIONS

UNITED STATES CODE ANNOTATED
26 U.S.C.A.—Internal Revenue Code

TABLE OF INTERNAL REVENUE CODE SECTIONS

UNITED STATES CODE ANNOTATED
26 U.S.C.A.—Internal Revenue Code

TABLE OF INTERNAL REVENUE CODE SECTIONS

UNITED STATES CODE ANNOTATED
26 U.S.C.A.—Internal Revenue Code

UNITED STATES CODE ANNOTATED
26 U.S.C.A.—Internal Revenue Code

UNITED STATES CODE ANNOTATED
26 U.S.C.A.—Internal Revenue Code

UNITED STATES CODE ANNOTATED
26 U.S.C.A.—Internal Revenue Code

TABLE OF INTERNAL REVENUE CODE SECTIONS

UNITED STATES CODE ANNOTATED
26 U.S.C.A.—Internal Revenue Code

UNITED STATES CODE ANNOTATED
26 U.S.C.A.—Internal Revenue Code

UNITED STATES CODE ANNOTATED
26 U.S.C.A.—Internal Revenue Code

UNITED STATES CODE ANNOTATED
26 U.S.C.A.—Internal Revenue Code

TABLE OF INTERNAL REVENUE CODE SECTIONS

UNITED STATES CODE ANNOTATED
26 U.S.C.A.—Internal Revenue Code

UNITED STATES CODE ANNOTATED
26 U.S.C.A.—Internal Revenue Code

TABLE OF INTERNAL REVENUE CODE SECTIONS

UNITED STATES CODE ANNOTATED
26 U.S.C.A.—Internal Revenue Code

UNITED STATES CODE ANNOTATED
26 U.S.C.A.—Internal Revenue Code

UNITED STATES CODE ANNOTATED
26 U.S.C.A.—Internal Revenue Code

UNITED STATES CODE ANNOTATED
26 U.S.C.A.—Internal Revenue Code

TABLE OF INTERNAL REVENUE CODE SECTIONS

UNITED STATES CODE ANNOTATED
26 U.S.C.A.—Internal Revenue Code

UNITED STATES CODE ANNOTATED
26 U.S.C.A.—Internal Revenue Code

TABLE OF INTERNAL REVENUE CODE SECTIONS

UNITED STATES CODE ANNOTATED
26 U.S.C.A.—Internal Revenue Code

UNITED STATES CODE ANNOTATED
26 U.S.C.A.—Internal Revenue Code

UNITED STATES CODE ANNOTATED
26 U.S.C.A.—Internal Revenue Code

UNITED STATES CODE ANNOTATED
26 U.S.C.A.—Internal Revenue Code

TABLE OF INTERNAL REVENUE CODE SECTIONS

UNITED STATES CODE ANNOTATED
26 U.S.C.A.—Internal Revenue Code

UNITED STATES CODE ANNOTATED
26 U.S.C.A.—Internal Revenue Code

TABLE OF INTERNAL REVENUE CODE SECTIONS

UNITED STATES CODE ANNOTATED
26 U.S.C.A.—Internal Revenue Code

TABLE OF INTERNAL REVENUE CODE SECTIONS

TEMPORARY TREASURY REGULATIONS

PROPOSED TREASURY REGULATIONS

PROPOSED TREASURY REGULATIONS

TABLE OF INTERNAL REVENUE CODE SECTIONS

PROPOSED TREASURY REGULATIONS

TREASURY REGULATIONS

TREASURY REGULATIONS

TABLE OF INTERNAL REVENUE CODE SECTIONS

TREASURY REGULATIONS

TREASURY REGULATIONS

TREASURY REGULATIONS

TABLE OF INTERNAL REVENUE CODE SECTIONS

TREASURY REGULATIONS

TABLE OF INTERNAL REVENUE CODE SECTIONS

TREASURY REGULATIONS

LVII

TREASURY REGULATIONS

TABLE OF INTERNAL REVENUE CODE SECTIONS

TREASURY REGULATIONS

REVENUE PROCEDURES

TABLE OF INTERNAL REVENUE CODE SECTIONS

REVENUE PROCEDURES

REVENUE RULINGS

REVENUE RULINGS

*

FEDERAL INCOME TAXATION OF PARTNERS AND PARTNERSHIPS

IN A NUTSHELL

Second Edition

*

CHAPTER 1

INTRODUCTION TO PARTNERSHIP TAXATION

§ 1. Aggregate and Entity Concepts

The statutory framework for the federal income taxation of partners and partnerships is set forth in §§ 701–777 of the Code (Subchapter K). One of the recurrent themes of Subchapter K is the blending of aggregate and entity concepts. A pure aggregate approach would look through the partnership, treating each partner as if he owned an undivided interest in the partnership assets and conducted a proportionate share of the partnership business. A pure entity approach, by contrast, would treat the partnership as a separate entity for tax purposes, with each partner owning an interest in the partnership rather than in the underlying assets.

Subchapter K adopts an aggregate approach to partnerships for some purposes and an entity approach for other purposes. For example, under the aggregate approach, a partnership is treated as a conduit which passes income through to the partners to be reported on their individual returns. A partnership is considered an entity, however, for purposes of determining the amount, character and

1

timing of partnership items. Subchapter K occasionally adopts a modified aggregate or entity approach in determining the tax consequences to the individual partners.

The hybrid entity-aggregate approach to partnerships accounts for much of the complexity of Subchapter K, but generally produces sensible results. As a policy matter, there may be a tendency to favor the aggregate approach, at least where it can be implemented without undue administrative cost or potential abuse. This approach reflects the underlying notion that the partnership form generally should affect the tax treatment of the partners as little as possible. Thus, it is often useful to compare the treatment of a transaction under Subchapter K with the treatment of a similar non-partnership transaction under general income tax principles.

§ 2. Transactional Approach

(a) General. Subchapter K is organized around four types of transactions: (i) partnership operations (§§ 701–709), (ii) contributions to a partnership (§§ 721–724), (iii) distributions from a partnership (§§ 731–737) and (iv) transfers of partnership interests (§§ 741–743). The remaining provisions contain operative rules for more than one type of transaction (§§ 751–755), general definitions (§ 761), and special rules for electing large partnerships (§§ 771–777).

(b) Partnership Operations. Although a partnership as such is not subject to income tax, it is treated as a separate entity for accounting purposes. §§ 701–703, 706; see Chapter 3. Items of income, gain, loss and deduction from partnership operations for each taxable year of the partnership are initially determined at the entity level; under conduit principles, these items are allocated among the partners and are passed through to them as distributive shares. The term "distributive share" refers not to actual distributions, but rather to each partner's allocable share of partnership items that must be reported. Both the amount and character of items included in a partner's distributive share are determined at the partnership level but are taxed to the partner on his individual return. Thus, the partnership serves as a conduit both quantitatively and qualitatively. See § 702. Electing large partnerships enjoy simplified conduit treatment. See § 9 below.

(c) **Inside and Outside Basis.** A partner's basis in his partnership interest ("outside basis") is separate and distinct from the partnership's basis in its assets ("inside basis"). Under § 722, a partner's outside basis is initially determined by reference to his investment in the partnership (i.e., the basis of any property and cash contributed in exchange for a partnership interest). Under § 723, the partnership takes a substituted basis in contributed property equal to its basis in the contributing partner's hands.

The relationship between inside and outside basis combines the entity and aggregate approaches. Although the separate computation of a partner's outside basis reflects an entity approach, §§ 722–

723 generally ensure that the partnership's aggregate inside basis will equal the sum of the partners' outside bases upon formation of the partnership. Moreover, parity between inside and outside basis is generally maintained through adjustments to outside basis reflecting partnership operations. Under § 705(a), a partner's outside basis is adjusted upward for his distributive share of income and any additional capital contributions, and is adjusted downward for his distributive share of partnership losses and any distributions from the partnership.

Under § 752, a partner's outside basis also includes his share of partnership liabilities. Section 752 ensures that increases and decreases in partnership-level liabilities are reflected in the partners' outside bases, thereby preserving parity of inside and outside basis. In addition, the allocation of partnership liabilities under § 752 determines whether a partner has sufficient outside basis to absorb his distributive share of items of loss and deduction. See Chapter 6. Under § 704(d), once a partner's outside basis has been reduced to zero, any further items of loss or deduction are suspended until his outside basis increases above zero. See Chapter 3.

(d) Contributions and Distributions. Under § 721, a contribution of cash or other property (but not services) in exchange for a partnership interest is generally tax free both to the partnership and the contributing partner. Traditionally, nonrecognition treatment has been justified on the theory that the partner is deemed to continue to own the contributed property, under an aggregate approach. The contribution of property to a partnership is viewed as a mere change in the form of ownership, rather than a substantive alteration in the nature of the partner's underlying investment. As a corollary to nonrecognition treatment, any unrealized gain or loss inherent in the contributed property is preserved in the partnership's inside basis as well as the contributing partner's outside basis. §§ 722–723; see Chapter 2. If the partnership subsequently disposes of contributed property, § 704(c) generally requires that any built-in gain or loss be allocated to the contributing partner. See Chapter 5.

Distributions of cash or property from a partnership to a partner are also generally tax free, unless the distributee partner receives cash in excess of his outside basis. See Chapter 9. The basis provisions ensure that any unrecognized gain or loss is preserved in the hands of the distributee partner, and his outside basis is reduced to reflect the distribution. §§ 731–733. Although contributions and distributions have traditionally enjoyed nonrecognition treatment, Congress has recently narrowed the scope of these principles. See §§ 704(c)(1)(B), 731(c) and 737; Chapters 5 and 9. It may also be important to distinguish transactions which are treated as contributions followed by distributions (under an aggregate approach) and those which are treated as disguised sales (under an entity approach). See § 707(a)(2)(B) and Chapter 7. Section 751(b) may also override nonrecognition treatment of certain distributions. See Chapter 9.

(e) Transfers of Partnership Interests. Under § 741, a partner who sells his partnership interest generally recognizes capital gain or loss equal to the difference between the amount realized and his outside basis. The collapsible partnership rules of § 751(a), however, may force the selling partner to recognize ordinary income if the partnership has ordinary income assets that have appreciated in value. See Chapter 8. Under § 742, a purchaser of a partnership interest takes a cost basis in the acquired interest. The entity approach reflected in §§ 741 and 742 treats a sale or exchange of a partnership interest as a disposition of a single unitary asset. By contrast, the quasi-aggregate approach reflected in § 751 looks through the partnership to the underlying partnership assets.

(f) Optional Adjustments to Inside Basis. Generally, the transfer of a partnership interest does not trigger any adjustment to the basis of partnership assets. If the partnership has a § 754 election in effect, however, a purchaser of a partnership interest is entitled to a special adjustment to his share of the partnership's inside basis to reflect his cost basis in the acquired partnership interest. §§ 743, 754; see Chapter 8. Similar adjustments are permitted to the basis of retained partnership property in connection with certain partnership distributions. §§ 734, 754; see Chapter 9. The special basis adjustment provisions preserve parity between inside and outside basis and thereby eliminate transitory distortions.

§ 3. Limits on Flexibility

(a) General. The rights and duties of the partners with respect to management of the partnership business are governed by state law and the terms of the partnership agreement. Under § 704(a), the partnership agreement also normally controls tax consequences, since it determines each partner's distributive share of partnership income, gain, loss and deduction. In an attempt to curb abusive partnership allocations, the regulations under § 704(b) set forth a complex set of rules intended to ensure that partnership allocations have "substantial economic effect." See Chapter 4.

(b) Form and Substance. In accordance with general income tax principles, a transaction may be recharacterized for tax purposes to reflect its economic substance. See, e.g., §§ 704(e) (family partnerships) and 707(a)(2) (disguised payments for property or services). The Treasury has also issued regulations that seek to curb transactions involving "abusive" partnerships. See § 11 below. In some situations, however, the partners have the flexibility to choose one form over another to determine the tax consequences of a transaction. For example, when a partner withdraws from a partnership, the parties have traditionally been permitted to choose between § 741 sale and § 736 liquidation treatment, even though certain tax advantages are available under one form but not the other.

(c) Tax Shelters. A typical tax-shelter investment enables a taxpayer to accelerate current tax benefits while deferring the corresponding tax liability; in addition, it may provide opportunities to convert ordinary income into capital gain. Until 1986, partnerships were unrivalled as tax-shelter vehicles because they permitted small investors to take full advantage of accelerated depreciation combined with leverage from nonrecourse borrowing. In the Tax Reform Act of 1986 (the "1986 Act"), however, Congress attacked the tax-shelter problem by enacting the passive loss rules of § 469, which limit the timing benefit of accelerated depreciation and other artificial deductions. See Chapter 3.

§ 4. Choice of Business Form

(a) General. The 1986 Act reinforced the corporate double-tax system and lessened the attractiveness of the corporate form of business. After the 1986 Act, the "master limited partnership" emerged as a means for active businesses previously conducted in corporate form to avoid the corporate-level tax. In 1987, however, Congress responded by requiring that certain publicly-traded partnerships be taxed as corporations. § 7704(a). Non-publicly-traded partnerships, however, continue to offer the advantage of a single-level tax. In effect, income passed through a partnership to its partners is taxed at a substantially lower effective rate than corporate distributions which are taxed once at the corporate level and again at the shareholder level.

(b) Hybrid Entities. In the late 1980's, limited liability companies (LLCs) emerged as a hybrid form of business organization that combines limited liability under state law with passthrough tax treatment under the federal income tax law. Members of an LLC who actively participate in business management ("member managers") are analogous to general partners; non-managing members are essentially passive investors, analogous to limited partners. Under state LLC statutes, all members enjoy limited liability, much like shareholders of a corporation. Flexible "default" rules allow the members of an LLC to custom tailor their business arrangement through an operating agreement. Since 1988 the Service has acknowledged that an LLC can qualify as a partnership for federal tax purposes. See Rev. Rul. 88–76. Other hybrid entities such as "limited liability partnerships" (LLPs) and "limited liability limited partnerships" (LLLPs) have also become increasingly popular. Partly in response to the emergence of such hybrid entities, the Treasury has greatly liberalized the entity classification rules. See § 7 below.

§ 5. Capital Accounts

(a) General. Typically, a partnership maintains capital accounts which reflect the value of each partner's equity interest in the partnership. In accounting terms, assets equal the sum of liabilities and capital (i.e., partners' equity). If all partnership assets were sold for fair market value and all liabilities were paid, the remaining cash, if any, would be equal to the partners' equity in the partnership (restated at current fair market value). If the partnership were then to wind up its business, those

partners with positive capital account balances
would be entitled to receive liquidating distributions
equal to their capital account balances. The
§ 704(b) regulations provide detailed rules concerning
the manner in which capital accounts must be
maintained if allocations under the partnership
agreement are to be respected for tax purposes. See
Chapter 4. The following discussion illustrates some
fundamental capital-accounting concepts in the context
of typical partnership transactions; unless otherwise
stated, capital accounts are assumed to be
maintained in accordance with the § 704(b) regulations.

(b) Partnership Contributions. When a partner
contributes property to a partnership, his capital
account must be credited with the fair market
(or "book") value of the contributed property, less
any liabilities secured by the property. Reg.
§ 1.704–1(b)(2)(iv)(b). The tax basis of the contributed
property does not affect the contributing partner's
"book" capital account, since the partners'
respective rights upon liquidation depend on the
fair market value (not the tax basis) of partnership
property. The partnership must keep track, however,
of any differences between the tax basis and
book value of contributed property for purposes of
tax accounting. The partnership will thus be required
to maintain two sets of capital accounts—a
tax capital account and a book capital account—
whenever property is contributed with a tax basis
different from its fair market value (or whenever
book capital accounts are restated to reflect the fair

market value of partnership property). A partner's tax capital account is initially credited with the amount of cash contributed plus the tax basis of any other contributed property (net of liabilities secured by such property).

Example (1): In exchange for equal 1/3 interests in the newly-formed ABC general partnership, A, B and C each contribute property of equal value. A contributes $30,000 cash; B contributes land with a basis of $10,000 and a value of $30,000; and C contributes securities with a basis of $45,000 and a value of $30,000. Immediately after the contribution, the partnership's balance sheet shows the following assets (left-hand side) and partners' capital (right-hand side):

	(1) Basis	(2) Value		(3) Basis	(4) Value
Assets			Capital		
Cash	$30,000	$30,000	A	$30,000	$30,000
Securities	45,000	30,000	B	10,000	30,000
Land	10,000	30,000	C	45,000	30,000
Total	$85,000	$90,000	Total	$85,000	$90,000

The partners' book capital accounts (Col. 4) reflect their equal contributions and equal rights to any liquidating distributions. The partners' tax capital accounts (Col. 3) reflect the basis of contributed property. The basis of the property in the partnership's hands (Col. 1) is the same as the basis of the property in the contributor's hands. § 723. The sum of the partners' book capital accounts ($90,-000) is equal to the total book value of the partnership's assets (Col. 2). The sum of the partners' outside bases—$30,000 (A), $10,000 (B), and $45,-000 (C)—equals the partnership's total inside basis ($85,000).

(c) Relationship to Outside Basis. A partner's capital account is adjusted (under rules similar to § 705(a)) to reflect partnership operations. Since a partner's distributive share of income and any additional contributions increase his investment in the partnership, they trigger corresponding increases in his capital account. Similarly, a partner's distributive share of losses and any distributions reduce his net investment in the partnership and trigger corresponding reductions in his capital account. A partner's capital account (but not his outside basis) may be reduced below zero by his distributive share of losses or by distributions. A deficit in a partner's book capital account normally represents the amount of cash that he would be obligated to contribute to the partnership upon liquidation. See, e.g., Park Cities Corp. (1976) (general partner liable for capital account deficit attributable to depreciation deductions). The value of partnership property, together with any partners' negative capital account balances, will equal the amount necessary to satisfy partnership liabilities and any other partners' positive capital account balances; thus, all partners' final capital accounts will be zero after liquidation of the partnership.

Another important difference between capital accounts and outside basis arises from the treatment of partnership liabilities. When a partnership borrows cash, the resulting partnership liability is matched by a corresponding increase in the value of partnership assets (i.e., cash or purchased property); conversely, when a partnership repays borrowed amounts, the reduction in partnership liabilities is matched by a corresponding decrease in the value of partnership assets (i.e., the cash used to repay the debt). Since partnership borrowing and principal repayments have no effect on the partnership's net asset value (i.e., partners' equity), increases and decreases in partnership liabilities are not reflected in the partners' capital accounts. By contrast, any increase or decrease in a partner's share of partnership liabilities triggers a corresponding increase or decrease in his outside basis. Section 752 adopts a pair of fictions to accomplish these outside basis adjustments: § 752(a) treats an increase in a partner's share of partnership liabilities as a deemed contribution of cash to the partnership, while § 752(b) treats a decrease in his share of partnership liabilities as a deemed cash distribution to the partner.

Often, a partner's outside basis may be determined indirectly by adding his share of partnership liabilities to his tax capital account. The relationship between outside basis and book capital account is much less straightforward because book capital account reflects differences between the basis and fair market value of contributed property.

(d) Taxable Income (Loss) and Cash Flow. The term "net cash flow" refers generally to the partnership's cash from operations available for distribution after paying (or setting aside reserves for) all necessary cash expenditures. It is important to distinguish net cash flow for a particular year from partnership taxable income (or loss), since deductions for certain non-cash items (e.g., depreciation allowance) are taken into account in calculating the latter but not the former. Net cash flow may be determined by subtracting actual cash expenditures (including principal payments on partnership debt) from partnership gross receipts (including borrowed proceeds). Net cash flow may be positive even though the partnership has a taxable loss for the year. From the partners' perspective, net cash flow is important because it may determine annual distributions under the partnership agreement. The following examples illustrate the relationship between capital accounts, outside basis and cash flow.

Example (2): The ABC partnership has the same initial balance sheet as in Example (1), above. Shortly after formation, ABC borrows $90,000 on a recourse basis to purchase a building on leased land. During Year 1, ABC has a tax loss of $6,000, computed by taking into account $9,000 depreciation, $3,000 of operating expenses and $6,000 of operating income; ABC does not repay any of the loan principal and distributes its available net cash flow of $3,000 ($6,000 operating income less $3,000 operating expense) to the partners in equal shares at the end of Year 1. The partnership's borrowing of $90,000 does not affect the partners' capital accounts, but increases each partner's outside basis by $30,000 (1/3 of the $90,000 liability). The depreciation (a non-cash item) reduces the basis and book value of the building from $90,000 to $81,000. Each partner's tax and book capital account (and outside basis) is decreased by her $1,000 tax-free cash distribution and her $2,000 distributive share of the partnership's tax loss. At the end of Year 1, the partnership's balance sheet is as follows:

	Basis	Value		Basis	Value
Assets			Liabilities	$ 90,000	$ 90,000
Cash	$ 30,000	$ 30,000	Capital		
Securities	45,000	30,000	A	27,000	27,000
Building	81,000	81,000	B	7,000	27,000
Land	10,000	30,000	C	42,000	27,000
Total	$166,000	$171,000	Total	$166,000	$171,000

The net increase in each partner's outside basis is $27,000 ($30,000 share of liabilities less $1,000 cash distribution less $2,000 distributive share of loss). Accordingly, the partners' respective outside bases are $57,000 (A), $37,000 (B), and $72,000 (C).

Example (3): During Year 2, ABC has taxable income of $3,000, computed by taking into account $9,000 depreciation, $3,000 of operating expenses and $15,000 of operating income; in addition, ABC repays $15,000 of the loan principal, reducing the outstanding liability to $75,000. The loan repayment does not affect the partners' capital accounts, but reduces each partner's outside basis by $5,000 (1/3 of $15,000 decrease in liabilities). The depreciation reduces the basis and book value of the building from $81,000 to $72,000. The partnership generates a negative cash flow of $3,000 ($15,000 operating income less $18,000 operating expenses and loan repayment), reducing partnership cash from $30,000 to $27,000. Each partner's tax and book capital account (and outside basis) is increased by her $1,000 distributive share of the partnership's taxable income. At the end of Year 2, the partnership's balance sheet is as follows:

	Basis	Value		Basis	Value
Assets			Liabilities	$ 75,000	$ 75,000
Cash	$ 27,000	$ 27,000	Capital		
Securities	45,000	30,000	A	$ 28,000	$ 28,000
Building	72,000	72,000	B	8,000	28,000
Land	10,000	30,000	C	43,000	28,000
Total	$154,000	$159,000	Total	$154,000	$159,000

The net decrease in each partner's outside basis is $4,000 ($5,000 decrease in share of liabilities plus $1,000 distributive share of income). Accordingly, the partners' respective outside bases are $53,000 (A), $33,000 (B), and $68,000 (C).

(e) Book/Tax Disparities. Whenever contributed property is properly reflected on the partnership's books at a value different from its tax basis, tax and book accounting entries will necessarily differ with respect to such property. The partners' book capital accounts are adjusted for items of "book" income, gain, loss and deduction determined by reference to the property's book basis. The partners' outside bases and tax capital accounts, however, are adjusted for items of income, gain, loss and deduction determined by reference to the property's tax basis. The separate accounting entries are necessary because tax and book capital accounts serve fundamentally different functions. Book capital accounts reflect contributed property at its fair market value at the time of contribution, while tax capital accounts reflect such property at its tax basis. When the partnership eventually disposes of the property, the amount of gain or loss for book or tax accounting purposes is determined by reference to the respective book or tax basis of the property.

Example (4): At the beginning of Year 3, ABC sells the land and securities when the land has increased in value to $33,000 and the securities have decreased in value to $27,000. The partnership recognizes a book gain of $3,000 ($33,000 amount realized less $30,000 book basis) with respect to the land and a book loss of $3,000 ($30,000 book basis less $27,000 amount realized) with respect to the securities, allocated equally among the partners. Since each partner's share of the book gain on the land ($1,000) equals her share of the book loss on the securities ($1,000), the partners' equity remains unchanged. Thus, each partner continues to have a balance of $28,000 in her book capital account, and the partnership's assets continue to have an aggregate book value of $159,000 ($72,000 book value of building plus $87,000 cash).

With respect to the land, the partnership recognizes a tax gain of $23,000 ($33,000 amount realized less $10,000 tax basis); the built-in gain ($20,-000) is allocated entirely to B (who contributed the land) and the balance ($3,000) is allocated equally among the partners. With respect to the securities, the partnership recognizes a tax loss of $18,000 ($45,000 tax basis less $27,000 amount realized); the built-in loss ($15,000) is allocated entirely to C (who contributed the securities) and the balance ($3,000) is allocated equally among the partners.

§ 704(c); see Chapter 5. B's tax capital account is increased by $20,000 (i.e., B's net tax gain) and C's tax capital account is decreased by $15,000 (i.e., C's net tax loss). After these adjustments, each partner's tax capital account equals her book capital account, leaving ABC with the following balance sheet:

	Basis	Value		Basis	Value
Assets			Liabilities	$ 75,000	$ 75,000
Cash	$ 87,000	$ 87,000	Capital		
Building	72,000	72,000	A	28,000	28,000
Total	$159,000	$159,000	B	28,000	28,000
			C	28,000	28,000
			Total	$159,000	$159,000

B's outside basis is increased by her $20,000 net tax gain, and C's outside basis is decreased her $15,000 net tax loss, leaving each partner with an outside basis of $53,000.

(f) Deemed–Sale Adjustment. After the initial contribution of property, the partners' book capital accounts will rarely reflect the current fair market value of the partners' equity. Unrealized appreciation or depreciation in the value of partnership property subsequent to contribution is generally not reflected on the partnership's books until the partnership sells the property or some other event (e.g., admission of a new partner) triggers a "revaluation." See Chapter 5. Before the partnership can wind up its business, however, the partners' book capital accounts must be adjusted to reflect their respective shares of any unrealized book gain or loss, determined as if the partnership property had been sold at fair market value. Thus, any remaining differences between the book value of partnership property and its fair market value will be eliminated immediately before liquidation of the partnership. The deemed-sale adjustment ensures that final book capital accounts accurately measure the partners' rights to liquidating distributions (or obligations to restore deficit balances). See Chapter 9.

§ 6.　Partnership Status

(a) General. Sections 761(a) and 7701(a)(2) both define a partnership to include any syndicate, joint venture or other unincorporated organization (other than a corporation, trust or estate) through which any business is carried on. Generally, a partnership exists only if two or more co-owners conduct a business for profit. See Uniform Partnership Act (UPA) § 6(1). Classification of an organization as a separate entity for federal tax purposes is governed by federal law. Reg. § 301.7701–1(a)(1). The regulations provide that a "joint venture or other contractual arrangement may create a separate entity for federal tax purposes if the participants carry on a trade, business, financial operation, or venture and divide the profits therefrom." Reg. § 301.7701–1(a)(2). Thus, existence of a separate entity is a threshold issue in classifying an arrangement as a partnership.

The regulations provide that "[m]ere co-ownership of property that is maintained, kept in repair, and rented or leased" does not give rise to a separate entity for federal tax purposes. Id. (same for expense-sharing arrangement). Such co-owners are capable of computing their individual incomes separately, without resorting to the intricacies of Subchapter K. If co-owners engage in any additional activity, however, they may be treated as partners. For example, the regulations provide that "a separate entity exists for federal tax purposes if co-owners of an apartment building lease space and in addition provide services to the occupants either directly or through an agent." Id.

In addition to record-keeping and reporting requirements, there may be other adverse tax consequences if an arrangement is classified as a partnership rather than some other relationship (e.g., tenancy-in-common or employer-employee). For example, an exchange of undivided interests in co-owned property is eligible for § 1031 nonrecognition treatment, but an exchange of partnership interests does not qualify. § 1031(a)(2)(D). If co-owners are treated as partners, most elections affecting taxable income must be made at the partnership level. § 703(b); see Chapter 3. Partnership status may also affect the character (i.e., capital or ordinary) of gain or loss recognized on sale of co-owned property. See, e.g., Podell (1970). If an individual is held to be an employee (rather than a partner), he will not be entitled to share in partnership losses and any cash distributed to him will be fully taxable as ordinary compensation. See, e.g., Luna (1964). The distinction between a payment for services and a distributive share of profits, however, is not always clear. § 707(a)(2)(A); see Chapter 7.

(b) Joint–Profit Motive. Generally, partners must intend to share profits for a partnership to exist. In *Allison*, the court held that a joint-profit motive was lacking where a purported partner received 75 out of 200 improved lots in exchange for providing direct loans and arranging financing necessary to improve the property. Allison (1976). The court found that joint division of profits from sale of the lots was never contemplated, noting the "specificity and certainty ... of the amount to be distributed" upon completion of the project. Compare *Madison Gas* (1979) (no distinction between a division of profits in kind and in cash). In *Allison*, the right to a relatively fixed return indicated a lack of the entrepreneurial risk-sharing generally associated with partner status. The court viewed the receipt of the lots merely as a payment in kind for the recipient's services in the course of its regular commercial loan business.

Often, one partner furnishes capital and another partner provides services; in such cases, partnership classification may depend upon whether the service provider is treated as a co-owner for tax purposes. In *Wheeler*, the court held that a "joint venture" agreement constituted a partnership, even though the service partner contributed no capital and the other partner was entitled to all profits (and bore the risk of any loss) until he recovered his capital (plus interest). Wheeler (1978). The court emphasized that the parties managed the business jointly and reported all transactions consistently as if a partnership existed.

(c) Election Out. Section 761(a) permits certain unincorporated organizations to elect to be excluded from all or part of Subchapter K. The election is available with respect to (i) investing partnerships, (ii) joint operating agreements for production, extraction or use of property, and (iii) certain short-term arrangements among dealers in connection with securities offerings. The election can be made only if the income of the organization's members can be "adequately determined without the computation of partnership taxable income." § 761(a). An electing organization is not subject to Subchapter K, but may be treated as a partnership for other tax purposes. See, e.g., Madison Gas (1979) (§ 162 deduction).

Although the statute refers to an election by "all the members" of the organization, the regulations allow the partnership itself to make the election. Reg. § 1.761–2(b)(2). The regulations also provide that an organization will be deemed to have elected out of Subchapter K "if it can be shown from all the surrounding facts and circumstances" that the members intended from the outset to be treated as co-owners rather than partners. Reg. § 1.761–1(b)(2)(ii). The requisite intent may be shown by the fact that members owning substantially all of the capital interests report their respective distributive shares "in a manner consistent with exclusion of the organization from Subchapter K." Id. The deemed election is designed to protect taxpayers who never intended to be treated as partners.

§ 7. Partnership Versus Corporation

(a) General. The "check-the-box" regulations, issued in 1996, greatly simplify and liberalize the entity classification rules. Reg. §§ 301.7701–1 through 301.7701–3. Under this elective regime, most newly-formed domestic unincorporated business entities will automatically be classified as partnerships unless they elect to be treated as associations taxable as corporations. Thus, such entities will generally have the flexibility to choose between double-tax and passthrough treatment. While some lingering questions remain concerning the Treasury's authority to issue these "interpretive" regulations, the elective regime has met with widespread approval.

(b) Historical Overview. The pre–1997 regulations sought to distinguish a partnership from an association taxable as a corporation based on a "resemblance" test. See Morrissey (1935). The former § 7701 regulations classified a state-law partnership as a corporation for federal income tax purposes only if it possessed more than two of four distinctively corporate characteristics: (i) continuity of life, (ii) centralized management, (iii) limited liability, and (iv) free transferability of interests. Former Reg. § 301.7701–2(a). Two other characteristics—associates and an objective to carry on business for joint profit—were considered common to corporations and partnerships, and hence not taken into account. Each of the four corporate characteristics was accorded equal weight, and the existence of other factors was generally irrelevant.

The mechanical approach of the prior regulations was heavily weighted in favor of partnership classification. Historically, this approach reflected the government's unsuccessful efforts in the 1960's to treat professional corporations as partnerships for federal tax purposes, in order to limit the availability of qualified pension and profit-sharing plans. Later, in the 1970's, the government belatedly attempted to curb tax-shelter limited partnerships by classifying them as associations taxable as corporations but was hindered by its own regulations. The significance of classification issues temporarily receded with the enactment of the passive loss rules of § 469 and the publicly-traded partnership rules of § 7704.

In the 1980's, the rise of LLCs called into question the appropriateness of distinguishing between double-tax and passthrough entities based on factors such as limited liability. The prior classification criteria, which depended largely on state-law differences between partnerships and corporations, were viewed as excessively formalistic. By choosing an appropriate organizational form and including appropriate terms in the governing instruments, most unincorporated businesses could obtain the desired tax classification. Thus, partnership classification was available for many non-publicly-traded entities that were virtually indistinguishable from corporations.

Making partnership classification available on an elective basis reduces unnecessary costs of business planning and tax administration. The current regime is not entirely elective, however, since state-law corporations cannot elect to be treated as partnerships for federal tax purposes. Because § 7701(a)(2) refers to "unincorporated organizations" in defining partnerships, any further expansion of the elective regime would presumably require a statutory amendment. Until such change, entity classification will continue to turn on relatively formalistic state-law distinctions. Moreover, the liberal classification rules lead to close scrutiny of other provisions of the Code that depend on partnership status.

(c) General Classification Rules. In applying the classification rules, the first step is to determine whether a particular arrangement is treated as a separate entity for federal tax purposes. See § 6 above. Separate entities other than trusts or estates are generally referred to as "business entities" under the regulations. Reg. § 301.7701–2(a). Business entities are further divided between those which are automatically classified as corporations ("per se corporations") and those which are eligible to make an election ("eligible entities"). Reg. § 301.7701–3(a). Per se corporations include (i) state-law corporations, (ii) certain foreign-law entities, and (iii) entities classified as corporations under other Code provisions. Reg. § 301.7701–2(b).

If an eligible entity does not make an express election, its status is determined under default rules. An entity with at least two members can elect corporate or partnership status; otherwise, all such domestic entities are classified as partnerships by default. Reg. § 301.7701–3(a), (b)(1). An eligible entity with a single owner can elect corporate status. Id. In the absence of such an election, an eligible single-owner entity is treated, for federal tax purposes, as a sole proprietorship, branch or division. Reg. § 301.7701–2(a).

(d) Foreign Organizations. Certain enumerated foreign entities are treated as per se corporations based on their resemblance to domestic corporations. Reg. § 301.7701–2(b)(8). In the case of foreign eligible entities, the default rules are intended to match the parties' likely expectations. By default, a foreign eligible entity is treated as a corporation if all of its members have limited liability; if any member is personally liable for the entity's debts, the entity is treated as a partnership (or disregarded in the case of a single-owner entity). Reg. § 301.7701–3(b)(2).

The check-the-box regulations facilitate the creation and use of "hybrid" arrangements, e.g., an entity which is taxable in one country but eligible for passthrough treatment in another country. Such entities may be used to secure more advantageous treatment under applicable U.S. foreign-tax-credit limitations. See generally §§ 901, 904(d). They may also undermine the elaborate "subpart F" anti-deferral rules of the Code which require certain U.S. shareholders to include in income currently the earnings (whether or not distributed) of "controlled foreign corporations'' (CFCs). See generally §§ 951–952, 954 and 957. The Service is likely to monitor closely the use of partnerships in the international area. IRS Notice 98–35.

(e) Change in Classification. Once an election has been made, an entity is generally barred from making a new entity election for a 60–month period unless the Service permits such an election following a substantial change of ownership. Reg. § 301.7701–3(b)(iv). Proposed regulations provide guidance concerning the tax consequences of an elective change of classification (e.g., conversion of a corporation into a partnership and vice versa). Prop. Reg. § 301.7701–3(g). An elective change from corporate to partnership status is treated as a taxable liquidation of the corporation, followed by an asset transfer by the shareholders to a newly-formed partnership in exchange for partnership interests. Prop. Reg. § 301.7701–3(g)(1)(ii); §§ 331, 336. Similarly, elective conversion of a partnership into a corporation is treated as a deemed contribution by the partnership of its assets to a newly-formed corporation in exchange for stock, followed by a deemed distribution of stock in liquidation of the partnership. Prop. Reg. § 301.7701–3(g)(1)(i).

(f) Future Direction. As a practical matter, the current system appears to be moving toward double-tax treatment for ''public'' entities and pass-through treatment for ''private'' entities. Apart from considerations of liquidity and access to capital markets, however, there seems to be relatively little policy justification for making the tax classification turn solely on whether ownership interests are widely-held or closely-held. Some commentators maintain that the dividing line between double-tax and passthrough entities should be based on the relative size of the business or active participation of owners. The emerging public/private distinction places great stress on the publicly-traded partnership rules as a bulwark against further erosion of the corporate tax base. Recent trends also increase pressure to identify and remedy provisions within Subchapter K that give rise to unexpected or unwarranted results.

§ 8. Publicly–Traded Partnerships

(a) **General.** A publicly-traded partnership (PTP) is generally treated as a corporation for federal tax purposes. § 7704(a). A PTP is defined as any partnership whose interests are (i) traded on an established securities market, or (ii) readily tradable on a secondary market (or the substantial equivalent thereof). § 7704(b). The regulations provide that these tests are satisfied "if, taking into account all of the facts and circumstances, the partners are readily able to buy, sell or exchange their partnership interests in a manner that is comparable, economically, to trading on an established securities market." Reg. § 1.7704–1(c)(1). The Taxpayer Relief Act of 1997 Act (the "1997 Act") provides that certain "grandfathered" PTPs (so-called "1987 partnerships") will not be reclassified as corporations provided they pay a tax of 3.5% on gross income from active conduct of a trade or business. § 7704(g); IRS Notice 98–3.

(b) Safe Harbors. Because the range of partnerships classified as PTPs is potentially quite broad, the regulations under § 7704 provide a series of safe harbors. The most important safe harbor relates to "private placements," i.e., partnerships in which all interests are issued in transactions exempted from registration under the Securities Act of 1933. Privately-placed partnerships are exempt from PTP status if the partnership does not have more than 100 partners at any time during the taxable year. Reg. § 1.7704–1(h)(1).

(c) Passive–Income Exception. Even if a partnership is a PTP, it will not be taxed as a corporation if nearly all of its income is derived from "passive" sources. § 7704(c). Section 7704(c) exempts from corporate treatment any PTP if at least 90% of its gross income for the taxable year constitutes "qualifying income," i.e., interest, dividends, rent and gain from real property, and income or gain derived from exploiting natural resources. Since real-estate and natural-resource activities have traditionally been conducted in noncorporate form, Congress considered that a statutory exception was appropriate. As a corollary to § 7704, however, § 469(k) imposes harsher passive loss rules with respect to qualifying PTPs. Under § 469(k), passive losses from such PTPs may be applied only against income or gain from the same PTP until the taxpayer disposes of his entire interest.

§ 9. Electing Large Partnerships

(a) General. In connection with enactment of § 7704, Congress directed the Treasury to undertake a broad study of compliance issues related to widely-held partnerships. In 1997, Congress enacted simplified reporting and administrative rules for "electing large partnerships," i.e., partnerships with 100 or more partners. § 775(a)(1). Most service partnerships are excluded from the application of these rules. § 775(b)(2).

(b) Passthrough Treatment. The electing large partnership rules provide for "simplified" passthrough treatment. Most items of income or loss are netted and reported to each partner as a single item, except for a limited number of separately-stated items (e.g., taxable income or loss from passive activities and other activities, net capital gain or loss, and tax-exempt income). § 772(a). Any limitations in computing taxable income are generally applied at the partnership level; most elections are also made by the partnership. § 773(a)(2), (3). An electing large partnership is allowed to deduct 30% of certain miscellaneous itemized deductions (including § 212 deductions); the remaining 70% is disallowed at the partnership level in lieu of applying the 2% floor of § 67. §§ 772(c)(3)(B), 773(b)(3) and 67. Electing large partnerships are also subject to special audit procedures. §§ 6240–6242.

§ 10. Corporate Passthrough Entities

(a) General. The two-level corporate tax applies to most incorporated business entities, commonly referred to as "C Corporations" because they are governed by Subchapter C (§§ 301–385). Nevertheless, specific provisions authorize passthrough treatment for certain types of incorporated entities. In some instances, these entities may provide an attractive alternative to partnerships.

(b) S Corporations. Although Subchapter S (§§ 1361–1378) permits certain "small business corporations" to elect to be taxed as conduits for tax purposes, the analogy between passthrough treatment of S corporations and partnerships is imperfect. An S corporation represents a hybrid of corporate and partnership characteristics, and remains subject to the normal corporate tax rules to the extent they are not preempted by the special rules of Subchapter S. § 1371(a). For example, a distribution of appreciated property by an S corporation triggers taxable gain at the corporate level. §§ 311, 336. An S corporation may have no more than 75 shareholders and one class of stock; in addition, shareholders of an S corporation are generally not permitted to include corporate-level liabilities in the basis of their stock. §§ 1361(b)(1), 1366(d) and 1367.

The relative simplicity of the Subchapter S conduit model comes at the cost of some of the flexibility available under Subchapter K. It has been suggested that Subchapter S may become obsolete if Subchapter K becomes the passthrough regime of choice for unincorporated entities. Quite apart from comparison with Subchapter K, there are important reasons for retaining Subchapter S. In the case of start-up businesses that contemplate going public or undergoing a reorganization, the S form offers significant advantages. Another advantage is that under current law an existing C corporation may elect S status without a deemed taxable liquidation.

(c) RICs, REITs and REMICs. Modified conduit treatment is available under Subchapter M (§§ 851–860G) for certain types of entities: Regulated Investment Companies (RICs, or mutual funds in common parlance), Real Estate Investment Trusts (REITs), and Real Estate Mortgage Investment Conduits (REMICs). Unlike Subchapter S, these entities are not limited to a relatively small number of shareholders, but instead typically provide passive investment vehicles for large numbers of investors. Subchapter M avoids much of the complexity of Subchapter K by generally requiring such entities to distribute virtually all of their income currently, while restricting the passthrough of losses. Under this modified conduit treatment, distributed earnings are taxed to the beneficial owners according to the amounts actually distributed, with any undistributed earnings taxed at the entity level.

§ 11. Anti–Abuse Rules

(a) General. In 1994, the Treasury proposed a set of anti-abuse regulations which drew harsh criticism on grounds of vagueness and overbreadth. In an attempt to allay taxpayer concerns, the Treasury refined and narrowed the scope of the anti-abuse rules. Reg. § 1.701–2. The final regulations contain two separate rules, a "general anti-abuse rule" and an "abuse-of-entity rule." These rules supplement the Service's ability to challenge abusive transactions under "nonstatutory principles and other statutory and regulatory authorities." Reg. § 1.701–2(i). To remedy abuses, the Service has broad discretion to disregard partnership (or partner) status, modify accounting methods, and reallocate income or loss. Reg. § 1.701–2(b). The Service may recast an abusive transaction even though it complies with the literal language of the statute or the regulations. Specific applications of the anti-abuse rules will be considered later, but it is useful here to sketch the general principles.

(b) General Anti–Abuse Rule. In order for the general anti-abuse rule to apply, two requirements must be satisfied. First, "a principal purpose" of the transaction must be to achieve a substantial reduction, in present value terms, of the partners' aggregate tax liability. Second, the transaction must be inconsistent with the intent of Subchapter K (the "abuse-of-intent" test). Since many partnership transactions are tax-motivated, determining the "intent of Subchapter K" is crucial in deciding whether a transaction will be respected. The regulations observe that "Subchapter K is intended to permit taxpayers to conduct joint business (including investment) activities through a flexible economic arrangement without incurring an entity-level tax." Reg. § 1.701–2(a). According to the regulations, several requirements are "implicit in the intent of Subchapter K": (i) the partnership must be bona fide and each partnership transaction (or series of transactions) must have a substantial business purpose, (ii) substance-over-form principles must be satisfied, and (iii) the tax consequences to each partner and the partnership "must accurately reflect the partners' economic agreement and properly reflect the partners' income" (the "proper-reflection-of-income" test). Id.

The general anti-abuse rule requires a determination based on all of the facts and circumstances. Reg. § 1.701–2(c). Specifically, the purported business purpose for a transaction be weighed against the claimed tax benefits. See id. (listing relevant factors). The regulations also contain examples illustrating the application of the general anti-abuse rule. Four of these examples demonstrate that merely choosing the partnership form in order to achieve an overall tax savings or even to circumvent restrictions outside Subchapter K will not necessarily run afoul of the general anti-abuse rule. See Reg. § 1.701–2(d) (Ex. 1–4). Other examples illustrate that the anti-abuse regulations are intended to backstop the principles of § 704(b) concerning allocation of partnership income or loss in accordance with the partners' economic arrangement. Id. (Ex. 5–7).

The regulations recognize that certain provisions of Subchapter K are intended primarily to promote administrative convenience or other objectives, sometimes at the expense of accurate measurement of income. Such provisions include the substituted basis rules of § 732(c) for distributed property and the elective basis adjustment rules of § 754. See

Chapters 8 and 9. Common transactions involving these provisions might technically violate the proper-reflection-of-income test because they frequently yield "non-economic" results. To prevent this result, the regulations generally deem the proper-reflection-of-income test to be satisfied if the tax results are "clearly contemplated" by the simplifying, administrative provision. Reg. § 1.701–2(a)(3). The Service reserves the right, however, to challenge "prearranged" transactions deliberately designed to exploit these non-economic rules. Reg. § 1.701–2(d) (Ex. 8–11).

(c) Abuse-of-Entity Rule. The separate abuse-of-entity rule permits the Service to treat a partnership as an aggregate, rather than an entity, in order to carry out the purpose of any provision of the statute or the regulations. Reg. § 1.701–2(e)(1). Unlike the general anti-abuse rule, the abuse-of-entity rule does not depend on the taxpayer's motive, but rather on the use of entity status to frustrate the purpose of tax provisions outside Subchapter K. Even if the relevant non-Subchapter K provision mandates entity treatment, the Service can impose aggregate treatment to the extent that the attendant tax consequences were not "clearly contemplated." Reg. § 1.701–2(e)(2); see also Reg. § 1.701–2(f) (Ex. 1–3).

CHAPTER 2

ORGANIZATION OF A PARTNERSHIP

§ 1. Overview

Section 721 provides generally that no gain or loss is recognized by a partnership or any of its partners when property is contributed to a partnership in exchange for a partnership interest. Despite the closely analogous policy considerations underlying the nonrecognition treatment of contributions to partnerships and corporations under §§ 721 and 351, § 721 imposes no restriction similar to the "control" requirement of § 351. Thus, a transfer of property to a newly-formed or existing partnership is generally tax free, even if the contributor holds only an insignificant partnership interest after the transfer. Any unrecognized gain or loss is preserved by the basis provisions of §§ 722 and 723, which generally prescribe the basis of the partnership interest (in the partner's hands) and the basis of the contributed property (in the partnership's hands) by reference to the basis of the property in the contributing partner's hands before the contribution.

Notwithstanding § 721, a contribution of encumbered property may trigger recognition of gain to

36

the extent that § 752 treats the partnership as assuming (or taking subject to) the contributing partner's liabilities. Furthermore, nonrecognition treatment does not apply to the receipt of a partnership interest in exchange for services, since § 721 addresses only contributions of property. In the case of contributions of property to an investment partnership, § 721(b) provides another exception to nonrecognition treatment. See also § 721(c), (d) (certain transfers to foreign partnerships). Other statutory provisions or judicially-developed doctrines may also limit the scope of nonrecognition treatment under § 721.

§ 2. Contributions of Unencumbered Property

(a) General. Section 721 applies only to a contribution of property in exchange for a partnership interest. The term "property," while not specifically defined in the statute, has been construed broadly, by analogy to § 351, to include cash, tangible property, accounts receivable, nonexclusive licenses and industrial know-how. In distinguishing between contributions of property and services, the regulations under § 721 serve a purpose similar to § 351(d). See Reg. § 1.721–1(b)(1). Even though receipt of a partnership interest in exchange for services falls outside § 721, in some cases it may be possible to characterize a claim for services as property. See, e.g., Stafford (1984); Frazell (1964).

An installment obligation is "property" which may be contributed tax free under § 721. Reg.

§§ 1.721–1(a), 1.453–9(c)(2). Although not addressed directly by the § 721 regulations, a partner's own note may be viewed as zero-basis property or as an obligation to make an additional capital contribution to the partnership. Oden (1981); Bussing (1987). The contributing partner should generally be permitted to increase his outside basis only to the extent that actual payments are made on the note. See Rev. Rul. 80–235; Reg. § 1.704–1(b)(2)(iv)(d)(2).

A contribution of property should be distinguished from a loan or sale. See § 707(a)(1). If a partner retains ownership of property and merely permits the partnership to use the property, § 721 does not apply. Reg. § 1.721–1(a). Moreover, a purported "loan" that actually represents equity placed at the risk of the venture may be recharacterized as a capital contribution in accordance with the substance of the transaction. Rev. Rul. 72–350; see Rev. Rul. 72–135 ("nonrecourse" loan to limited partner or to partnership by the general partner treated as capital contribution). Under the disguised-sale rules of § 707, a purported "contribution" may be partially taxable if the contributor receives cash or other property (boot) in addition to a partnership interest. See Chapter 7. If the transaction is not treated as a disguised sale, the contributing partner may be able to receive boot as a tax-free distribution under § 731. See Chapter 9.

(b) Basis Consequences. Under § 722, a contributing partner's substituted basis in a partnership interest acquired in a § 721 exchange is equal to the amount of cash contributed plus the contributor's adjusted basis (determined as of the time of contribution) of any other property contributed. Under § 723, the partnership takes a substituted basis in the contributed property equal to the contributor's adjusted basis at the time of contribution. (If the contribution triggers gain under § 721(b) because the partnership is an investment partnership, the contributor's outside basis and the partnership's inside basis are increased by the amount of gain recognized. §§ 722, 723; see § 6 below.)

Under §§ 722 and 723, the contributor's basis in the contributed property is essentially preserved both in the partnership's inside basis in the property and in the contributor's outside basis in his partnership interest. If the partnership sells property that was contributed with a built-in gain or loss, § 704(c)(1)(A) generally requires that the entire built-in gain or loss be allocated to the contributing partner, with a corresponding adjustment to the contributor's outside basis. See Chapter 5. Thus, the contributor will not recognize the built-in gain or loss a second time when he sells his partnership interest. If the contributing partner instead sells his partnership interest while the partnership still holds the contributed property, however, the built-in gain or loss will continue to be preserved in the partnership's inside basis. Thus, the built-in gain or loss may be recognized when the partnership sells the contributed property, unless the partnership's inside basis is adjusted upon a sale of the contributor's partnership interest. See Chapter 8.

Example (1): A, B and C receive equal 1/3 partnership interests upon formation of a general partnership. A contributes land with a fair market value of $100,000 and a basis of $80,000; B and C each contribute $100,000 cash. Under § 721, no gain or loss is recognized on formation of the partnership. Under § 722, the partners' respective bases in their partnership interests are $80,000 (A), $100,000 (B) and $100,000 (C). Under § 723, the partnership takes a basis of $80,000 in the land. If the partnership subsequently sells the land for $100,000, the $20,000 of gain will be allocated to A under § 704(c), increasing A's outside basis from $80,000 to $100,000. If A then sells his partnership interest for $100,000, he will recognize no further gain or loss on the sale.

(c) Holding Period. A partner's holding period for a partnership interest acquired in a § 721 exchange is determined by reference to his holding period for the contributed property (a "tacked" holding period), provided that the contributed property is capital gain property (i.e., capital assets or § 1231 property). § 1223(1). Regardless of the character of the transferred assets (i.e., ordinary or capital), the partnership interest will generally be a capital asset in the contributor's hands. If a partner contributes both ordinary and capital gain property, the holding period of his partnership interest is unclear. In the corporate context, the Service has held that each share of stock received in a § 351 transfer takes a split holding period in proportion to the fair market value of the transferred assets. Rev.

Rul. 85–164. This treatment would give rise to complications under Subchapter K, however, because of the unitary nature of a partnership interest. See Rev. Rul. 84–53 (different classes of partnership interests, i.e., general and limited, have a single unitary basis in partner's hands). Fortunately, the problem is of limited significance because a partner rarely sells his partnership interest shortly after contribution. A partnership may tack the contributor's holding period in each transferred asset for purposes of determining the partnership's holding period for the asset. § 1223(2). Tacking is permitted regardless of the character of the asset in the contributor's hands.

§ 3. Contributions of Encumbered Property

When a partner contributes encumbered property to a partnership, the § 752 adjustments for liabilities affect both the contributor's outside basis and the amount of any gain recognized. Section 752(b) treats any decrease in a partner's individual liabilities by reason of the partnership's assumption of such liabilities as a deemed distribution of cash from the partnership to the partner. Conversely, § 752(a) treats any increase in a partner's share of partnership liabilities as a deemed contribution of cash by the partner to the partnership. Finally, § 752(c) treats a liability to which property is subject as a liability of the property owner to the extent of the property's fair market value. For example, if a partnership receives contributed property subject to a liability (e.g., a mortgage) without becoming personally liable for the underlying obligation, the partnership is nevertheless treated as having assumed the liability, subject to the fair-market-value limitation of § 752(c). Reg. § 1.752–1(e).

For purposes of § 752, any decrease in a partner's share of individual liabilities as a result of a contribution of encumbered property is netted against any increase in his share of partnership liabilities arising from the same transaction; only the net increase or decrease triggers a deemed contribution or distribution of cash. Reg. § 1.752–1(f). Therefore, in determining the amount of gain (if any) recognized by a partner on a contribution of encumbered property, only the net decrease in the contributor's liabilities (i.e., the decrease in his individual liabilities less any increase in his share of partnership liabilities) is counted. Under § 733, the deemed cash distribution resulting from a net relief of liabilities reduces the contributor's basis in his partnership interest (but not below zero); to the extent the deemed cash distribution exceeds outside basis, the contributor recognizes gain (generally capital) under §§ 731(a)(1) and 741. The interaction of the netting rules of § 752 and the basis rules of §§ 722 and 733 is illustrated below.

Example (2): C acquires a 1/3 general partnership interest in exchange for a contribution of property with a basis of $15,000 and a fair market value of $60,000, subject to a recourse liability of $30,000 which the partnership assumes; the partnership has no other liabilities. Under § 752(b), the partnership's assumption of the liability reduces C's individual liabilities by $30,000. Under § 752(a), C's share of partnership liabilities simultaneously increases by $10,000 (1/3 of the $30,000 liability assumed by the partnership). Under the netting rules of § 752, only the net decrease in C's liabilities ($20,000) is treated as a deemed cash distribution. Under § 733, the deemed distribution reduces C's basis in her partnership interest from $15,000 (the pre-contribution basis of the property in C's hands) to zero; under §§ 731(a) and 741, the balance of the deemed distribution triggers $5,000 of capital gain to C.

C could avoid recognition of gain either by contributing property with a basis of at least $20,000 or by making an additional cash contribution of at least $5,000. In either case, her outside basis would be sufficient to absorb the $20,000 deemed distribution. C could also avoid recognition of gain if she agreed to remain personally liable to the creditor (and no other partner bore any economic risk of loss for the liability). As a result of the contribution, C's share of individual liabilities would decrease by $30,000, but her share of the partnership's recourse liabilities would simultaneously increase by $30,-000. Since only the net increase or decrease in liabilities is taken into account, there would be no deemed distribution under § 752; thus, C would recognize no gain and, under § 722, her outside basis would be $15,000. See Reg. § 1.752–1(g).

In illustrating the mechanics of the basis adjustments, the example assumes that (in the absence of a different agreement) each partner is allocated an equal 1/3 share of the partnership's recourse liabilities. The liability-sharing rules of § 752, which are discussed in Chapter 6, generally reach this result by allocating recourse liabilities based on a partner's share of the economic risk of loss for such liabilities. Reg. § 1.752–2(a). Equal general partners typically share the economic risk of loss for recourse liabilities equally, since each would be personally liable for his proportionate share of the partnership's debts. By contrast, limited partners generally bear the economic risk of loss for recourse liabilities only to the extent that they agree to contribute additional capital to the partnership. Thus, if C were a limited partner with no obligation to contribute additional capital, C's share of the partnership's recourse liabilities would be zero. Accordingly, C would recognize $15,000 of gain on the contribution ($30,000 net liability relief less $15,000 outside basis) and would end up with a basis of zero in her partnership interest.

Under § 752, subject to certain special rules, both general and limited partners typically share nonrecourse liabilities in accordance with their share of partnership profits. A nonrecourse liability is defined, for purposes of § 752, as any liability for which no partner bears the economic risk of loss. Reg. § 1.752–1(a)(2). If a partner contributes built-in gain property subject to a nonrecourse liability, the § 752 liability-sharing rules minimize the amount of gain recognized by the contributor. Under these rules, the portion of the liability allocated to the contributing partner can never be less than the excess of the liability over the tax basis of the property. This minimum amount corresponds to the built-in gain ("§ 704(c) minimum gain") that would be allocated to the contributing partner on a hypothetical sale of the property for no consideration other than relief of the nonrecourse liability. Reg. § 1.752–3(a); see Chapter 6. The "excess" nonrecourse liability (i.e., the portion not allocated under the built-in gain rule) is then allocated among the partners in accordance with their profit-sharing ratios. Thus, at the time property is contributed subject to a nonrecourse liability, the contributor's share of the liability is equal to the sum of his share of the § 704(c) minimum gain and his share of the excess liability.

Example (3): A acquires a 20% partnership interest in exchange for a contribution of property with a basis of $200 and a fair market value of $1,000, subject to a nonrecourse liability of $500; the partnership has no other liabilities. A's share of the partnership's nonrecourse liability is $340, i.e., $300 under the built-in gain rule ($500 liability less $200 basis) plus $40 (20% of the $200 excess liability). The remaining $160 of the nonrecourse liability (80% of the $200 excess liability) is shifted to the other partners. Since the net decrease in A's individual liabilities ($160) does not exceed A's basis in the contributed property ($200), A recognizes no gain on the contribution, and takes a basis of $40 in his partnership interest ($200 less $160).

The partnership's basis in contributed property is not adjusted to reflect any gain recognized by a contributing partner as a result of a net decrease in individual liabilities (unless a § 754 election is in effect). The other partners will increase their outside bases, however, to reflect any liabilities shifted to them under § 752. For example, if A has a $20,000 net decrease in individual liabilities in connection with a contribution of property subject to a recourse liability of $30,000 to the equal ABC general partnership, the $20,000 of liabilities shifted away from A will be allocated equally to B and C, who will each increase outside basis by $10,000. If a contribution alters the ratio in which the partners share profits and losses, the § 752 liability-sharing rules may also trigger an increase or decrease in the noncontributing partners' shares of existing partnership liabilities. See Chapter 6.

§ 4. Effect on Capital Accounts

The capital account rules of § 704(b) require that a contributing partner's book capital account be increased by the fair market value (rather than the adjusted tax basis) of contributed property at the time of contribution. Reg. § 1.704–1(b)(2)(iv)(d)(1). Upon a contribution of encumbered property, only the net value of the property (fair market value less liabilities secured by the property) is credited to the contributor's book capital account. Reg. § 1.704–1(b)(2)(iv)(c). This adjustment is appropriate because a partner's share of partnership liabilities is not included in his book capital account; the book capital account measures the partner's right to receive proceeds of partnership property after satis-

faction of partnership liabilities. For tax a͙
purposes, the contributor's tax capital acʮ
credited with the adjusted tax basis of the contributed property (at the time of contribution) less any
liabilities secured by the property. If the liabilities
exceed the adjusted basis of the contributed property (but not its fair market value), the contributor
may have a negative tax capital account even
though he has a positive book capital account.

Example (4): A, B and C form an equal general
partnership. A and B each contribute $10,000 cash;
C contributes land with a basis of $12,000 and a fair
market value of $25,000, subject to a nonrecourse
liability of $15,000. C is credited with a book capital
account of $10,000 ($25,000 fair market value of
contributed property less $15,000 liability) and a
tax capital account of negative $3,000 (the excess of
the $15,000 liability over the $12,000 basis of the
contributed property). A and B are credited with tax
and book capital accounts of $10,000 each. The ABC
partnership has the following balance sheet at inception:

	Basis	Value		Tax	Book
Assets			Liabilities	$15,000	$15,000
Cash	$20,000	$20,000	Capital		
Land	12,000	25,000	A	10,000	10,000
Total	$32,000	$45,000	B	10,000	10,000
			C	(3,000)	10,000
			Total	$32,000	$45,000

C's share of the partnership's nonrecourse liability is $7,000, i.e., $3,000 under the built-in gain rule
($15,000 liability less $12,000 basis) plus $4,000 (1/3

of the $12,000 excess liability). C's outside basis of $4,000 ($12,000 basis of the contributed property less $8,000 net decrease in individual liabilities) is equal to the sum of her share of partnership liabilities ($7,000) and her negative tax capital account ($3,000). A and B each have an outside basis of $14,000, i.e., $10,000 cash contributed plus a $4,000 share of the partnership's nonrecourse liability (1/3 of the $12,000 excess liability).

§ 5. Character of Contributed Property

(a) General. The character of contributed property in the partnership's hands is generally determined, under an entity approach, by reference to the partnership's purpose for holding the property. Section 724, however, preserves the character of gain or loss on specific categories of contributed property (unrealized receivables, inventory items, and capital loss property) in the hands of the partnership. Section 724 is intended to discourage the use of partnerships as vehicles for converting ordinary income property into capital gain property (or built-in capital losses into ordinary losses). If a partnership disposes of property subject to § 724 in a nonrecognition transaction, the § 724 taint generally applies to any "substituted basis" property resulting from the transaction. § 724(d)(3).

The "taint" of ordinary gain or loss treatment is permanent for unrealized receivables (as defined in § 751(c)). § 724(a). If a partner contributes inventory, any gain or loss recognized by the partnership on the disposition of the property within five years after the contribution is treated as ordinary; thereafter, the character of the property is determined at the partnership level. § 724(b). For this purpose, inventory is defined broadly to include not only § 1221(1) assets, but any other property that would not be considered a capital asset or § 1231 property if sold by the contributor (except that the § 1231(b) holding period requirement is disregarded). §§ 724(d)(2), 751(d). If a partner contributes a capital asset with a built-in loss, any loss recognized by the partnership from sale of the property within five years after the contribution is treated as a capital loss to the extent of the built-in loss; thereafter the character of the property is determined at the partnership level. § 724(c).

Example (5): A, a real estate investor, contributes undeveloped land with a basis of $12,000 and a fair market value of $10,000 to a partnership which is a real estate dealer. If the partnership sells A's property for $11,000 within five years of the contribution, the built-in loss of $1,000 is treated as a capital loss (and allocated entirely to A under § 704(c) principles). If the partnership instead sells the land for $7,000, the recognized loss of $5,000 is treated as a capital loss only to the extent of the built-in portion ($2,000); the remaining $3,000 loss is treated as an ordinary loss because the partnership is a dealer. If the partnership instead sells the land for more than $12,000, the entire gain is ordinary.

(b) Recapture Property. A contribution of § 1245 or § 1250 recapture property triggers depreciation recapture only to the extent of any gain recognized by the contributor (i.e., from a net decrease in individual liabilities exceeding basis). §§ 1245(b)(3), 1250(d)(3); see Reg. § 1.1245–4(c)(4) (Ex. 3). Notwithstanding § 741, a portion of the contributor's gain may thus be treated as ordinary income attributable to depreciation recapture. Any remaining depreciation recapture inherent in the contributed property continues in the partnership's hands, and will generally be recognized when the partnership sells or otherwise disposes of the property. The § 1245 regulations generally require that depreciation recapture be allocated to the partner who received the benefit of the prior depreciation (including pre-contribution depreciation). See Reg. § 1.1245–1(e)(2); see Chapter 4.

§ 6. Investment Partnerships

Section 721(b) denies § 721(a) nonrecognition treatment for transfers to "a partnership which would be treated as an investment company (within the meaning of section 351) if the partnership were incorporated." This provision is aimed at so-called "swap funds" in which taxpayers seek to achieve a tax-free diversification of their investment by transferring appreciated stock, securities, or similar assets to a partnership in exchange for a partnership interest. Like § 351(e)(1) in the corporate context, § 721(b) applies only if (i) the transfer results (directly or indirectly) in diversification of the transferors' interests and (ii) more than 80% of the transferee's assets consist of stock, securities, and other enumerated assets which are treated as stock and securities for this purpose. See § 351(e)(1); Reg. § 1.351–1(c)(1). If § 721(b) applies, the contributing partner recognizes gain (but not loss) on the exchange. Under §§ 722 and 723, the contributor's basis in his partnership interest and the partnership's basis in the contributed property are both increased by the amount of any gain recognized under § 721(b).

§ 7. Receipt of a Partnership Interest for Services

(a) **Overview.** The transfer of a partnership interest in exchange for services may be a taxable event for both the service partner and the partnership itself. Although this area remains unsettled, the Service has issued general guidance concerning such compensatory transfers. See Rev. Proc. 93–27. If a partner receives an interest in partnership capital (a capital interest) as compensation for services, the fair market value of the interest constitutes ordinary income to the partner under § 61. By contrast, receipt of an interest in partnership profits (a profits interest) for services rendered "in a partner capacity or in anticipation of being a partner" is generally nontaxable, subject to certain exceptions. Id. If receipt of the partnership interest is taxable, the timing rules of § 83 (the general provision governing transfers of property in connection with services) may be applicable.

(b) **Capital or Profits Interest.** Since the tax treatment depends on the type of partnership interest received, it is important initially to determine whether a service partner has received an interest in partnership capital or profits (or both). Under the deemed-liquidation test, the partnership is deemed to sell all of its assets for their fair market value and to distribute the proceeds in liquidation immediately after the interest is acquired. Rev. Proc. 93–27. If the service provider would be entitled to receive a share of the liquidating distribution, the transferred interest is a capital interest. Conversely, if the service provider has only a right to participate in future profits and would not receive any distribution upon an immediate liquidation, the transferred interest is a profits interest. Id.

A purported "profits" interest may actually be a disguised capital interest to the extent that the partnership's assets have unrealized appreciation (including goodwill) when the service partner is admitted. For example, assume that A and B each contribute $250 to form a partnership which purchases land worth $500; when the land has appreciated in value to $750, C is admitted as a partner and receives a 1/3 profits interest in exchange solely for a contribution of services. To prevent a capital shift from the existing partners to C, the partnership property should be revalued, in connection with C's admission, to reflect its fair market value; the revaluation ensures that any pre-admission unrealized appreciation inherent in the partnership property will eventually be allocated entirely to A and B under § 704(c) principles. In the absence of a revaluation (or equivalent special allocations), C will be treated as having received a capital interest worth $83 (⅓ of the $250 pre-admission gain), i.e., the amount that C would receive upon a deemed liquidation of the partnership immediately after C's admission. The § 704(b) regulations warn that such a capital shift may have adverse tax consequences. Apparently, the capital shift may be treated either as a gift or as taxable compensation under § 83. Reg. § 1.704–1(b)(2)(iv)(f).

(c) Contributions of Property and Services. A service provider may be able to avoid recognition of gain by converting services into property and contributing the property in exchange for a partnership interest. See, e.g., Stafford (1984) (real estate developer's letter of intent treated as property for purposes of § 721); Frazell (1964) (geological maps prepared by taxpayer). Nonrecognition treatment is generally available only if the service provider acted on his own behalf (rather than on behalf of the partnership) in creating the property. See, e.g., James (1969) (pre-existing agreement to transfer property to partnership). If a partnership interest is acquired in exchange for a combination of services and self-created property, only a portion of the partnership interest is tax free under § 721. See Frazell (1964) (allocation between services and geological maps prepared by the contributing partner).

(d) Receipt of a Vested Capital Interest. If a partner receives a capital interest in exchange for services, the value of the interest is includible in the recipient's gross income as compensation. §§ 61, 83;

Reg. § 1.721–1(b)(1). It is not entirely clear, however, whether the amount and timing of the inclusion is governed by § 83 or the regulations under § 721. Under § 83(a), if property is transferred as compensation for services, the recipient must include in gross income the fair market value of the property (determined without regard to any restrictions other than restrictions that will never lapse) less the amount, if any, paid for the property. The fair-market-value determination and the taxable event occur when the property first becomes substantially vested, i.e., when it is either "transferable" or "not subject to a substantial risk of forfeiture." Reg. § 1.83–3(b); see Reg. §§ 1.83–3(c)(1), (d). Proposed regulations that would have expressly made § 83 applicable to a transfer of a partnership interest for services have never been finally adopted or withdrawn. See Prop. Reg. § 1.721–1(b)(1). The language of § 83 is sufficiently broad, however, to encompass compensatory transfers to a partner.

Section 83 apparently also governs the tax treatment of the transferor of the capital interest (i.e., the partnership). Except as provided in § 1032 (relating to issuance of corporate stock), the regulations require the transferor to recognize gain or loss as a result of a § 83 transfer. Reg. § 1.83–6(b). Under general principles of income taxation, a transfer of appreciated property in satisfaction of an obligation is treated as a taxable event to the transferor. See, e.g., Davis (1962). Although there is no case authority directly in point, § 83 and *Davis* arguably require a partnership to recognize gain (or loss) when a service partner receives a capital interest as compensation. In an analogous case, the transfer of an undivided one-half interest in a race horse as compensation for services triggered gain recognition to the transferor and the resulting co-ownership was treated as a partnership. McDougal (1974).

If a service partner acquires his capital interest from an existing partnership, the transaction may be viewed as if the partnership transferred an undivided interest in its assets to the service partner, who then recontributed such assets to the partnership in exchange for his capital interest. The partnership's gain or loss should be measured by the difference between the partnership's basis in the assets deemed transferred and the fair market value of those assets. Any recognized gain or loss should be allocated to the other partners. See § 706(d)(2). Some commentators have suggested, however, that the partnership should be treated as if it paid cash compensation to the service partner, who then recontributed that cash to the partnership in exchange for a partnership interest. The transfer of the partnership interest would be nontaxable to the partnership as long as it held (or borrowed) cash equal to the value of the service partner's interest, even if it also held appreciated property. Since the partnership could easily avoid gain recognition simply by borrowing sufficient cash, the cash-compensation analogy seems appropriate only if it is conceded that a nonrecognition policy is justified.

The fictional exchange provides a mechanism for giving the service partner a cost basis in the assets deemed transferred to him and recontributed to the partnership in a tax-free § 721 transfer. Under § 723, the partnership should take a cost basis in the recontributed assets equal to their basis in the service partner's hands. If the partnership elects to revalue its assets in connection with the service partner's admission, any remaining unrealized gain or loss inherent in the partnership's assets will be allocated to the other partners in accordance with § 704(c) principles. See Chapter 5.

Finally, the regulations under § 83 provide that the transferor is entitled to a deduction (to the extent otherwise allowable under § 162 or § 212) equal to the amount includible in the service provider's income. Reg. § 1.83–6(a)(1), (4) (capital expenditures). If the expense is currently deductible, § 83 allows the deduction for the transferor's taxable year "in which or with which ends the taxable year of the service provider in which such amount is includible as compensation." Reg. § 1.83–6(a)(1); but cf. Reg. § 1.721–1(b)(2) (treating the property transfer as a "guaranteed payment" deductible under § 707(c) for the partnership's taxable year in which paid or incurred). Under § 704(b), the amount of the deduction (or capital expenditure) should be specially allocated entirely to the other partners. See § 706(d)(2).

Example (6): In exchange for services, C receives a vested 1/3 capital interest in the AB general partnership which has the following balance sheet:

	Basis	Value		Basis	Value
Assets			Capital		
Cash	$3,000	$3,000	A	$3,000	$4,500
Land	3,000	4,500	B	4,800	4,500
Accounts			Total	$7,800	$9,000
Receivable	1,800	1,500			
Total	$7,800	$9,000			

In exchange for their respective partnership interests, A contributed land with a basis of $3,000 and a fair market value of $4,500, and B contributed cash of $3,000 and accounts receivable with a basis of $1,800 and a fair market value of $1,500. The AB partnership's income and expenses have been equal in each year since inception, and the value of its assets has remained constant. Since C's 1/3 capital interest is received in exchange for services rather than property, C must recognize ordinary income under § 61 equal to the fair market value of her partnership interest, or $3,000 (1/3 of the $9,000 fair market value of the partnership's assets). Under § 83(a), this amount is includible in C's income in the year in which she receives the interest, since it is not subject to a substantial risk of forfeiture.

Under the cash-compensation analogy, the partnership would recognize no gain or loss on the deemed transfer of $3,000 cash to C. The prevailing view, however, is that the deemed transfer triggers recognition of gain or loss to the partnership, which is treated as transferring an undivided 1/3 interest in the land, accounts receivable and cash. Under § 704(c), the partnership's built-in gain of $500 on the deemed sale of 1/3 of the land ($1,500 fair market value less $1,000 basis) is allocated entirely to A, increasing A's outside basis to $3,500. § 705(a)(1)(A). Similarly, the partnership's built-in loss of $100 on the deemed sale of 1/3 of the accounts receivable ($600 basis less $500 fair market value) is allocated entirely to B, decreasing B's outside basis to $4,700. § 705(a)(2)(A).

C is treated as receiving assets in the deemed transfer with a basis equal to their fair market value ($3,000) and recontributing the same assets to the partnership in a tax-free § 721 transfer in exchange for a 1/3 partnership interest. Under § 722, C's outside basis is $3,000 (the adjusted basis of the contributed property). Under § 723, the partnership takes a fair-market-value basis in the recontributed assets ($1,000 cash, land worth $1,500 and accounts receivable worth $500). If the cost of C's services is currently deductible to the partnership, the $3,000 deduction is allocated equally to A and B, leaving them with outside bases of $2,000 and $3,200, respectively.

Immediately after C's admission, the ABC partnership has the following balance sheet:

		Basis	Value		Basis	Value
Assets				Capital		
Cash		$3,000	$3,000	A	$2,000	$3,000
Land	(⅔)	2,000	3,000	B	3,200	3,000
	(⅓)	1,500	1,500	C	3,000	3,000
Accounts				Total	$8,200	$9,000
Receivable	(⅔)	1,200	1,000			
	(⅓)	500	500			
Total		$8,200	$9,000			

Each partner's book capital account is restated to reflect an equal 1/3 share of the fair market value of the partnership's assets ($3,000). If the partnership sold the land for $4,500, immediately after C's admission, A would recognize the remaining $1,000 of built-in gain, increasing A's outside basis (and tax capital account) to $3,000. Similarly, if the partnership immediately sold the accounts receivable for $1,500, B would recognize the remaining built-in loss of $200, decreasing B's outside basis (and tax capital account) to $3,000. Under § 704(c) principles, no portion of the built-in gain or loss would be allocated to C.

The deductibility of the partnership's deemed payment to C depends upon the nature of C's services (i.e., ordinary and necessary business expenses or capital expenditure). For example, if C performed legal services incident to the creation of the partnership, the partnership would be required to capitalize the payment to C and could elect, under § 709(b), to amortize it over a 60–month period. See Chapter 3. Any amortization deductions attributable to the capital expenditure should be specially allocated to A and B, and would reduce their outside bases (and tax capital accounts) when taken into account for the partnership's tax accounting purposes. To balance the partnership's books, it may be necessary to reflect the capital expenditure as an increase in the book value of the partnership's fixed assets or as a separate partnership asset.

(e) Receipt of a Vested Profits Interest. Prior to *Diamond* (1974), receipt of a profits interest was generally treated as an open transaction. See Hale (1965). Since the service partner would be taxed on his share of partnership profits as earned, open-transaction treatment avoided valuation difficulties. Commentators viewed the negative implication of the parenthetical in the § 721 regulations as persuasive support for not taxing receipt of a "mere" profits interest. See Reg. § 1.721–1(b)(1) (distinguishing transfer of a capital interest). In *Diamond*, however, the analogy to compensation income was sufficiently compelling to warrant immediate taxation of the service partner's profits interest. *Diamond* involved a partnership that held a contract to purchase an office building; the taxpayer contributed no capital but obtained financing for the purchase in exchange for a 60% share of the profits to be realized from the building (after repayment of capital contributions). The taxpayer sold his 60% profits interest for $40,000 almost immediately after the formation of the partnership. Relying on the argument that the receipt of a profits interest was nontaxable under § 721, the taxpayer reported a $40,000 short-term capital gain on the sale of his interest which he used to offset capital losses from other sources.

Both the Tax Court and the Seventh Circuit, however, held that the taxpayer recognized ordinary income under § 61 on receipt of the profits interest. Noting the "opaque draftsmanship" of Reg. § 1.721–1(b)(1), the Tax Court concluded that nothing in the § 721 regulations shielded a partner from immediate taxation on receipt of a profits interest for *past* services. In affirming the Tax Court's decision, the Seventh Circuit observed that the value of the particular profits interest in question could be readily determined (in light of its prompt resale for $40,000), but stated that "[s]urely in many if not the typical situation [a profits interest] will have only a speculative value, if any," and urged the government to issue regulations to address this area.

For several years after *Diamond*, the Service failed to clarify the treatment of a service partner who receives a profits interest. The proposed § 721 regulations, issued shortly after *Diamond*, merely reiterated the relevant language from the former regulations. See Prop. Reg. § 1.721–1(b)(1). A subsequent General Counsel Memorandum indicated that *Diamond* might be inapplicable if a partner received a profits interest as compensation for *future* services. GCM 36346. The General Counsel Memorandum analogized a profits interest to an "unfunded, unsecured promise to pay deferred compensation," which is not considered "property" for purposes of § 83 and is thus not taxable when received. Reg. § 1.83–3(e). Courts generally treated a profits interest as property for purposes of § 83, but arrived at a taxable value of zero under the deemed-liquidation test. See St. John (1983); Kenroy, Inc. (1984).

In *Campbell*, however, the Tax Court applied § 83 to receipt of a profits interest and required immediate recognition of income. Campbell (1990). The taxpayer in *Campbell* received "special limited partnership interests" as compensation for services in connection with the formation and syndication of several partnerships. The Tax Court held that the partnership interests were taxable upon receipt and determined their value based on the terms of other sales and on the discounted present value of projected future tax benefits and cash flow.

On appeal, the Eighth Circuit reversed the Tax Court's decision, holding that the profits interests were "without fair market value" because of their speculative nature. Campbell (1991). The court also expressed "doubt" that the taxpayer's profits interests were taxable on receipt, but failed to resolve the issue as a matter of law. It found "some justification" for treating receipt of capital and profits interests differently for nonrecognition purposes. The court's narrow holding on valuation may be less important than its dictum concerning the interplay of §§ 721 and 707. According to the court, § 707(a)(2)(A) would arguably be unnecessary if profits interests were taxable upon receipt.

The Eighth Circuit's *Campbell* decision allayed widespread concern that receipt of a profits interest would be treated as a taxable event; it left the substantive law unsettled, however. The Eighth Circuit did not expressly adopt the taxpayer's theory that receipt of a profits interest is a nonrealization event and therefore nontaxable under §§ 61 and 83. This approach would permit the general nonrecognition principles of § 721 to override the § 83 treatment of compensatory transfers, and would leave § 707 as the exclusive means of taxing a service-related transfer of a partnership profits interest that falls outside the normal distributive share rules of § 702. See Chapter 7.

In *Campbell*, the government argued unsuccessfully that the taxpayer had received the profits interests for services rendered in his capacity as an employee of his corporate employer (a real estate brokerage and consulting firm). The *Campbell* decision nevertheless leaves open the possibility of imposing an immediate tax, under § 83, on a service provider who receives a vested profits interest as an employee or independent contractor. Section 83 would defer the taxable event only if the profits interest were treated as an "unfunded, unsecured" obligation to pay deferred compensation. Moreover, a purported profits interest might be treated as a disguised capital interest if the service provider received an interest in partnership capital. See Diamond (1974); GCM 36346.

In response to *Campbell*, the Service reconsidered its position and issued Revenue Procedure 93–27. Although this guidance does not purport to represent the Service's view of the substantive law, it ensures that most transfers of profits interests will escape immediate taxation. Accordingly, the Service will treat as a nontaxable event (for both the recipient and the partnership) receipt of a profits interest "for the provision of services to or for the benefit of a partnership in a partner capacity or in anticipation of being a partner." Rev. Proc. 93–27. This general rule is subject to three exceptions. Thus, receipt of a profits interest will be taxable if (i) the interest relates to a "substantially certain and predictable" income stream, (ii) the recipient disposes of the interest within two years of receipt, or (iii) the interest is a limited partnership interest in a publicly-traded partnership (within the meaning of § 7704(b)). Whether services are rendered in a partner capacity will presumably be determined by reference to the rules of § 707. See Chapter 7. If the services are performed in a nonpartner capacity (e.g., as an employee or an independent contractor), receipt of the interest will be taxable under the normal rules of §§ 61 and 83.

In the unlikely event that receipt of a vested profits interest is taxable, the consequences at the partner and partnership levels should be determined by analogy to receipt of a vested capital interest. The service partner should be treated as receiving compensation equal to the fair market value of the profits interest. Under *P.G. Lake* principles, the partnership may be treated as having made an anticipatory assignment of income (i.e., a share of future profits), triggering immediate recognition of gain to the other partners. P.G. Lake (1958). If the partnership is entitled to a current deduction for the value of the services, the partnership's gain and deduction will wash. The partnership should also be permitted to amortize the basis of the income interest which has already been taxed to the service partner. Under § 704(c) principles, the amortization deductions (up to the previously taxed amount) should be allocated entirely to the service partner.

(f) Receipt of a Nonvested Capital or Profits Interest. If a partnership capital or profits interest is subject to a substantial risk of forfeiture (e.g., because the recipient's rights are conditioned upon performance of future services), the taxable event is deferred until the interest becomes substantially vested. Until the service provider recognizes income, the § 83 regulations treat the transferor as the owner of the transferred property for tax purposes. Reg. § 1.83–1(a)(1); see Reg. § 1.83–6(a)(1) (deferring the transferor's deduction until the recipient's inclusion). Under § 83(b), however, the recipient may elect (within 30 days of the transfer) to include the value of nonvested property in income at the time of receipt. A recipient who makes a § 83(b) election does not recognize any additional compensation income when the property becomes substantially vested. Reg. § 1.83–2(a). If the property is subsequently forfeited before it becomes substantially vested, no deduction is allowed to the recipient. § 83(b)(1) (flush language). A § 83(b) election limits the amount recognized as compensation income and ensures that subsequent appreciation in the transferred property is eligible for favorable capital gain treatment. The restoration of a significant capital gain preference enhances the importance of making a § 83(b) election if the transferred property is expected to increase in value prior to vesting. In the absence of a § 83(b) election, the fair-market-value determination and the taxable event will occur when the transferred interest becomes substantially vested.

Example (7): In exchange for services, C receives a 1/3 nonvested capital interest in the AB partnership in 2000, when the partnership's only asset is a building with a basis of $90,000 and a fair market value of $150,000. In 2006, when C's interest vests, the building has a basis of $30,000 and a fair market value of $225,000. If C makes a § 83(b) election, she will recognize $50,000 ordinary income (1/3 of the $150,000 fair market value of the building) in 2000. In the same year, the partnership will recognize $20,000 of gain (1/3 of the $60,000 appreciation in the building), and deduct (or capitalize) the $50,000 paid to C. If C forfeits her interest in 2001, the partnership will be required to include $50,000 in gross income and C will receive no deduction. See Reg. § 1.83–6(c) (transferor must include amount of prior deduction in income in the year of forfeiture). If C does not make a § 83(b) election, the taxable event will be deferred until 2006 when C's interest becomes substantially vested. At that time, C will recognize $75,000 of ordinary income (1/3 of the $225,000 fair market value of the building). In 2006, the partnership will recognize $65,000 of gain (1/3 of the $195,000 appreciation in the building), and deduct (or capitalize) the $75,000 paid to C.

Unless the recipient makes a § 83(b) election, the § 83 regulations treat the transferor as the "owner" of the transferred property until the time of vesting. This treatment may make a § 83(b) election attractive as a means of avoiding the potentially harsh consequences resulting from the interaction of Subchapter K and § 83. If the service provider is not treated as a partner until his interest vests, his distributive share of income and loss must be reallocated to the other partners. Any cash distributions from the partnership to the service provider will constitute ordinary income (rather than potentially tax-free basis recovery under the distribution rules of § 731).

CHAPTER 3

PARTNERSHIP TAX ACCOUNTING

§ 1. Overview

The rules for determining a partner's share of taxable income or loss from partnership operations represent a blend of entity and aggregate principles. Although a partnership is not taxed as a separate entity, partnership taxable income is computed in a manner similar to that of an individual. §§ 701, 703(a). Under § 702, each partner is taxed separately on his distributive share of partnership income, gain, loss, deduction and credit. The character of items included in a partner's distributive share is determined at the partnership level. § 702(b). Most elections affecting the computation of partnership income must be made by the partnership. § 703(b). Moreover, the partnership's taxable year is determined as if the partnership were a separate taxpayer. § 706(b).

A partner's basis in his partnership interest is initially determined by reference to his investment in the partnership and subsequently adjusted to reflect his distributive share of partnership income or loss and distributions from the partnership. § 705(a). Since outside basis cannot fall below zero, any excess losses allocated to a partner are suspended until the partner's outside basis rises above zero. § 704(d). In addition, a partner's ability to deduct his distributive share of partnership losses may be subject to further restrictions under the at-risk and passive loss rules. §§ 465, 469.

§ 2. Determining Taxable Income

(a) **Partnership Taxable Income.** In computing a partnership's taxable income, § 703(a)(2) disallows deductions for certain items, including personal exemptions, foreign taxes, charitable contributions, net operating losses and additional itemized deductions. Since these items are allowed directly to the partners on their separate returns, § 703(a)(2) is necessary to prevent a "double" deduction. For example, charitable contributions made by a partnership do not reduce partnership taxable income but instead pass through to the partners on their separate returns. §§ 703(a)(2)(C), 702(a)(4). Similarly, § 212 investment expenses are not deductible at the partnership level but may be allowed to the individual partners (subject to the 2% floor for "miscellaneous itemized deductions"). §§ 703(a)(2)(E), 702(a)(7) and 67.

In computing its taxable income, a partnership must state separately certain items which may have different effects on a partner's taxable income depending on the partner's particular tax posture. Such separately-stated items include capital gains and losses, § 1231 gains and losses, charitable contributions, dividends eligible for the corporate dividends-received deduction, foreign taxes and any other item prescribed by regulations. § 702(a)(1)-(7). The regulations require separate statement of various specific items (e.g., § 111 tax-benefit recoveries, § 165(d) wagering gains and losses, and § 212 investment expenses). Proposed regulations would clarify that an item must be separately stated if such treatment "would result in an income tax liability for that partner, or any other person, different from that which would result if that partner did not take the item into account separately." Prop. Reg. § 1.702–1(a)(8)(ii). Items of partnership taxable income or loss which are not required to be separately stated fall into a residual category referred to as "bottom-line" items. § 702(a)(8). On his individual return, each partner reports his distributive share of separately-stated and bottom-line items as shown on the partnership information return for the partner (Schedule K–1).

A partner must include his distributive share of partnership income in gross income whether or not he has received any distributions from the partnership. § 702(c). He is taxable on his distributive share even though his right to receive distributions may be contingent or forfeitable. See Basye (1973) (nonvested contributions to retirement plan). Assignment-of-income principles may be relevant in determining whether income should be treated as earned by the partnership or an individual partner. In *Schneer*, a retired law partner was entitled to certain fees from his former firm for client referrals and consulting services; upon joining two other firms, he was required to turn over the fees to the new partnerships. Schneer (1991). The court found that the fees were not "accruable" by the partner prior to the assignment; accordingly, the new partnerships properly treated the fees as partnership income allocable among the partners in accordance with their distributive shares.

(b) Entity–Level Characterization. Any item of partnership income, loss, deduction or credit included in a partner's distributive share has the same character "as if such item were realized directly from the source from which realized by the partnership, or incurred in the same manner as incurred by the partnership." § 702(b). While somewhat opaque, this provision has been interpreted to require that the character of partnership items be determined at the partnership level, without regard to the partners' individual characteristics. See Reg. § 1.702–1(b). For example, if a partnership sells property which is a non-capital asset in the hands of the partnership but would be a capital asset in the hands of a partner, any gain which is ordinary in character at the partnership level will retain its character when passed through to the partner. See, e.g., Podell (1970); see also Rev. Rul. 68–79 (§ 1231 gain determined at partnership level and passed through as separately-stated item). Entity-level characterization is subject, however, to the special rules of § 724 with respect to certain categories of contributed property. See Chapter 2. A partnership is not allowed a net operating loss under § 172, since it is not a taxable entity. Instead, partnership losses pass through to the partners, subject to the limitations of §§ 704(d), 465 and 469. If a partner's share of partnership business losses exceeds his other income, the excess is treated as a net operating loss carryback or carry-forward at the partner level.

Significant tax consequences may turn on whether income is determined at the partnership level or the partner level. In *Brown Group*, the issue was whether a partner's distributive share of income from a foreign partnership should be characterized as "controlled-foreign-corporation" (CFC) income (as defined in subpart F of the Code). Brown Group (1996). The income would clearly have been CFC income if earned directly by the partner (Brown Cayman) and therefore includible in income by Brown Cayman's parent (a U.S. corporation). In a controversial decision, however, the Eighth Circuit held that the income was not CFC income; it refused to ignore the foreign partnership as an entity or attribute its activities directly to each of its partners. The Service has rejected *Brown Group* as inconsistent with the purpose of subpart F, which limits U.S. deferral of certain CFC income. See I.R.S. Notice 96–39. *Brown Group* illustrates one type of transaction that may be challenged under the abuse-of-entity rule of the § 701 regulations.

(c) Partnership Elections. To ensure consistency, § 703(b) generally requires that any elections affecting taxable income be made at the partnership level. For example, if partnership property is involuntarily converted, the partnership must make the § 1033 election to acquire replacement property and must take title to such property. See Demirjian (1972) (attempted § 1033 election by partners invalid; receipt of conversion proceeds treated as a taxable event). The operation of § 703(b) may be especially harsh if the partners are unaware of the existence of a partnership for federal tax purposes. If the partners properly elect out of partnership status under § 761(a), however, they should be able to make independent elections.

Section 703(b) provides that each partner must make separately the elections under § 108(b)(5) and (c)(3) relating to discharge of indebtedness. Income from discharge of partnership indebtedness is not excludible at the partnership level even if the partnership is insolvent. § 108(d)(6); cf. Stackhouse (1971) (superseded by § 108(d)(6)). Instead, the discharge income passes through to the partners as an item of partnership income and each partner then applies the rules of § 108 based on his particular circumstances. Each partner's outside basis is increased by his distributive share of the discharge income, and decreased by the deemed § 752 cash distribution resulting from the reduction in his share of partnership liabilities. §§ 705(a)(1)-(2), 733. These upward and downward basis adjustments will exactly offset each other only if the discharge income is allocated among the partners in the same ratio as the partners share the discharged debt under § 752. Rev. Rul. 92–97. If a partner's deemed § 752(b) cash distribution exceeds his distributive share of the discharge income, gain may be triggered under the distribution rules of § 731. See Chapter 9.

Under § 108(c), a taxpayer may elect to exclude from income his share of debt discharge from "qualified real property business indebtedness." § 108(a)(1)(D), (c). If 108(c) applies, the amount of the debt discharge reduces the basis of the taxpayer's depreciable real property. § 108(c)(1)(A), (c)(3). For this purpose, an electing partner's partnership interest is treated as depreciable real property to the extent of his share of the basis of the partnership's depreciable real property, provided that the partnership agrees to a corresponding reduction in its inside basis. § 1017(b)(3)(C); Reg. § 1.1017–1(g). Similar rules apply if a bankrupt or insolvent partner makes an election under § 108(b)(5) to reduce the basis of depreciable property (in lieu of reducing other tax attributes). § 108(b)(5).

§ 3. Adjustments to Outside Basis

(a) General. A partner's outside basis is subject to upward and downward adjustments which reflect partnership operations. Outside basis is increased by additional capital contributions from a partner and by his distributive share of partnership taxable income and tax-exempt income; it is decreased (but not below zero) by distributions to the partner and by his distributive share of partnership losses and partnership expenditures that are neither deductible in computing partnership taxable income nor properly chargeable to capital account ("nondeductible noncapital expenditures''). §§ 705(a), 722 and 733. Nondeductible noncapital expenditures include illegal bribes and kickbacks, expenses relating to tax-exempt income, and disallowed losses between related parties. In addition, the partnership's charitable contributions and § 212 investment expenses reduce outside basis even though the partner may not be able to use the deduction on his individual return. See Rev. Rul. 96–11 (outside basis reduced by partner's share of the partnership's basis in appreciated property contributed to charity).

These adjustments are necessary to ensure that the partner's share of economic gain or loss will not give rise to a double benefit or burden for tax purposes. The upward adjustment for a partner's distributive share of partnership taxable and tax-exempt income ensures that the partner will not be taxed again on the same amount when he subsequently receives distributions or sells his partnership interest. Conversely, the downward adjustment for a partner's distributive share of partnership losses and nondeductible noncapital expenditures prevents such items from artificially reducing the partner's gain (or increasing his loss) when he subsequently sells his partnership interest.

A current expenditure (whether or not deductible) reduces partnership assets available for distribution, and a corresponding reduction in outside basis preserves parity with the partnership's inside basis in the remaining partnership assets. Outside basis is reduced under § 705(a)(2)(A) by the amount of any deductible current expenditure (e.g., an operating loss) and under § 705(a)(2)(B) for any nondeductible current expenditure (e.g., a fine under § 162(f)). By contrast, a capital expenditure represents a mere change of form rather than a reduction of assets held by the partnership. For example, if a partnership purchases a building for $100,000, the cost of the building is capitalized; the partnership's balance sheet will show that $100,000 of partnership assets previously held in the form of cash are now held in the form of a building. If a capital expenditure generates cost recovery deductions (e.g., depreciation), however, the deductions will be reflected in the basis of the capital asset on the partnership's books and in the partners' outside bases.

Example (1): In exchange for a 1/3 partnership interest in the ABC general partnership, A contributes land with an adjusted basis of $50,000 and a fair market value of $100,000. During the first year, ABC receives $60,000 of taxable income and $30,000 of tax-exempt income, and pays $75,000 of deductible current expenditures and $21,000 of nondeductible noncapital expenditures. A receives a cash distribution of $5,000 at year end, which is treated as a tax-free recovery of basis under § 731. See Chapter 9. A's outside basis is adjusted as follows:

Initial outside basis (§ 722):	$50,000
Increases for A's distributive share of	
taxable income (§ 705(a)(1)(A))	20,000
tax-exempt income (§ 705(a)(1)(B))	10,000
Decreases for cash distribution (§ 733)	(5,000)

Decrease for A's distributive share of
   deductible expenditures (§ 705(a)(2)(A))   (25,000)
   nondeductible expenditures (§ 705(a)(2)(B))   (7,000)
Adjusted outside basis: $43,000

For purposes of the basis adjustment rules, gains and losses are taken into account only when recognized by the partnership. Thus, a partner's outside basis is not increased by his share of the realized gain on nonrecognition transactions (e.g., a § 1031 like-kind exchange) until the partnership recognizes such gain. If a basis adjustment were permitted immediately, a partner could avoid tax on his share of the gain by selling his partnership interest (with an inflated basis) before the partnership recognized any gain.

(b) Organization and Syndication Expenses. Under § 709(a), no current deduction is allowed to the partnership or any partner for "any amounts paid or incurred to organize a partnership or to promote the sale of (or to sell) an interest in such partnership." Section 709(b) provides, however, that a partnership may elect to amortize organizational expenses over a 60–month period. Organizational expenses are defined as any expenditures which (i) are incident to creation of the partnership, (ii) are chargeable to capital account, and (iii) would otherwise be amortizable if the partnership had an ascertainable life. The regulations provide as examples of organizational expenses "[l]egal fees for services incident to organization of the partnership, such as negotiation and preparation of a partner-

ship agreement; accounting fees for services incident to the organization of the partnership; and
filing fees." Reg. § 1.709–2(a).

The regulations specifically provide that amortizable organizational expenses do not include (i) expenses connected with acquiring assets for the partnership or transferring assets to the partnership, or
(ii) syndication expenses. Id. Syndication expenses
are defined as expenses connected with issuing and
marketing partnership interests, including brokerage and registration fees, legal fees incurred by the
underwriter or issuer for securities or disclosure
advice, and the costs of preparing and printing
offering material. Reg. § 1.709–2(b). The Service
has ruled that the cost of a tax opinion included in
the offering material is a syndication expense. Rev.
Rul. 88–4. Syndication expenses (and organizational
expenses which the partnership does not elect to
amortize under § 709(b)) are properly chargeable to
capital account and hence should not reduce outside
basis under § 705(a)(2)(B). See Rev. Rul. 87–111;
Rev. Rul. 85–32.

(c) Alternative Rule of § 705(b). As an alternative to the mechanical adjustments of § 705(a), a
partner's outside basis may in unusual circumstances be determined "by reference to his proportionate share of the adjusted basis of partnership
property" upon a termination of the partnership.
§ 705(b). The alternative rule reflects the underlying principle that the partnership's aggregate inside
basis will generally equal the partners' aggregate
outside bases. At the inception of the partnership,

the substituted basis provisions of §§ 722 and 723 generally ensure that inside basis and outside basis will initially be equivalent. See Chapter 2. The basis adjustment rules generally preserve this relationship, since the events that give rise to changes in the partners' outside bases under § 705(a) reflect corresponding changes in the partnership's inside basis. Under the alternative rule, adjustments may be necessary to reflect any § 704(c) allocations and other events such as transfers of partnership interests and distributions of partnership property. Reg. § 1.705–1(b).

(d) Events Requiring Basis Determination. Although a partner's outside basis is constantly subject to adjustment, a partner is required to determine his outside basis "only when necessary for the determination of his tax liability or that of any other person." Reg. § 1.705–1(a). If the partnership has losses, a partner generally must determine his outside basis at the end of the partnership's taxable year in order to apply the § 704(d) loss limitation, discussed below. Outside basis determinations may also be necessary if a partner's interest is sold or liquidated or if a partner receives a current distribution of property or cash.

§ 4.   Limitations on Losses

(a) Section 704(d) Loss Limitation. Under § 704(d), a partner may deduct his distributive share of partnership loss only to the extent of his outside basis at the end of the partnership's taxable year in which the loss was incurred. The § 704(d) loss limitation operates in conjunction with § 705(a)(2), which prohibits reduction of a partner's outside basis below zero. If a partnership's overall loss for the taxable year comprises items of different classes (e.g., capital and ordinary losses), a proportionate share of each class is suspended under § 704(d). Reg. § 1.704–1(d)(2). For example, if a partner's distributive share of losses consists of $7,500 ordinary losses and $2,500 capital losses and the partner's outside basis is only $6,000, the $4,000 suspended losses will comprise $3,000 ordinary losses and $1,000 capital losses.

Any losses suspended under § 704(d) are carried forward indefinitely until they can be used in a subsequent year. Suspended losses can be deducted at the end of the next succeeding partnership year in which the partner's outside basis rises above zero (before taking current losses into account). Reg. § 1.704–1(d)(1). For example, a partner's outside basis may be increased above zero by additional capital contributions, undistributed partnership profits, or increases in his share of partnership liabilities. A partner generally cannot increase his outside basis by contributing his own note, since such a note has a zero basis. See Chapter 2. However, an obligation to contribute additional capital may increase a partner's share of partnership liabilities under § 752, thereby indirectly increasing outside basis. See Chapter 6.

Example (2): At the beginning of the partnership's taxable year, A has a suspended ordinary loss of $1,500 and a suspended long-term capital loss of

$500. A's distributive share for the partnership's current year consists of a long-term capital loss of $1,000, a short-term capital loss of $1,500 and taxable income of $3,000. A's outside basis at year end (before taking into account losses for the current year) is increased to $3,000 to reflect A's distributive share of the partnership's taxable income. For purposes of applying the § 704(d) limitation, A's total losses for the taxable year are the sum of A's distributive share of the losses for the current year plus her suspended losses. Reg. § 1.704–1(d)(2) (last sentence). Thus, A's total losses of $4,500 comprise $1,500 ordinary loss (carried forward), $1,500 long-term capital loss ($1,000 current and $500 carried forward) and $1,500 short-term capital loss (current). A offsets a total of $3,000 of losses against her outside basis, leaving A with an outside basis of zero. One-third of A's total losses in each class ($500 ordinary loss, $500 long-term capital loss, and $500 short-term capital loss) are suspended and carried forward to subsequent years.

(b) Ordering Rules. The ordering rules for basis adjustments are important in determining the treatment of distributions and losses. The upward and downward adjustments for a partner's distributive share of partnership income and loss are taken into account as of the last day of the partnership's taxable year; the downward adjustment for each distribution, by contrast, is taken into account as of the date of the distribution. If the partner receives a cash distribution in excess of his outside basis at the time of the distribution, the excess amount is generally taxable under § 731(a)(1). See Chapter 9. The regulations, however, treat "advances" or "drawings" against the partner's distributive share as current distributions made on the last day of the partnership's taxable year rather than the date of payment. Reg. § 1.731–1(a)(1)(ii); Rev. Rul. 94–4 (deemed § 752(b) cash distribution treated as advance or draw). In effect, a partnership advance or drawing is treated as a "loan" from the partnership to the partner. If the amount of the loan exceeds the partner's distributive share of partnership profits, the partner must repay the excess at year end to avoid triggering gain under § 731.

Example (3): At the beginning of the partnership's taxable year, partner A has an outside basis of zero and receives monthly "advances" of $1,000 totalling $12,000 for the year. A's distributive share of partnership profits for the year is $14,000. At year end, A's outside basis is first increased to $14,000 to reflect A's distributive share of partnership profits, and then decreased to $2,000 to reflect the $12,000 distribution. §§ 705(a), 733. If A's distributive share of partnership profits for the year were only $9,000, A could retain no more than $9,000 of advances without triggering taxable gain.

In summary, as of the last day of the partnership's taxable year, each partner's outside basis is first increased by his distributive share of partnership income and then decreased for year-end distributions to him, and finally decreased (subject to the § 704(d) limitation) by his distributive share of losses and any losses carried forward from previous years. Reg. § 1.704–1(d)(2); Rev. Rul. 66–94. If a partner lacks sufficient outside basis (after upward adjustment for his distributive share of current partnership income) to cover year-end cash distributions and his distributive share of partnership losses, the ordering rule maximizes the amount of cash that can be distributed tax free to the partner and minimizes the amount of losses that he can deduct in the current year.

Example (4): At the beginning of the partnership's taxable year, partner A has an outside basis of $10,000; A's share of partnership income for the year is zero and his share of partnership losses is $5,000; and A receives a cash distribution of $10,-000 on the last day of the partnership's taxable year. Under the ordering rules, the $10,000 distribution reduces A's outside basis before the loss is taken into account. Thus, A's outside basis is reduced to zero as a result of the distribution, and the entire $5,000 of loss is suspended.

(c) Transfer of § 704(d) Suspended Losses. Upon a sale or exchange of a partnership interest, a partner should not be permitted to deduct losses suspended under § 704(d). A suspended loss often means that a partner's capital account has a deficit balance which he may be required to restore. See Chapter 4. If a partner restores his negative capital account by contributing additional cash, he should be allowed to use the suspended loss. But see Sennett (1985) (loss carryover denied where partner repaid amount after withdrawing from partnership).

The purchaser, who takes a cost basis in his partnership interest under § 1012, is not permitted to use the seller's suspended losses. See § 742. The consequences to the transferee should be the same if the interest is acquired upon the transferor's death, since the basis of the partnership interest will be stepped up (or down) to fair market value. §§ 742, 1014. Under §§ 743 and 754, the partnership may elect to adjust the aggregate basis in its assets to reflect the § 1012 or § 1014 basis of the transferee partner.

If a partner instead disposes of his partnership interest by gift, the transferee should arguably be permitted to use the suspended loss. In effect, the transferee steps into the transferor's shoes for purposes of determining the transferee's proportionate share of inside basis. Since the suspended loss has already reduced the partnership's basis in its assets, it may be necessary to permit the transferee to use the suspended loss in order to avoid a permanent disparity between inside and outside basis. The policy underlying § 1015, restricting transfers of built-in losses from a donor to a donee, should not apply since the transferred partnership interest is likely to have a fair market value in excess of its zero basis.

(d) Other Limitations. The at-risk and passive loss limitations impose additional restrictions on a partner's ability to deduct losses passed through from a partnership. Even if a partner has sufficient outside basis to absorb his share of partnership loss under § 704(d), the loss may nevertheless be suspended under the at-risk rules of § 465 or the passive loss rules of § 469. Any losses suspended under § 465 or § 469 are carried over indefinitely to subsequent years until a deduction is allowed. A partner's distributive share of losses reduces his outside basis under § 705(a)(2) even though the loss is suspended under § 465 or § 469.

§ 5. At–Risk Rules

(a) General. Under § 465, an individual partner may deduct losses from business and investment activities (including real estate activities) only to the extent of the aggregate amount the taxpayer has "at risk" in the activity at the close of the taxable year. A partner's amount at risk is initially equal to the amount of personal funds and the adjusted basis of unencumbered property which he contributes to the activity. § 465(b)(1); see Prop. Reg. §§ 1.465–22(a), 1.465–23(a). A partner's amount at risk is increased by his distributive share of partnership income (including tax-exempt income) and decreased by distributions and his distributive share of partnership losses. Prop. Reg. §§ 1.465–22(b)–(c), 1.465–23(c) and 1.465–24(b)(2)(i). Amounts borrowed for use in an activity increase a partner's amount at risk only to the extent that he is personally liable for repayment of the borrowed amount or has pledged property not used in the activity as security. § 465(b)(2). Amounts borrowed with respect to certain activities are not considered at risk if the lender has an interest (other than as a creditor) in the activity or is related to a person (other than the taxpayer) who has such an interest. § 465(b)(3). In addition, the partner must not be "protected against loss through ... guarantees, stop loss agreements, or other similar arrangements." § 465(b)(4).

Under a special rule applicable to the holding of real property, a partner is considered at risk to the extent of his share of "qualified nonrecourse financing" (e.g., a commercial loan) which is secured by real property used in the activity. § 465(b)(6). Qualified nonrecourse financing does not include any amount borrowed from (i) a related person, (ii) a person from whom the taxpayer acquired the real property held in the activity (or a related person), or (iii) a person who receives a fee with respect to the taxpayer's investment (or a related person). § 465(b)(6)(B)(ii), (D)(i); see § 49(a)(1)(D)(iv). These rules are intended to discourage overvaluation of property by means of inflated nonrecourse acquisition debt from related parties, sellers, promoters and brokers. A loan from a related party may nevertheless be considered qualified nonrecourse borrowing if the loan is "commercially reasonable and on substantially the same terms as loans involving unrelated persons." § 465(b)(6)(D)(ii).

A partner's share of qualified nonrecourse financing is determined under the § 752 liability-sharing rules. § 465(b)(6)(C). See Chapter 6. An entity such as an LLC may be personally liable for a liability, even though none of the individual members have personal liability. Since the personal liability of the entity may be meaningless in this situation, such a liability may nevertheless be treated as qualified nonrecourse financing. Reg. § 1.465–27. A portion of a liability for which no person has personal liability may be treated separately. Id.

If losses exceed the partner's amount at risk at the end of the taxable year, such excess losses are suspended and carried forward indefinitely to subsequent years until the partner's amount at risk is sufficient to absorb them. § 465(a)(2); Prop. Reg. § 1.465–2. If a partner's amount at risk falls below zero (e.g., as a result of a cash distribution), the partner must include in gross income an amount equal to his negative amount at risk. § 465(e)(1)(A). The "recaptured" amount is treated as a suspended loss and a deduction is allowed in subsequent years to the extent that the taxpayer's amount at risk rises above zero. § 465(e)(1)(B).

(b) Ultimate Liability Standard. In determining a partner's amount at risk, courts have looked to ultimate liability. For example, a guarantee of an otherwise nonrecourse liability increases the guarantor's amount at risk to the extent that he is ultimately liable. See, e.g., Abramson (1986). By contrast, a limited partner's guarantee of a partnership recourse debt does not increase the limited partner's amount at risk if he is subrogated to the creditor's rights against the general partner. See, e.g., Brand (1983). In *Melvin*, the court held that the taxpayer was at risk for his share of a partnership liability to the extent of his deferred obligation to contribute additional funds to the partnership. Melvin (1987).

In *Pritchett*, the Ninth Circuit rejected the government's argument that the limited partners' deferred contribution obligations in several oil and gas partnerships were "too contingent" to generate amounts at risk with respect to a partnership recourse promissory note; according to the court, the limited partners were ultimately liable because "economic reality" indicated that the general partner would enforce the contribution obligation. Pritchett (1987). On remand to the Tax Court, however, the government was able to show that the limited partners were not at risk with respect to one of the five partnerships because the lender had an interest other than as a creditor in the partnership's activity. See Pritchett (1989).

The preamble to the § 752 regulations warns that no inference may be drawn for purposes of § 465 from the economic risk of loss analysis under the liability-sharing rules. While §§ 465 and 752 both focus on ultimate liability, some differences may remain. For example, the § 752 regulations require that a partner's deferred contribution obligation be discounted to present value in some situations. Reg. § 1.752–2(g)(1). Courts have refused, however, to apply time-value-of-money considerations in determining a partner's amount at risk. See Follender (1987); Pritchett (1989).

(c) Operation. In applying § 465, it is necessary to determine a partner's amount at risk in each separate activity conducted by the partnership. Section 465(c)(2) specifies that activities with respect to certain types of property (e.g., motion pictures, oil and gas, and equipment leasing) must be treated separately. Most other types of activities constituting a trade or business are subject to the broad aggregation rules of § 465(c)(3)(B). See § 465(c)(3)(C).

Example (5): A is a limited partner in a partnership which engages in three separate activities: equipment leasing, oil exploration and snow-mobile manufacturing. A contributed $15,000 cash to the partnership, which used $5,000 in each activity. A has pledged her own personal property (other than her partnership interest), with a fair market value of $12,000, to secure her $20,000 share of the partnership's otherwise nonrecourse debt incurred in the equipment-leasing activity. In addition, the partnership has borrowed $30,000 from a wholly-owned subsidiary of the general partner in connection with the oil exploration activity, and A has agreed to indemnify the general partner to the extent partnership assets are insufficient to pay the $30,000 recourse debt; under § 752, A bears the economic risk of loss for the entire $30,000. See Chapter 6. During the year, A's distributive share comprises $25,000 of losses from equipment leasing, $20,000 of losses from oil exploration and $15,000 income from snow-mobile manufacturing.

Before taking into account losses for the year, A's outside basis is $80,000, consisting of A's $15,000 cash contribution, $50,000 share of partnership liabilities, and $15,000 distributive share of income. Since A's outside basis exceeds her distributive share of losses, the § 704(d) limitation does not apply. Under § 705(a), A's outside basis at year end is $35,000 ($80,000 less $45,000 loss). With respect to the equipment-leasing activity, A has a § 465 suspended loss of $8,000, i.e., the amount by which her $25,000 share of losses exceeds her $17,000 amount at risk ($5,000 cash contribution plus the $12,000 fair market value of the pledged property). With respect to the oil exploration activity, A has a § 465 suspended loss of $15,000, i.e., the amount by which her $20,000 share of losses exceeds her $5,000 amount at risk ($5,000 cash contribution). Under § 465(b)(3), A is not entitled to increase her amount at risk for her share of the partnership recourse debt because the lender is related to the general partner. See §§ 465(b)(3), 267(b)(3), 267(f) and 1563(a). A's distributive share of income increases her amount at risk in the partnership's snow-mobile manufacturing activity to $20,000 ($5,000 cash contribution plus $15,000 income).

(d) Transfer of § 465 Suspended Losses. If a partner sells or otherwise disposes of his partnership interest, his share of § 465 suspended losses does not carry over to the transferee. A taxable disposition of the transferor's partnership interest generally triggers sufficient gain, however, to offset any suspended losses because his share of liabilities is included in the amount realized. See Chapter 8. The proposed regulations under § 465 treat gain from sale of a partnership interest as "income from the activity," thereby increasing the partner's amount at risk. Prop. Reg. § 1.465–66(a). Even a gift of a partnership interest is likely to trigger offsetting gain because of the deemed relief of liabilities.

Example (6): At the beginning of 2000, A has an outside basis of $15,000 which is entirely attributable to his share of partnership nonrecourse liabilities. During 2000, A's $10,000 distributive share of partnership losses reduces A's outside basis to $5,000 at year end. Under § 465, the entire $10,000 of losses is suspended because A is not considered at risk for his share of nonrecourse liabilities. At the beginning of 2000, A transfers his partnership interest to his daughter for no consideration. As a result of the gift, A is deemed to realize an amount equal to his share of partnership liabilities, triggering a gain of $10,000 ($15,000 amount realized less $5,000 basis) equal to the amount of his suspended loss.

§ 6. Passive Loss Limitations

(a) **General.** Section 469(a) disallows "passive activity losses" of individuals and certain other taxpayers. Under § 469(d)(1), a passive activity loss is defined as the excess, if any, of aggregate losses from all passive activities for the taxable year over aggregate income from all passive activities for such year. See Temp. Reg. § 1.469–2T(b)(1). Thus, losses from passive activities may generally be used only to offset income from passive activities, not income from active sources or portfolio income (e.g., dividends, interest and royalties). See § 469(e)(1). Passive losses disallowed for the current taxable year are suspended and carried over indefinitely to subsequent years. § 469(b); see Temp. Reg. § 1.469–1T(f).

(b) Material Participation. A passive activity generally includes any trade or business in which the taxpayer does not "materially participate." § 469(c). Under the temporary regulations, a taxpayer is treated as "materially participating" in an activity for the taxable year if he satisfies any one of seven alternative tests (e.g., participation for more than 500 hours in the year or on a "regular, continuous, and substantial basis"). Temp. Reg. § 1.469–5T(a). Generally, participation includes work done in any capacity (other than as an investor) in an activity in which the taxpayer owns an interest; participation by a spouse is attributed to the taxpayer. § 469(h)(5); Temp. Reg. § 1.469–5T(f). Rental activities (defined generally as any activity in which payments are principally for the use of tangible property) are treated as passive activities without regard to material participation. § 469(c)(2), (j)(8). Section 469(c)(7) provides limited relief for individuals who provide personal services mostly in real property trades or businesses and perform at least 750 hours of work in such activities during the taxable year.

The temporary regulations also provide exceptions to the general rule that a limited partner is not treated as materially participating in an activity. See § 469(h)(2). A limited partner is treated as materially participating if (i) he participates in the activity for more than 500 hours during the taxable year; (ii) he materially participated in the activity during five of the ten preceding taxable years; or (iii) the activity is a personal service activity in which he participated for any three preceding taxable years. Temp. Reg. § 1.469–5T(e)(2). A limited partnership interest held by an individual general partner is not treated as a limited partnership interest for purposes of § 469. Temp. Reg. § 1.469–5T(e)(3)(ii).

(c) Oil and Gas Interests; Rental Real Estate. A working interest in oil or gas property is not treated as a passive activity if the taxpayer holds the interest directly or through an entity which does not limit the taxpayer's liability. § 469(c)(3)(A). A limited partnership interest does not qualify under this exception unless the limited partner is also a general partner. Temp. Reg. § 1.469–1T(e)(4)(v)(A)(1). A special rule permits an individual to offset nonpassive income by up to $25,000 of losses from rental real estate activities in which the individual "actively participates." § 469(i). An individual cannot qualify as an active participant unless the taxpayer (or his spouse) owns at least 10% of all interests in the activity. § 469(i)(6)(A). In addition, a person who owns only a limited partnership interest cannot qualify as an active participant. § 469(i)(6)(C).

(d) Coordination With §§ 704(d) and 465. Any item of deduction or loss from a passive activity that is disallowed under § 704(d) or § 465 is not taken into account in determining a taxpayer's passive activity loss for the taxable year. Temp. Reg. § 1.469–2T(d)(6). Instead, the § 469 limitations apply to such losses in the taxable year in which they are subsequently allowable under §§ 704(d) and 465. The character of the loss (i.e., active or passive) is determined by reference to the taxpayer's participation in the subsequent year. Reg. § 1.469–2(d)(8).

Example (7): At the beginning of 2000, A has a suspended loss of $600 that was previously disallowed under §§ 704(d) and 465. In 2000, A's outside basis and amount at risk increase to $2,000 (before taking any losses into account), and A's distributive share of partnership loss is $1,000. During 2000, A does not materially participate in the partnership's trade or business. For purposes of § 469, A's share of current losses ($1,000) plus his suspended loss ($600) are treated as passive activity deductions arising in 2000, i.e., the year in which such losses are allowed under §§ 704(d) and 465.

(e) Significant Participation. The temporary regulations recharacterize net income from certain passive activities as nonpassive. See Temp. Reg. § 1.469–2T(f); § 469(*l*)(3). These rules are intended to prevent taxpayers from structuring transactions to generate passive income that would otherwise offset unrelated passive losses. The recharacterization rules apply to any "significant participation" activity, defined generally as any trade or business activity in which the taxpayer participates more than 100 hours during the taxable year but does not materially participate. Temp. Reg. §§ 1.469–2T(f)(2), 1.469–5T(c)(2).

(f) Scope of Activity. The passive loss rules generally apply on an activity-by-activity basis. Activities that represent "an appropriate economic unit" may be combined into a single activity, except that rental and non-rental activities must normally be kept separate. Reg. § 1.469–4(c)(1), (d)(1). A broad definition of an activity may be desirable to meet the material participation test. However, a narrow definition may be advantageous in determining whether a taxpayer has disposed of his interest in an activity, as discussed below. As long as the treatment is consistent, the taxpayer's grouping of particular activities will normally be of relatively little concern to the Service.

(g) Disposition. If a taxpayer disposes of his interest in an activity in a fully taxable transaction, any suspended passive losses from the activity are generally recognized and may be used to offset other income. § 469(g)(1)(A); but see § 469(g)(1)(B) (related-party disposition). If a partnership is engaged in more than one activity, gain or loss on a disposition of an interest in the partnership is treated as passive or active by looking through to the partnership's activities. Temp. Reg. § 1.469–2T(e)(3). Any gain on disposition of an interest in an activity is generally treated as passive only if the activity constitutes a passive activity in the year of disposition. Temp. Reg. § 1.469–2T(c)(2)(i)(A)(2).

§ 7. Accounting Method

For purposes of determining the timing of income and deductions, a partnership is treated as an entity and chooses its method of accounting pursuant to § 446. In order to prevent timing abuses, however, many partnerships are required to use the accrual method of accounting. A partnership may not use the cash method if (i) any partner is a C corporation or (ii) the partnership is a "tax shelter." § 448(a). The first rule is intended to reinforce the general prohibition against C corporations using the cash method. A C corporation (or a partnership having a C corporation partner) may use the cash method, however, if the C corporation is a "qualified personal service corporation" (as defined in § 448(d)(2)). See § 448(b)(2). A corporation is a qualified personal service corporation if (i) substantially all of its activities involve the performance of services in specified fields (including health, law, accounting and consulting) and (ii) substantially all of its stock is owned by employees, retired employees or their estates. § 448(d)(2). Moreover, the cash method may be used by any entity (other than a tax shelter) whose average annual gross receipts do not exceed $5,000,000 for the three-year period preceding the taxable year. §§ 448(b)(1), (3); 448(c).

A partnership may be prohibited from using the cash method, even if none of its partners is a C corporation, if the partnership is a tax shelter. For this purpose, a tax shelter is broadly defined to include any partnership if (i) interests in the partnership have been offered for sale in an offering subject to registration under federal or state securities law, (ii) more than 35% of partnership losses during the taxable year are allocated to limited partners or limited entrepreneurs who do not actively participate in management of the partnership, or (iii) the principal purpose of the partnership is avoidance or evasion of federal income tax. See §§ 448(d)(3), 461(i)(3).

§ 8. Taxable Year

(a) General. A partnership's income or loss flows through to a partner in his taxable year in which (or with which) the partnership's taxable year ends. § 706(a). For example, if a partnership's first taxable year begins on February 1, 2000 and ends on January 31, 2001, an individual partner will report his distributive share of partnership items for that period in his return for the calendar year 2001. In effect, the partnership's fiscal year permits a deferral of tax at the partner level on the first 11 months of partnership income. Unless a business purpose can be shown for a different fiscal year, a partnership must adopt the taxable year prescribed under § 706(b). See Rev. Proc. 87–32.

Section 706(b)(1) circumscribes the partnership's selection of a taxable year by reference to the partners' taxable years. Under § 706(b)(1)(B)(i), a partnership must use the "majority interest taxable year" if one exists, i.e., the taxable year (if any) which constitutes the taxable year of one or more partners having an aggregate interest in partnership capital and profits of more than 50%. See

§ 706(b)(4)(A)(i). If there is no majority interest taxable year, the partnership must adopt the same taxable year as all of its principal partners, i.e., those partners having an interest of 5% or more in partnership capital or profits. § 706(b)(1)(B)(ii), (b)(3). If neither of the foregoing rules applies, the partnership must adopt a calendar year or any other taxable year prescribed by regulations. § 706(b)(1)(B)(iii). If the taxable year of a partnership changes as a result of the majority interest rule, no further change is required for either of the two taxable years following the change. § 706(b)(4)(B).

If the majority interest and principal partner rules do not apply, temporary regulations require that the partnership adopt the taxable year used by one or more of its partners that results in the "least aggregate deferral of income to the partners." Temp. Reg. § 1.706–1T(a)(1). The taxable year prescribed by the temporary regulations thus overrides the calendar year as the default rule. The aggregate deferral for a particular year is determined by multiplying the months of deferral for each partner times his percentage interest in partnership profits, and then summing the products for all partners; the partner's year which produces the lowest total is the required taxable year for the partnership. Temp. Reg. § 1.706–1T(a)(2). For this purpose, deferral to each partner is measured in terms of the months from the end of the test year forward to the end of the partner's taxable year.

Example (8): A, B and C own 50%, 30%, and 20%, respectively, of the capital and profits interests in the newly-formed ABC partnership. A, B and C have fiscal years ending on April 30, June 30 and November 30, respectively. The majority interest rule does not apply because no partners owning more than 50% of the capital or profits in the aggregate have the same taxable year. Similarly, the principal partner rule does not apply because the principal partners (A, B and C) all have different taxable years. Thus, ABC must adopt a taxable year ending on April 30, i.e., the taxable year which produces the least aggregate deferral, determined as follows:

Taxable Year	Profits Interest × Months of Deferral			Aggregate Deferral
	A	B	C	
April 30	50% × 0	30% × 2	20% × 7	2.0
June 30	50% × 10	30% × 0	20% × 5	6.0
November 30	50% × 5	30% × 7	20% × 0	4.6

If different taxable years yield the same aggregate deferral, the partnership may generally elect any of such years; if one of the qualifying years coincides with the partnership's current taxable year, the partnership must maintain its existing year. Id.; see Temp. Reg. § 1.706–1T(d) (Ex. 3). If an ownership change results in another taxable year with less aggregate deferral, the partnership is generally required to adopt that year, subject to a de minimis exception. Temp. Reg. § 1.706–1T(a)(4).

(b) Election Out: §§ 444 and 7519. Even absent a business purpose, a partnership may elect a taxable year that results in no more than three months of deferral at the partner level (generally, a taxable year ending in September, October or November). § 444. The price of the election is that the partnership must pay a tax which is intended to compensate for the partner-level deferral attributable to the § 444 election. § 7519. The required payments under § 7519 are in the nature of a deposit and must be recomputed annually; payments for prior years are credited against the current year's liability and excess payments may be refunded.

CHAPTER 4

PARTNERSHIP ALLOCATIONS

§ 1. Overview

Section 704(a) provides that a partner's distributive share of partnership income, gain, loss or deduction is generally determined by the partnership agreement. If the partnership agreement fails to allocate an item among the partners or provides an allocation which lacks substantial economic effect, however, § 704(b) requires that a partner's distributive share be determined "in accordance with the partner's interest in the partnership," taking into account all facts and circumstances. Section 704(b) applies to "bottom-line" allocations of partnership net income or loss as well as to special allocations of specific items. Reg. § 1.704–1(b)(1)(vii). For example, if the partnership agreement specially allocates all depreciation to one partner and the remainder of the partnership's income is divided equally, both the special and residual allocations must be tested under § 704(b).

Under the detailed provisions of the § 704(b) regulations, an allocation by agreement is respected only if the allocation has "economic effect" and such economic effect is "substantial." Reg. § 1.704–1(b)(2)(i). Generally, an allocation has economic effect only if it is consistent with the underlying economic arrangement of the partners. This means that "in the event there is an economic benefit or economic burden that corresponds to an allocation, the partner to whom the allocation is made must receive such economic benefit or bear such economic burden." Reg. § 1.704–1(b)(2)(ii). In turn, the economic effect of an allocation generally is substantial if it will affect the ultimate dollar amounts to be received by the partners from the partnership, independent of tax consequences. Reg. § 1.704–1(b)(2)(iii)(a). The term "substantial" is used in a technical rather than a descriptive sense. The purpose of the substantiality test is to invalidate abusive allocations that seek to exploit the partners' outside tax attributes. For example, an allocation may be insubstantial if it is matched by other offsetting allocations which result in overall tax savings without affecting the dollar amounts allocated to the partners.

The requirement of substantial economic effect is intended to ensure, to the extent possible, that tax allocations follow the corresponding economic benefits and burdens. If an allocation under a partnership agreement is not respected, the items in question must be reallocated under § 704(b) in accordance with the partners' interests in the partnership. In approaching the § 704(b) regulations, it is essential to grasp the fundamental relationship between the concept of substantial economic effect and that of the partners' interests in the partnership. In both cases, the tax allocation of partnership items must correspond to the partners' economic sharing arrangement. The regulations underscore this point by providing that the partners' interests in the partnership reflect "the manner in which the partners have agreed to share the economic benefit or burden (if any)" corresponding to the allocated item. Reg. § 1.704–1(b)(3)(i). The primary difference is that the substantial economic effect test provides a "safe harbor" based on strict compliance with a relatively mechanical set of accounting rules, while the partners' interest in the partnership must be determined based on all facts and circumstances.

The § 704(b) regulations provide special rules for validating tax allocations for certain items that inherently lack economic effect. For example, items of tax credit and excess percentage depletion have no economic effect because they are not reflected in the partners' capital accounts. Similarly, nonrecourse deductions have no economic effect because the economic burden of any decline in value of the underlying property ultimately falls on the creditor rather than the partners. Finally, disparities between book value and adjusted tax basis may necessitate tax allocations of certain items under § 704(c) principles which differ from the corresponding book allocations. See Chapter 5. Despite the absence of economic effect, the tax allocations are "deemed to be in accordance with the partner's interest in the partnership" in these situations, if specified requirements are met. Reg. § 1.704–1(b)(1)(i).

In summary, an allocation will be respected under § 704(b) if it (i) has substantial economic effect, (ii) is in accordance with the partners' interests in the partnership, or (iii) is deemed to be in accordance with the partners' interests in the partnership under special rules. In turn, the § 704(b) regulations provide three alternative tests for economic effect: the primary test for economic effect, the alternate test for economic effect, and the economic effect equivalence test. See Exhibit I (infra pp. 106–107). If an allocation is not respected, it must be reallocated in accordance with the partners' interests in the partnership. Finally, § 704(e) prevents shifting of income in the context of family partnerships.

§ 2. Economic Effect

(a) Primary Test. The primary economic effect test is satisfied only if the partnership meets three requirements. First, the partners' capital accounts must be determined and maintained in accordance with the detailed rules of Reg. § 1.704–1(b)(2)(iv). Second, upon liquidation of the partnership (or any partner's interest in the partnership), liquidating distributions must be made in accordance with the partners' positive capital account balances. Third, if a partner has a deficit balance in his capital account following liquidation of his interest in the partnership, such partner must be unconditionally obligated to restore the deficit. Reg. § 1.704–1(b)(2)(ii)(b).

(b) Capital Account Analysis. The detailed capital account analysis establishes a link between the partnership's tax allocations and the partners' arrangement for sharing economic benefits and burdens. The focus on liquidating distributions is appropriate because liquidation furnishes an opportunity to determine whether a partner's aggregate distributions correspond in value to the partner's contributions increased by his distributive share of income and decreased by his distributive share of deductions. Upon liquidation, a partner is entitled to receive the value of his positive capital account balance or is obligated to restore the amount of his capital account deficit, as the case may be. The capital account balances thus serve to reconcile the entitlements and obligations of the partners on liquidation.

The *Orrisch* case illustrates an allocation that lacked substantial economic effect under the pre–1976 version of § 704(b). Orrisch (1970). In *Orrisch*, the partners (the Orrisches and the Crisafis) agreed orally to allocate all of the depreciation from two apartment buildings to the Orrisches who had substantial outside income. The partners were to share equally all other income and deductions, except that any gain on sale of the buildings would be allocated to the Orrisches up to the amount of the depreciation deductions allocated to them (a "gain chargeback"). The Orrisches argued that the special allocation of depreciation had substantial economic effect because it was reflected in their capital accounts. As of the end of 1967, the Orrisches had a capital account deficit totalling $25,187, while the Crisafis had a small positive capital account.

In *Orrisch*, if the partnership had sold the buildings for an amount equal to their original cost, the recognized gain would have been equal to the

EXHIBIT I
THE YELLOW BRICK ROAD OF §704(b)*

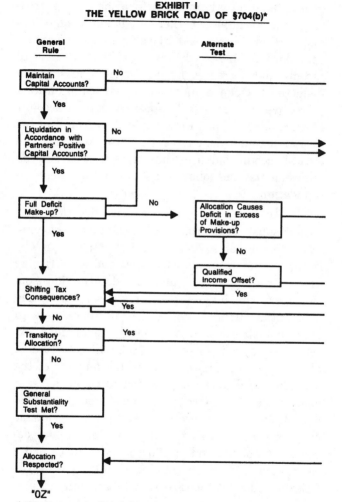

* This chart assumes that all debts of the partnership are on a recourse basis. Reprinted with permission from Taxation of Partners and Partnerships, 5–35. Copyright © 1989 by Ernst & Young.

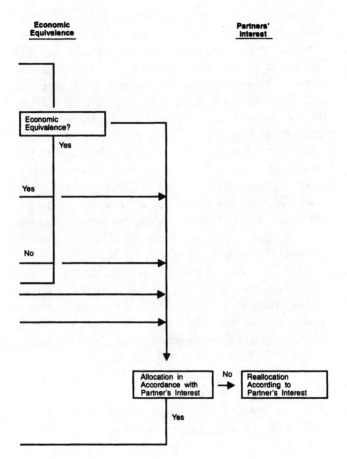

amount of the prior depreciation deductions. The Orrisches' capital account would have been increased by the gain allocated to them under the gain chargeback provision, leaving them in the same economic position as if the depreciation had not been specially allocated. The court, however, tested the economic effect of the partnership allocations by inquiring whether the Orrisches would bear the corresponding economic burden if the buildings were sold for less than their original cost. Under normal capital account rules, if the gain did not fully offset the prior depreciation deductions, the Orrisches should have been entitled to a lesser amount on liquidation or required to restore the remaining deficit in their capital account. The court, however, did not find that the Orrisches had agreed to restore a capital account deficit. Instead, it believed that the parties contemplated an equal division of assets upon liquidation of the partnership (regardless of capital account balances). Because the capital accounts did not govern liquidating distributions, the special allocation was disregarded.

The § 704(b) regulations adopt the *Orrisch* approach by focusing on the economic effect of an allocation if depreciated property is ultimately sold for less than its original cost. The regulations generally presume that the fair market value of property is equal to its adjusted book basis. Reg. § 1.704–1(b)(2)(iii)(c). Thus, depreciation deductions are treated as if they reflected an actual decline in the value of the underlying property. The § 704(b) capital account rules force a partner with an unlimited deficit restoration obligation to relinquish actual dollars to the extent that a special allocation of depreciation exceeds the amount of any gain chargeback. If the *Orrisch* agreement had satisfied these capital account requirements, the special allocation of depreciation and gain chargeback would have been respected.

(c) Operation. Under the § 704(b) regulations, the validity of partnership allocations is determined annually. Reg. § 1.704–1(b)(2)(i). Thus, an allocation may be respected one year, but not the next; if an allocation is respected only in part, "both the part that has economic effect and the portion that is reallocated shall consist of a proportionate share of all items that made up the allocation to such partner for such year." Reg. § 1.704–1(b)(2)(ii)(e). The following examples illustrate the mechanical operation of the primary economic effect test and its underlying principles.

Example (1): A and B each contribute $100 cash to the AB general partnership which purchases depreciable property (worth $500) for $200 cash and a $300 recourse note. The partnership is not required to pay principal on the note for three years. The partnership meets all of the requirements for economic effect under the § 704(b) regulations. Under the partnership agreement, all depreciation is allocated to A, and the remainder of the partnership income and loss is shared equally. During Year 1, the partnership has operating income of $180, operating expenses of $70, and depreciation of $100. To satisfy the capital account rules, the partners' capital accounts at the end of Year 1 must be as follows:

	Capital Accounts	
	A	B
Initial balance	$100	$100
Operating income	90	90
Less: operating expenses	(35)	(35)
depreciation	(100)	
Balance at end of Year 1	$ 55	$155

Since partnership liabilities are not reflected in the partners' capital accounts, each partner has an initial balance of $100 equal to her cash contribution. Each partner's capital account is increased by her $90 share of the partnership's operating income and decreased by her $35 share of the partnership's operating expenses. In addition, A's capital account is reduced by $100 of depreciation.

The economic effect of allocating the Year 1 depreciation to A can be shown by assuming a hypothetical sale of the partnership's property for an amount equal to its adjusted basis ($400) at the beginning of Year 2. Since the partnership would recognize no gain or loss on the sale, the partners' capital accounts would remain unchanged. After payment of the debt, the partnership would have cash of $210 ($400 sale proceeds plus $110 of cash flow from Year 1 less $300 debt repayment) available for distribution. Accordingly, each partner would be entitled to a distribution of cash equal to her capital account balance ($55 to A and $155 to B). The capital account rules force A to bear the economic burden of the $100 of depreciation by reducing her share of the proceeds on liquidation.

Example (2): The AB partnership has the same balance sheet at the end of Year 1 as in Example (1), above. During Year 2, the partnership again has depreciation of $100, and its operating income equals its operating expenses. The Year 2 allocation of depreciation produces a $45 deficit in A's capital account ($55 balance at the end of Year 1 less $100 depreciation). The allocation has economic effect, however, since A is required to restore any deficit in her capital account. Assume that the partnership sells the property for its adjusted basis ($300), pays off the liability and liquidates at the beginning of Year 3. After A contributed $45 (increasing her capital account to zero), the partnership would have cash of $155 available for distribution ($300 sales proceeds plus $45 contribution plus $110 cash flow from Year 1 less $300 debt repayment). B would be entitled to a distribution of the entire $155 of cash, satisfying her positive capital account balance. Thus, A bears the economic burden of the Year 2 depreciation since she would receive $100 less at the end of Year 2 ($45 deficit) than at the end of Year 1 ($55 positive balance).

Example (3): The facts are the same as in Example (1), above, except that the partnership agreement provides that A and B will share liquidating distributions equally (regardless of their capital account balances) and the partners are not obligated (under the partnership agreement or state law) to restore any deficit in their capital accounts. In this case, the Year 1 allocation of depreciation lacks economic effect because A would not bear the full economic burden corresponding to the depreciation deductions allocated to her. On a sale of the property for $400 at the beginning of Year 2, each partner would receive $105 on liquidation (after payment of the partnership debt) even though A's capital account is $55 and B's is $155. Accordingly, all items of partnership income and loss for Year 1 must be reallocated in accordance with the partners' interests in the partnership. See Reg. § 1.704–1(b)(5) (Ex. 1(i)).

Example (4): The facts are the same as in Example (1), above, except that partnership agreement also provides for a gain chargeback upon sale of the property. At the beginning of Year 2, the partnership sells the property for its original cost and recognizes a gain of $100 ($500 amount realized less $400 adjusted basis), which is allocated entirely to A. A's capital account is increased to $155 ($55 balance at the end of Year 1 plus $100 gain chargeback). After payment of the debt, the partnership has cash of $310 ($500 sales proceeds plus $110 cash flow from Year 1 less $300 debt). A and B would each be entitled to a distribution of $155, reducing their capital accounts to zero. In effect, the gain chargeback offsets the effect of the special allocation of depreciation and restores equality between the partners' capital accounts. If the partnership agreement did not contain a gain chargeback, the $100 gain would be divided equally, leaving A with a capital account balance of $105 ($55 balance at the end of Year 1 plus $50 share of gain) and B with a capital account balance of $205 ($155 balance at the end of Year 1 plus $50 share of gain). But for the gain chargeback, A would thus receive $100 less than B on liquidation, a result that the partners probably did not intend. The special allocation of depreciation to A is valid whether or not it is accompanied by a gain chargeback. See Reg. § 1.704–1(b)(5) (Ex. 1(xi)).

(d) Economic Effect Equivalence. In limited circumstances, an allocation may be deemed to have economic effect under the "economic effect equivalence" test even though it fails to satisfy the detailed capital account rules. Under the economic effect equivalence test, an allocation will be respected if the partners can show that a liquidation of the partnership at the end of any partnership year would produce the same economic results as would occur if all three requirements of the primary economic effect test had been satisfied. Reg. § 1.704–1(b)(2)(ii)(i). For example, assume that two members of a general partnership contribute capital in the ratio 75:25 and agree to share profits, losses and distributions according to the same ratio; the partnership does not maintain capital accounts, but (under a state law right of contribution) each general partner would ultimately be liable for the partnership's debts in the ratio 75:25. The allocations are valid under the economic effect equivalence test because the economic results to the partners are the same as if the primary economic effect test had been satisfied. See Reg. § 1.704–1(b)(5) (Ex. 4 (ii)).

If the partners' deficit restoration obligations are limited (e.g., in the case of limited partners), however, the economic effect equivalence test cannot sustain an otherwise invalid allocation.

§ 3. Maintenance of Capital Accounts

(a) Basic Rules. An allocation can satisfy the primary (or alternate) economic effect test only if the partnership maintains capital accounts in accordance with the detailed rules of the § 704(b) regulations. Under the § 704(b) regulations, a partner's capital account must be increased by (i) the amount of money contributed by the partner to the partnership, (ii) the fair market value of property contributed by the partner to the partnership (net of any liabilities secured by such property which the partnership is considered to assume or take subject to under § 752) and (iii) the partner's distributive share of "book" income and gain (including tax-exempt income and gain). Reg. § 1.704–1(b)(2)(iv)(b). A partner's capital account must be decreased by (i) the amount of money distributed to the partner by the partnership, (ii) the fair market value of property distributed to the partner by the partnership (net of liabilities secured by such property which the partner is considered to assume or take subject to under § 752), (iii) the partner's distributive share of § 705(a)(2)(B) expenditures, and (iv) the partner's distributive share of the partnership's other items of "book" loss and deduction. Id.

The fair market value of property as determined by the partnership will be respected if "such value is reasonably agreed to among the partners in arm's-length negotiations" and "the partners have sufficiently adverse interests." Reg. § 1.704–1(b)(2)(iv)(h). Generally, the partners will have sufficiently adverse interests because the valuation for capital account purposes ultimately affects their respective rights to liquidating distributions.

(b) Book/Tax Disparities. For purposes of the economic effect test, the partners' capital accounts are maintained on a "book" basis (i.e., in accordance with the capital account rules set forth in the § 704(b) regulations, as distinguished from tax or financial accounting rules). Disparities between a partner's book account and his tax account may arise from differences between the capital account rules which govern book accounts and tax accounting principles which apply to tax accounts. For example, contributed property is reflected at its fair market value in the contributing partner's capital account for book purposes, but is reflected at its adjusted tax basis in the partner's tax account. See Chapter 2; see also Chapter 9 (distributions). Other adjustments for items of income, gain, loss and deduction are also reflected in capital accounts on a book basis. In certain circumstances, the § 704(b) regulations permit an optional adjustment to the partners' capital accounts to reflect a general revaluation of the partnership property "made principally for a substantial non-tax business purpose." Reg. § 1.704–1(b)(2)(iv)(f)(5). In the case of revalued

property, the partnership must follow § 704(c) principles in order to minimize disparities between each
partner's tax and book accounts. See Chapter 5.

(c) Transfers of Partnership Interests. When
a partner transfers his partnership interest, his
capital account generally carries over to the transferee, who steps into the transferor's shoes for
capital account purposes. Reg. § 1.704–
1(b)(2)(iv)(l); see Chapter 8.

§ 4.   Alternate Economic Effect Test

(a) General. The primary test for economic effect can be satisfied only if a partner has an unlimited deficit restoration obligation. Under state law,
general partners are personally liable for the partnership's obligations to creditors, but may agree to
limit their obligation to repay losses attributable to
another partner's capital contributions or undistributed share of profits. Since limited partners and
LLC members (by definition) lack an unlimited
obligation to restore capital account deficits, the
§ 704(b) regulations provide an alternative means
of satisfying the economic effect test. Under the
"alternate economic effect" test, the first two requirements of the primary test (capital account
maintenance and governance) must be satisfied, but
an unlimited deficit restoration is not required. An
allocation to a partner will nevertheless be respected if (i) the allocation does not cause or increase a
deficit balance in the partner's capital account (after taking any limited deficit restoration obligation
of such partner into account) and (ii) the partner-

ship agreement contains a "qualified income offset." Reg. § 1.704–1(b)(2)(ii)(d).

A partner is treated as having a limited deficit restoration obligation to the extent of (i) the outstanding principal balance of the partner's own promissory note (other than a readily tradeable note) contributed to the partnership and (ii) the amount of any other unconditional obligation under the partnership agreement or applicable state law to make subsequent contributions to the partnership. Reg. § 1.704–1(b)(2)(ii)(c). Generally, the partner must be required to satisfy the note or obligation no later than the end of the partnership's taxable year in which his interest is liquidated (or, if later, within 90 days after liquidation). The regulations warn that an obligation will be disregarded if it is not legally enforceable or if there is a plan to avoid or circumvent the obligation. Id.

Example (5): A and B each contribute $50,000 to a limited partnership. The partnership agreement meets the first two requirements of the primary economic effect test for maintaining capital accounts and distributing liquidating proceeds in accordance with positive capital accounts. B, the limited partner, is not required to restore any deficit in his capital account, but the partnership agreement contains a qualified income offset. The partnership uses the $100,000 cash to purchase property which the partnership will depreciate over a 10–year period under the straight-line method ($10,000 annually). Under the partnership agreement, income and losses are shared equally by A and B, except that all depreciation deductions are allocated to B. The partnership expects that annual operating income will equal annual operating expenses in Years 1–10, and does not intend to make any distributions prior to liquidation. Under the alternate economic effect test, the allocation of depreciation deductions in Years 1–5 is valid and reduces B's capital account to zero at the end of Year 5. The depreciation deductions in Year 6 and thereafter must be reallocated to A, however, unless B agrees to be liable for the limited amount of any deficit in his capital account. See Reg. § 1.704–1(b)(5) (Ex. 1(iv), (viii)).

(b) Expected Distributions. The alternate economic effect test reflects the notion that an allocation of loss or deduction to a partner has economic effect to the extent it does not reduce his adjusted capital account balance (after taking into account any limited deficit restoration obligation) below zero. For purposes of the alternate economic effect test, the partner's capital account must be adjusted for expected future distributions and certain other items. The § 704(b) regulations provide that the partner's capital account must be adjusted downward for "[d]istributions that, as of the end of [the] year, reasonably are expected to be made to such partner to the extent they exceed offsetting increases to such partner's capital account that reasonably are expected to occur during (or prior to) the partnership taxable years in which such distributions are reasonably expected to be made.... " Reg. § 1.704–1(b)(2)(ii)(d)(6).

This requirement is intended to ensure that reductions in a partner's capital account as a result of expected distributions are taken into account (to the extent not offset by increases from other items) in determining whether an allocation of loss or deduction would produce an impermissible deficit in the partner's capital account. Since the fair market value of partnership property is deemed to equal its adjusted book basis, projected gains or losses on disposition of property cannot be taken into account in determining reasonably expected increases or decreases in a partner's capital account. Reg. § 1.704–1(b)(2)(iii)(c). An allocation of loss or deduction will be respected only to the extent that it does not cause the partner to have a deficit in his adjusted capital account, after taking any limited deficit restoration into account.

Example (6): The facts are the same as in Example (5), above, except that the partnership expects to borrow $40,000 recourse and distribute $20,000 to each partner in Year 5. B's capital account must be adjusted to take into account the expected distribution (which is not offset by reasonably expected increases to his capital account). Before any allocations for Year 1, B's actual capital account is $50,000 but his adjusted capital account is only $30,000 ($50,000 less $20,000 expected distribution). As a result, only the allocations for Years 1 through 3 are respected, and depreciation deductions in Year 4 and subsequent years must be allocated to A. See Reg. § 1.704–1(b)(5) (Ex. 1(vi)). The adjustment for expected distributions thus reduces the total amount of depreciation deductions that can be validly allocated to B from $50,000 to $30,000. The difference ($20,000) is equal to the amount of the expected distribution in Year 5 which reduces B's actual (and adjusted) capital account to zero ($50,-000 less $30,000 depreciation less $20,000 distribution) but does not create a deficit.

(c) Qualified Income Offset. Although reasonably expected distributions are taken into account under the alternate economic effect test in determining whether an allocation will produce a deficit in a partner's capital account, there can be no assurance that an unexpected distribution will not give rise to a deficit exceeding any limited deficit restoration obligation. In the event of an unexpected distribution, the alternate economic effect test requires that the distributee partner be allocated items of income or gain sufficient to eliminate the resulting capital account deficit "as quickly as possible" (a "qualified income offset"). Reg. § 1.704–1(b)(2)(ii)(d). The qualified income offset makes it unlikely that an unexpected distribution will result in an impermissible capital account deficit upon liquidation and thus serves as a backstop to the adjustment for expected distributions.

Example (7): The facts are the same as in Example (6), above, except that the distribution of recourse borrowing in Year 5 was not reasonably expected. The allocations of depreciation deductions in Years 1 through 4 reduce B's actual (and adjusted) capital account to $10,000 at the end of Year 4. The $20,000 unexpected distribution in Year 5, however, triggers the qualified income offset: B must be allocated sufficient gross income to eliminate the resulting $10,000 deficit as quickly as possible. Assuming that the partnership has $50,-000 of operating income and $50,000 of operating expenses (net of $10,000 of depreciation) in Year 5, the required allocation of the first $10,000 of gross income to B eliminates the deficit in his capital account. The gross income allocation to B creates a bottom-line loss of $20,000 ($40,000 balance of operating income less $50,000 operating expenses less $10,000 depreciation) that must be allocated entirely to A, since it cannot be allocated to B without creating an impermissible deficit in his capital account. At the end of Year 5, the partners' capital accounts are as follows:

| | Capital Accounts | |
	A	B
Initial	$50,000	$50,000
Years 1–4: depreciation		(40,000)
End of Year 4	50,000	10,000
Year 5: distribution	(20,000)	(20,000)
gross income allocation		10,000
loss allocable to A	(20,000)	
End of Year 5	$10,000	$ 0

In effect, the qualified income offset triggered in Year 5 "recaptures" the $10,000 of depreciation allocated to B in the preceding year. The deferral of the offsetting income allocation thus produces a limited timing advantage to the partner who receives an unexpected distribution.

§ 5. Substantiality

(a) General. The § 704(b) regulations require not only that allocations have economic effect, but also that such effect be "substantial." In general, the test for substantiality is met only if "there is a reasonable possibility that the allocation (or allocations) will affect substantially the dollar amounts to be received by the partners from the partnership, independent of tax consequences." Reg. § 1.704–1(b)(2)(iii)(a). An allocation lacks economic effect if it is in effect neutralized by an offsetting allocation in the same year (a "shifting" allocation) or a different year (a "transitory" allocation). Reg. § 1.704–1(b)(2)(iii)(b)–(c). Under the overall-tax-effect rule, allocations may also be disregarded if they enhance the after-tax position of at least one partner without adversely affecting any other partner. Reg. § 1.704–1(b)(2)(iii)(a).

(b) Shifting Allocations. A shifting allocation is an allocation that reduces the partners' total tax liabilities for a particular year without substantially affecting the partners' capital account balances for the same year. Under the § 704(b) regulations, a shifting allocation is not substantial if, at the time the allocation becomes part of the partnership agreement, there is a "strong likelihood" that the net increases and decreases in the partners' capital accounts for the year "will not differ substantially" from the net increases and decreases that would occur without the allocation, and the total tax liability of the partners will also be reduced as a result of the allocation (taking into account the partners' outside tax attributes). Reg. § 1.704–1(b)(2)(iii)(b). If the allocation actually produces an overall tax savings coupled with no substantial effect on capital account balances, the § 704(b) regulations raise a rebuttable presumption that "there was a strong likelihood that these results would occur." Id.

Shifting allocations often involve attempts to specially allocate partnership items of a particular character in a manner that reduces total taxes without affecting the pre-tax dollar amount of any partner's distributive share. For example, the partners might try to achieve an overall tax saving by allocating a specific dollar amount of taxable income to a low-bracket partner while allocating an equal dollar amount of tax-exempt income to a high-bracket partner. Assuming that the partnership realizes sufficient taxable and tax-exempt income to satisfy the special allocations, there is no significant economic risk. The allocations are insubstantial because they shift the character but not the amount of the income reported by the partners. In this situation, the § 704(b) regulations generally reallocate the items ratably among the partners in accordance with the economic sharing arrangement. See Reg. § 1.704–1(b)(5) (Ex. 7(ii)).

The § 704(b) regulations also illustrate a shifting allocation in the case of an equal two-person partnership which expects to incur a loss on the sale of § 1231 property. The partnership agreement allocates the § 1231 loss to the partner who expects to have no § 1231 gains for the year and allocates an equal amount of ordinary loss to the partner who expects to have § 1231 gains for the year. The allocation is not substantial because it reduces the partners' total tax liability by changing the character but not the amount of each partner's distributive share. Therefore, the § 704(b) regulations disregard the special allocation and reallocate the § 1231 loss equally between the two partners. Reg. § 1.704–1(b)(5) (Ex. 6).

If there is significant risk concerning the effect of an allocation on the amount of net increase or decrease in a partner's capital account, the allocation should be respected even if it also affects the character of the partners' distributive shares. For example, a non-resident partner who performs services in a foreign country may receive an allocation of all income from operations in that country. The allocation of foreign-source income to the non-resident partner will be respected, at least if the amount of such income "cannot be predicted with any reasonable certainty," since the non-resident partner bears the economic risk of fluctuations in the amount of the allocated item. Reg. § 1.704–1(b)(5) (Ex. 10(i)). The result would be different if the special allocation affected only the character and not the amount of income derived by the non-resident partner. See id. (Ex. 10(ii)).

(c) Transitory Allocations. A transitory allocation is similar to a shifting allocation, except that the effect of the original allocation on a partner's capital account is neutralized by an offsetting allocation in a subsequent year rather than in the same year. Under the § 704(b) regulations, transitory allocations are generally not substantial if, at the time the allocations become part of the partnership agreement, there is a "strong likelihood" that the net increases and decreases in the partners' capital accounts "will not differ substantially" from the net increases and decreases that would occur without the allocations, and the total tax liability of the partners for the years involved will also be reduced as a result of the allocations (taking into account the partners' outside tax attributes). Reg. § 1.704–1(b)(2)(iii)(c). As in the case of shifting allocations, the regulations raise a rebuttable presumption that there was a strong likelihood that the prohibited results would occur if they do in fact occur.

The § 704(b) regulations illustrate a transitory allocation in the case of an equal two-person partnership in which one partner has a net operating loss due to expire in the current year. The partnership agreement allocates the partnership's income for the current year to the partner with the net operating loss and allocates partnership income in subsequent years to the other partner until the original allocation is offset. The partnership expects to produce sufficient income within the next five years to offset the original allocation. Apart from the net operating loss, both partners expect to be in the same tax bracket for the next several years. There is a strong likelihood that the original and offsetting allocations, when viewed together, will reduce the partners' total tax liability without substantially affecting their respective capital accounts. The original allocation reduces the loss partner's total taxes by accelerating income that can be sheltered by his expiring net operating loss. The allocations also defer the other partner's share of partnership income but do not change the total dollar amounts reflected in the partners' capital accounts over the entire period. Therefore, the allocations lack substantial economic effect because they affect only the timing but not the amount of income reported by the partners. Reg. § 1.704–1(b)(5) (Ex. 8(ii)).

The § 704(b) regulations provide an important exception where the offsetting allocation will not occur within five years after the original allocation. A transitory allocation may be respected if, at the time it becomes part of the partnership agreement, "there is a strong likelihood that the offsetting allocation(s) will not, in large part, be made within five years after the original allocation(s) is made (determined on a first-in, first-out basis)." Reg. § 1.704–1(b)(2)(iii)(c). The five-year exception applies regardless of whether the allocation reduces the partners' total tax liability or has any net effect on the partners' capital accounts.

The § 704(b) regulations illustrate the five-year exception in the context of a two-person partnership which owns and leases five-year recovery property. The partnership agreement allocates losses 90% to C and 10% to D until the partnership has taxable income, and then income 90% to C and 10% to D until each partner has been allocated taxable income equal to the losses previously allocated to him. Thereafter, partnership income and losses are allocated equally. The partnership enters into a 12–year lease and expects to have tax losses in years 1–5 (due to accelerated depreciation) and taxable income in years 6–12. There is a strong likelihood that the allocations for years 1–5 will not be "largely offset" within the following five-year period (determined on a first-in, first-out basis). In the example, 40% of the first year's loss is offset in year 6, 50% in year 7 and 10% in year 8. Since the offsetting allocations are spread over more than five years, the transitory allocation rule is inapplicable. See Reg. § 1.704–1(b)(5) (Ex. 2). The regulations leave open the possibility, however, that the allocations lack substantial economic effect under the overall-tax-effect rule.

The value-equals-basis rule imposes another important limitation on the transitory allocation rule. Because the § 704(b) regulations conclusively presume that the fair market value of property is equal to its adjusted book basis, a partner who has received allocations of depreciation deductions may also receive offsetting allocations of gain on disposition of the underlying property without running afoul of the transitory allocation rule: a gain chargeback can never render an allocation transitory. Reg. § 1.704–1(b)(2)(iii)(c). The value-equals-basis rule apparently shields only gain chargebacks, not allocations of operating income, from the transitory allocation rule. Moreover, partnership property may be expected to produce income even though its basis has been fully depreciated. See Reg. § 1.704–1(b)(5) (Ex. 2). Certain activities may be sufficiently speculative, however, that there is no strong likelihood of offsetting allocations of future income. See Reg. § 1.704–1(b)(5) (Ex. 3) (research and development); id. (Ex. 19(ii)) (oil drilling).

(d) Overall–Tax–Effect Rule. Even though an allocation may affect the actual dollar amounts to be received by the partners, it may nevertheless be invalid if the overall after-tax benefit more than offsets any pre-tax economic detriment. The overall-tax-effect rule applies if, as a result of an allocation, the "after-tax economic consequences of at least one partner may ... be enhanced" and there is also a "strong likelihood that the after-tax economic consequences of no partner will ... be substantially diminished." Reg. § 1.704–1(b)(2)(iii)(a). Thus, it is necessary to compare the after-tax consequences of the allocation to the partners in present value terms, at the time the allocation becomes part of the partnership agreement, with the results if the partnership agreement had not contained the allocation. The overall-tax-effect rule looks behind the dollar amounts reflected in the partners' capital accounts to determine the effect of the allocation on the partners' outside tax attributes. The rule is triggered only if an allocation exploits different outside tax attributes of the partners in order to achieve a net after-tax benefit for one or more partners at the expense of the government.

Example (8): A and B make equal contributions to an investment partnership and agree to share equally any gains or losses from sale of investment securities. The partnership agreement meets the capital account maintenance and governance requirements of the § 704(b) regulations, and each partner is obligated to restore any deficit in her capital account. Over the next several years, A and B expect to have marginal income tax rates of 15% and 30%, respectively, and the partnership expects to have roughly equal amounts of taxable and tax-exempt income. The partnership allocates the taxable income entirely to A and the tax-exempt income 10% to A and 90% to B.

Assuming that the partnership earns $100 of taxable income and $100 of tax-exempt interest, the allocation lacks substantial economic effect as compared with the results if the partners shared taxable and tax-exempt income equally. In effect, the allocation shifts $50 of taxable income from B to A, resulting in an overall tax savings of $7.50 (the difference between a tax on $50 at B's 30% rate and A's 15% rate). If the allocation were respected, each partner would benefit at the expense of the government. The after-tax consequences to the partners can be illustrated as follows:

	Special Allocation		No Special Allocation	
	A	B	A	B
Tax-exempt income	$ 10	$ 90	$ 50	$ 50
Plus: taxable income	100	0	50	50
Less: tax at marginal rate	(15)	(0)	(7.50)	(15)
Net income after-tax	$ 95	$ 90	$92.50	$ 85

The overall-tax-effect rule applies only if there is a "strong likelihood," at the time the allocation is entered into, that the allocation will leave no partner in a substantially worse after-tax position than if the allocation were not made. If an allocation fails under the overall-tax-effect test, the tax consequences must be reallocated to reflect the partners' economic sharing arrangement. The dollar amounts allocated to the partners' respective capital accounts remain unchanged, but the character of the items is reallocated ratably. In the preceding example, for instance, since the partnership's total income is allocated 55% ($110/$200) to A and 45% ($90/$100) to B, each item of partnership income would be reallocated 55% to A and 45% to B. See Reg. § 1.704–1(b)(5) (Ex. 5(ii)).

§ 6. Partner's Interest in the Partnership

(a) General. If an allocation lacks substantial economic effect, the item in question must be reallocated in accordance with the partner's interest in the partnership. The § 704(b) regulations provide that a partner's interest in the partnership is determined by "taking into account all facts and circumstances relating to the economic arrangements of the partners." Reg. § 1.704–1(b)(3)(i). In the absence of facts and circumstances to the contrary, all partners' interests are presumed to be equal. Id. In applying the partner's interest standard, the following factors are considered relevant: (i) the partners' relative contributions to the partnership, (ii) the partners' interests in economic profits and losses (if different from their interests in taxable income or loss), (iii) the partners' interests in cash flow and other non-liquidating distributions, and (iv) the partners' rights to distributions of capital upon liquidation. Reg. § 1.704–1(b)(3)(ii).

The partner's interest test is intended to reallocate tax items in accordance with the partners' underlying economic sharing arrangement. If the partners have generally agreed to share items in a fixed ratio (e.g., a simple 50/50 partnership) subject only to an invalid special allocation of a particular item (e.g., cost recovery deductions), the specially allocated item will be reallocated in accordance with the partners' overall sharing ratio. See Reg. § 1.704–1(b)(5) (Ex. 1(i)). In more complex sharing arrangements, however, the partner's interest test quickly becomes more difficult to apply.

(b) Special Partner's Interest Test. Fortunately, the § 704(b) regulations provide a special test for identifying a partner's interest where the partnership agreement satisfies the first two requirements of the primary economic effect test (relating to maintenance of capital accounts and distributions on liquidation) but an allocation lacks economic effect solely because of the absence of an unlimited deficit restoration obligation. Under the special partner's interest test, the item in question is reallocated based on a comparison of the distributions (and contributions) which would be made if the partnership were liquidated immediately following a deemed sale of the partnership's assets for book value (i) at the end of the taxable year to which the allocation relates and (ii) at the end of the prior taxable year, respectively. Reg. § 1.704–1(b)(3)(iii). The results of this calculation must then be adjusted in a manner similar to the adjustments required under the alternate economic effect test (e.g., anticipated distributions). Essentially, the special partner's interest test reallocates the item in question based on the difference in the dollar amounts that each partner would receive if the partnership were liquidated at the beginning or at the end of the current year. See Reg. § 1.704–1(b)(5) (Ex. 15(ii)-(iii)).

§ 7. Nonrecourse Deductions

(a) General. With respect to recourse deductions, the § 704(b) regulations generally ensure that the deductions are allocated to the partner who bears the corresponding economic burden. Allocations of nonrecourse deductions (i.e., deductions attributable to partnership nonrecourse liabilities within the meaning of the § 752 regulations) pose special problems, however, because the corresponding economic burden falls on the creditor rather than the partners. Therefore, allocations of nonrecourse deductions can never have economic effect. Nevertheless, the § 704(b) regulations provide that an allocation of nonrecourse deductions is deemed to be in accordance with the partners' interests in the partnership if certain conditions are satisfied. In general terms, the § 704(b) regulations require that a partner who receives a nonrecourse deduction must also receive a matching allocation of income or gain when the partnership disposes of the underlying property or repays the nonrecourse liability. In turn, the liability-sharing rules under

§ 752 ensure that the outside basis attributable to partnership nonrecourse liabilities is allocated in the same manner as the corresponding nonrecourse deductions. See Chapter 6.

(b) Nonrecourse Debt Safe Harbor. An allocation of nonrecourse deductions is valid only if: (i) the partnership agreement satisfies the first two requirements of the primary economic effect test (relating to maintenance of capital accounts and distributions on liquidation) and partners with deficit capital accounts agree to an unlimited deficit restoration obligation or qualified income offset; (ii) the partnership agreement provides for allocations of nonrecourse deductions among the partners in a manner that is reasonably consistent with allocations, which have substantial economic effect, of some other significant partnership item attributable to the property securing the nonrecourse liability; (iii) the partnership agreement contains a "minimum gain chargeback"; and (iv) all other material allocations are valid. Reg. § 1.704–2(e). If the safe harbor rule is not met, nonrecourse deductions are allocated in accordance with the partners' overall economic interests in the partnership. Reg. § 1.704–2(b)(1).

Allocations of nonrecourse deductions must be reasonably consistent with some other significant partnership item attributable to the property securing the nonrecourse liability (other than a minimum gain chargeback). The consistency requirement restricts the opportunity to shift tax benefits by requiring that allocations of nonrecourse deductions must follow some other significant allocation which has substantial economic effect. For example, if a partnership allocates profits and losses to its partners in an initial ratio of 90:10 which subsequently flips to a 50:50 ratio, an allocation of nonrecourse deductions in any ratio between 90:10 and 50:50 would be respected, but a 99:1 allocation ratio would be invalid. See Reg. § 1.704–2(m) (Ex. 1(ii)–(iii)).

The safe harbor for nonrecourse deductions is analogous to the tax treatment of an individual owner who acquires property subject to nonrecourse debt. Under *Crane*, the owner of property includes nonrecourse acquisition debt in basis even though the lender bears the corresponding economic burden. Crane (1947). As long as the property is worth more than the amount of the outstanding debt, the owner has an incentive to repay the debt in order to retain the property. When the owner repays the outstanding principal balance with after-tax dollars, he makes an additional equity investment in the property which validates the tax benefit derived from the prior nonrecourse deductions. If the value of the property falls below the amount of the debt, however, the owner may decide to extinguish the debt by surrendering the property to the creditor. On relief of the debt, the outstanding balance of the debt will be included in the owner's amount realized, triggering *Tufts* gain (i.e., the excess of the extinguished nonrecourse debt over the basis of the property) and validating the tax benefit derived from the prior nonrecourse deductions. Tufts (1983).

Example (9): A (the general partner) and B (the limited partner) each contribute $100,000 cash to a limited partnership which purchases a building (worth $1,000,000) for $200,000 cash and an $800,-000 nonrecourse note. The partnership agreement complies with all of the requirements under the alternate economic effect test and provides for a minimum gain chargeback. In Year 1, the partnership's operating income equals its operating expenses. The partnership also has $200,000 of depreciation deductions which are allocated $100,000 each to A and B, reducing their respective capital accounts to zero. The partnership's allocations for Year 1 are valid under the alternate economic effect test because they are attributable to the partners' equity investment. At the end of Year 1, if the property were sold for its adjusted basis ($800,000), the sales proceeds would be sufficient to pay the creditor, leaving nothing for A and B.

Once the adjusted basis of the property falls below the amount of the nonrecourse debt, any further depreciation will generate nonrecourse deductions and drive the partners' capital accounts negative. Thus, at the end of Year 2, the aggregate deficit in the partners' capital accounts will be equal to the excess of the debt ($800,000) over the property's adjusted basis ($600,000). Since the debt is nonrecourse, however, neither partner is obligated to contribute additional capital to repay the debt even if the property is worth less than the amount of the outstanding debt. Thus, if the value of the property actually declined to $600,-000 and the partnership surrendered it in satisfaction of the $800,000 debt, the creditor would suffer a $200,000 economic loss while the partnership would recognize $200,000 of *Tufts* gain. This minimum amount of gain ("partnership minimum gain"), representing the tax cost of the nonrecourse deductions previously allocated to the partners, is sufficient to eliminate the aggregate deficit in the partners' capital accounts. The regulations require that the minimum gain (sometimes called "phantom gain") be allocated to the partners who received the corresponding nonrecourse deductions (a "minimum gain chargeback") in order to offset the prior tax benefit. Thus, the minimum gain would be allocated equally to A and B, restoring their capital accounts to zero.

(c) Partnership Minimum Gain. With respect to nonrecourse deductions, the concept of partnership minimum gain replaces economic effect in determining the validity of allocations. Under the regulations, partnership minimum gain is the amount of gain that the partnership would realize on a taxable disposition of the property subject to the nonrecourse liability in full satisfaction thereof (and for no other consideration). Reg. § 1.704–2(d). A partner's share of partnership minimum gain at the end of any year is generally equal to the cumulative nonrecourse deductions allocated to him (increased by certain distributions to him attributable

to nonrecourse liabilities and decreased by any reductions in his share of partnership minimum gain
up to that time). Reg. § 1.704–2(g)(1).

The regulations determine the amount of nonrecourse deductions for the partnership's taxable year
by reference to the net increase, if any, in partnership minimum gain for such year (reduced by certain distributions attributable to nonrecourse liabilities). Reg. § 1.704–2(c). Nonrecourse deductions
are deemed to consist first of depreciation deductions with respect to partnership property subject to
nonrecourse liabilities to the extent of any increase
in minimum gain attributable to such property; any
excess nonrecourse deductions are deemed to consist of a ratable share of the partnership's other
items of loss, deduction and § 705(a)(2)(B) expenditure for the year. Id. If there is a net *decrease* (or no
net increase) in partnership minimum gain for the
taxable year, none of the partnership's deductions
are nonrecourse and the minimum gain chargeback
may apply.

The net increase (or decrease) in partnership
minimum gain is determined by comparing the
amounts of partnership minimum gain at the end of
the current year and at the end of the immediately
preceding year. Reg. § 1.704–2(d). A net increase in
partnership minimum gain may be attributable to
(i) depreciation deductions in excess of principal
repayments, (ii) a nonrecourse refinancing in excess
of basis or (iii) conversion of a partnership liability
from recourse to nonrecourse. A net decrease in
partnership minimum gain may be attributable to

(i) a taxable disposition of the underlying property securing the nonrecourse liability, (ii) principal payments on the nonrecourse liability in excess of depreciation deductions for the year or (iii) conversion of a partnership liability from nonrecourse to recourse.

Subject to certain exceptions, a net decrease in partnership minimum gain triggers a minimum gain chargeback to the partners who received the underlying nonrecourse deductions. Reg. § 1.704–2(f)(1). A partner's minimum gain chargeback is equal to his share of the net decrease in partnership minimum gain, i.e., the net decrease multiplied by the partner's share of total partnership minimum gain at the end of the preceding year. Reg. § 1.704–2(g)(2). For example, if a partner's share of total partnership minimum gain is 20% and the net decrease is $100, the partner's share of the net decrease is $20.

A minimum gain chargeback must be made before any other allocation of partnership items for the year. Reg. § 1.704–2(j). The required allocation consists first of gains recognized from disposition of property subject to nonrecourse liabilities and thereafter of a ratable share of other items of partnership income and gain for the year. Reg. § 1.704–2(f)(6). If the partnership has insufficient items of income and gain to satisfy the required allocation, such items must be allocated in subsequent years to cure the deficiency as soon as possible. Id.

The regulations provide several important exceptions to the mandatory minimum gain chargeback. First, a partner is not subject to a minimum gain chargeback to the extent that his share of the net decrease in partnership minimum gain is attributable to conversion of a nonrecourse liability to a recourse liability (e.g., as result of a guarantee or refinancing) for which he bears the economic risk of loss under the § 752 regulations. Reg. § 1.704–2(f)(2), (f)(7) (Ex. 2). Second, a partner is not subject to a minimum gain chargeback to the extent that he contributes capital to the partnership to repay a nonrecourse liability and his share of the net decrease is attributable to the repayment. Reg. § 1.704–2(f)(3); Reg. § 1.704–2(m) (Ex. 1(iv)). These exceptions reflect the fact that the partner's share of prior nonrecourse deductions is "restored" through a capital contribution (or obligation to pay the creditor), so that a minimum gain chargeback is unnecessary. The partnership may also request a waiver of the chargeback requirement if it would lead to unintended economic distortions. Reg. § 1.704–2(f)(3). The waiver provision is intended to provide flexibility in situations where a minimum gain chargeback is unnecessary due to prior adjustments to the partners' capital accounts (e.g., offsetting income allocations). See Reg. § 1.704–2(f)(7) (Ex. 1). In some circumstances, the chargeback may be deferred until the occurrence of a subsequent triggering event. See Reg. § 1.704–2(i)(4).

Example (10): A (the general partner) contributes no capital and B (the limited partner) contributes

$200,000 cash to the AB partnership which purchases a building (worth $1,000,000) for $200,000 cash and an $800,000 nonrecourse note. The partnership agreement satisfies the requirements of the alternate economic effect test and contains a minimum gain chargeback provision. Only A is required to restore any deficit in her capital account. During Years 1–3, the partnership has annual operating income of $150,000, annual operating expenses of $130,000, and annual depreciation deductions of $200,000. The partnership uses its annual cash flow of $20,000 to repay a portion of the loan principal at the end of each year. The partnership does not intend to make any distributions before liquidation.

In Year 1, the entire depreciation deduction is allocated to B, and the net operating income of $20,000 is allocated equally to A and B. The Year 1 allocations have economic effect, leaving each of the partners with a positive capital account balance ($10,000) at year end. There are no nonrecourse deductions in Year 1 because at year end the basis of the property ($800,000) exceeds the amount of the debt ($780,000).

At the end of Year 2, there is partnership minimum gain of $160,000 ($760,000 debt less $600,000 basis). Accordingly, the $200,000 depreciation deduction comprises $40,000 of recourse deductions and $160,000 of nonrecourse deductions. Without regard to the nonrecourse deductions, the partnership has a taxable loss of $20,000 for Year 2 ($150,000 operating income less $130,000 operating expenses less $40,000 depreciation). Allocation of the

$20,000 loss equally to A and B has economic effect, and reduces each partner's capital account to zero.

The $160,000 of nonrecourse deductions for Year 2 may be allocated in any manner that is "reasonably consistent" with valid allocations of other significant items attributable to the underlying property. A 50/50 allocation, for example, would correspond to the partners' equal division of other significant items that have economic effect, and should therefore be respected. Can the entire nonrecourse deduction be allocated to B, on the ground that it corresponds to the allocation to B of the entire Year 1 depreciation (consisting of $200,000 of recourse deductions attributable to B's investment in the property)? If the allocation of Year 1 depreciation represents a "significant item," then an allocation of the entire nonrecourse deduction to B should be respected. At the end of Year 2, B would have a negative capital account balance of $160,000 which corresponds to her share of the partnership minimum gain. For purposes of the alternate economic effect test, a partner's share of partnership minimum gain is added to her actual deficit restoration obligation, if any. Reg. § 1.704–2(g)(1); Reg. § 1.704–1(b)(2)(ii)(d). Thus, B is deemed to have a deficit restoration obligation of $160,000.

At the end of Year 3, there is partnership minimum gain of $340,000 ($740,000 debt less $400,000 basis), a net increase of $180,000 from the end of Year 2. Accordingly, the $200,000 depreciation deduction for Year 3 comprises $20,000 of recourse deductions and $180,000 of nonrecourse deductions. Without regard to the nonrecourse deductions, the partnership has no taxable income or loss for Year 3 ($150,000 operating income less $130,000 operating expenses less $20,000 depreciation). If the nonrecourse deductions of $180,000 for Year 3 are validly allocated entirely to B, she will have a negative capital account balance (and a deemed deficit restoration obligation) of $340,000 at year end.

If the partnership sells the building at the beginning of Year 4 for no consideration other than relief of nonrecourse liabilities, the net decrease in partnership minimum gain will be $340,000. B's share of the net decrease attributable to the disposition will be $340,000, which is also the amount necessary to eliminate the deficit in her capital account. Accordingly, the entire *Tufts* gain of $340,000 will be allocated to B, leaving her with a capital account balance of zero. If the partnership's nonrecourse deductions were instead allocated 50% to A and 50% to B in Years 1–3, the partners would share the minimum gain chargeback equally. A's 50% share of the net decrease in Year 4 would trigger a minimum gain chargeback even though A has an unlimited deficit restoration obligation.

Example (11): The facts are the same as in Example (10), above, except that the partnership does not sell the building. During Year 4, the partnership has operating income of $350,000, operating expenses of $130,000, and a depreciation deduction of $200,000. The partnership uses its net cash flow ($220,000) and an additional capital contribution from A ($60,000) to repay $280,000 of the debt. At the end of Year 4, there is partnership minimum gain of $260,000 ($460,000 liability less $200,000 basis), a net decrease of $80,000 from the end of Year 3. Therefore, the minimum gain chargeback rules require that gross income and gain be allocated to B as soon as possible in an amount sufficient to eliminate the deficit in her capital account (after taking into account B's $260,000 share of the remaining partnership minimum gain). The $80,000 gross income allocation to B creates a bottom-line loss of $60,000 ($270,000 balance of operating income less $130,000 operating expenses less $200,000 depreciation). The entire bottom-line loss is a recourse deduction, since there is no net *increase* (only a net *decrease*) in partnership minimum gain for the year. Under the economic effect rules, the $60,000 loss must be allocated entirely to A, since any recourse deduction allocated to B would drive her capital account impermissibly negative. At the end of Year 4, the partners' capital accounts will be as follows:

	Capital Accounts	
	A	B
Balance at end of Year 3:	$ 0	($340,000)
Year 4: capital contribution	60,000	
minimum gain chargeback		80,000
recourse deductions	(60,000)	
Balance at end of Year 4:	$ 0	($260,000)

By requiring an allocation to B of $80,000 of gross income in Year 4, the minimum gain chargeback serves a similar function as a qualified income offset. Both provisions seek to ensure that a partner will not wind up with a capital account deficit in excess of any limited restoration obligation.

Assume that the facts are the same as in Example (11), above, except that B (rather than A) contributes the additional $60,000 to repay a portion of the nonrecourse debt. The net decrease in partnership minimum gain for Year 4 would still be $80,000, but the minimum gain chargeback would be limited to B's share of the net decrease in excess of his additional capital contribution ($20,000). Reg. § 1.704–2(f)(3); Reg. § 1.704–2(m) (Ex. 1(iv)). The $20,000 gross income allocation to B would leave the partnership with no bottom-line income or loss ($330,-000 balance of operating income less $130,000 operating expenses less $200,000 depreciation). At the end of Year 4, A would have a capital account of zero and B would have a deficit of $260,000 ($340,-000 less $60,000 capital contribution less $20,000 chargeback), the same result as above.

(d) Distributions of Nonrecourse Liability Proceeds. An increase in partnership minimum gain may also be attributable to a nonrecourse refinancing in excess of the adjusted book basis of partnership property. If the partnership uses the nonrecourse liability proceeds to pay deductible expenses, the payment will generate additional nonrecourse deductions, triggering a corresponding increase in the partners' shares of partnership minimum gain. If the partnership instead promptly distributes the proceeds, some mechanism is necessary to ensure that the distribution increases the distributee partners' shares of partnership minimum gain. Otherwise, the partnership would have an increase in partnership minimum gain, but no partner would be allocated a share of that minimum gain due to the absence of additional nonrecourse deductions. Mechanically, the regulations accomplish this result by including in a partner's share of partnership minimum gain all distributions to such partner of the proceeds of nonrecourse liabilities allocable to an increase in partnership minimum gain. Reg. § 1.704–2(h)(1). The amount so allocated may be determined under "any reasonable method" but may not exceed the increase in partnership minimum gain for the year. Reg. § 1.704–2(h)(2); Reg. § 1.704–2(m) (Ex. 1(vi)).

Example (12): In Years 1–4, the AB partnership has the same operating results as in Example (11), above. At the beginning of Year 5, when the value of the building has unexpectedly increased due to rezoning, the partnership incurs a $40,000 nonrecourse second mortgage secured only by the building; the partnership promptly distributes the nonrecourse liability proceeds equally to A and B. During Year 5, the partnership's operating income equals operating expenses, and it has $200,000 of depreciation allocable entirely to B. The partnership does not make any principal payments during Year 5.

At the end of Year 5, there is partnership minimum gain of $500,000 ($460,000 first mortgage plus $40,000 second mortgage less zero basis of the building), a net increase of $240,000 from the end of

Year 4. Of this amount, $40,000 is treated as attributable to the distribution of nonrecourse liability proceeds and the remaining $200,000 gives rise to nonrecourse deductions (i.e., $200,000 of depreciation deductions). At the end of Year 5, the partners' capital accounts will be as follows:

	Capital Accounts	
	A	B
Balance at end of Year 4:	$ 0	($260,000)
Year 5: distribution	(20,000)	(20,000)
depreciation		(200,000)
Balance at end of Year 5:	($20,000)	($480,000)

The unexpected distribution in Year 5 increases the deficit in B's capital account, but does not trigger a qualified income offset under the alternate economic effect test, since B is deemed to have a deficit restoration obligation equal to her share of partnership minimum gain. At the end of Year 5, B's share of partnership minimum gain is $480,000, i.e., the cumulative nonrecourse deductions allocated to B ($160,000 in Year 2, $180,000 in Year 3, and $200,000 in Year 5), increased by her share of distributions attributable to nonrecourse liability proceeds ($20,000 in Year 5), and decreased by prior reductions in her share of partnership minimum gain ($80,000 in Year 4). At the end of Year 5, A's share of partnership minimum gain is $20,000.

Assume that, at the beginning of Year 6, A guarantees the partnership's nonrecourse debt, converting the first and second mortgages to recourse liabilities allocable entirely to A. See Chapter 6. The loan conversion triggers a $500,000 net decrease in partnership minimum gain and a corresponding minimum gain chargeback. To eliminate the impermissible deficit in her capital account, B must be allocated, as soon as possible, $480,000 of gross income equal to her share of the net decrease in partnership minimum gain ($480,000 share of partnership minimum gain/$500,000 total partnership minimum gain x $500,000 net decrease in partnership minimum gain). Even though the loan conversion also reduces A's share of partnership minimum gain, no minimum gain chargeback is required since A bears the economic risk of loss for the guaranteed nonrecourse debt under the § 752 regulations. See Reg. § 1.704–2(f)(2) and Chapter 6. A's $20,000 share of the net decrease in partnership minimum gain will be charged back, however, if the partnership later repays the guaranteed debt. See Reg. § 1.704–2(f)(7) (Ex. 2).

(e) Partner Nonrecourse Debt. Special rules apply if a partner (or a related person) makes or guarantees a nonrecourse loan to the partnership or otherwise bears the economic risk of loss with respect to a nonrecourse liability of the partnership ("partner nonrecourse debt"). Reg. § 1.704–2(i). In general, deductions attributable to partner nonrecourse debt ("partner nonrecourse deductions") must be allocated to the partner who bears the economic risk of loss for such debt. Any decrease in minimum gain attributable to partner nonrecourse debt may trigger a minimum gain chargeback. This treatment reflects the hybrid character of partner nonrecourse debt, which is classified as a recourse liability for purposes of § 752 but is nevertheless subject to the minimum gain rules for nonrecourse debt under § 704(b).

(f) Conversion of Recourse Debt. The conversion of a liability from recourse to nonrecourse may reduce or eliminate a partner's obligation to restore his deficit capital account. In effect, the deductions allocated to the partner who bore the economic risk of loss prior to the conversion are transformed from recourse deductions to nonrecourse deductions. Accordingly, the regulations allocate to that partner a share of the increase in partnership minimum gain arising from the debt conversion. Reg. § 1.704–2(g)(3). If partner nonrecourse debt is converted to a nonrecourse liability (e.g., because the partner's guarantee lapses), the minimum gain chargeback is deferred until the partnership repays the debt or disposes of the property. Id.; Reg. § 1.704–2(i)(4).

(g) Limited Liability. A business entity classified as a partnership may provide limited-liability protection for all of its members. For example, even recourse liabilities of an LLC may be treated as nonrecourse liabilities for purposes of § 752, because no member bears the economic risk of loss for the entity's liabilities. See Chapter 6. Despite the ostensibly recourse character of the debt, the creditor's state-law right to repayment is limited to the LLC's assets, assuming no member has guaranteed or assumed the underlying debt. Deductions attributable to "limited liabilities" of an LLC or similar entity should be governed by the § 704(b) rules for allocating nonrecourse deductions, including the safe harbor rules. The concept of a minimum gain chargeback may give rise to technical difficulties, however, since the § 704(b) regulations generally assume that nonrecourse debt is secured by specific assets, rather than by all of an entity's assets. Given the liberal consistency requirement under the § 704(b) safe harbor rule, limited-liability entities should have considerable flexibility in allocating nonrecourse deductions.

§ 8. Anti–Abuse Rules

The § 701 anti-abuse rules backstop the detailed mechanical rules of § 704(b). An allocation should nevertheless be respected if it has potential economic consequences and is otherwise valid under the § 704(b) regulations. For example, the § 701 regulations clarify that § 704(b) special allocations may be valid, even though the partners anticipate significant tax benefits as a result of such allocations. Reg. § 1.701–2(d) (Ex. 5–6). The § 701 regulations also recognize that the § 704(b) regulations clearly contemplate the application of certain rules that do not necessarily reflect economic benefits and burdens, e.g., the value-equals-basis rule and the safe harbor rules for allocating nonrecourse deductions. Allocations that rely upon these non-economic rules will not be treated as abusive even if such allocations would otherwise fail the "proper-reflection-of-income" test. Reg. § 1.701–2(a)(3); Reg. § 1.701–2(d) (Ex. 6).

The § 701 regulations also provide an example of an abusive arrangement. Reg. § 1.701–2(d) (Ex. 7). The example involves a three-person partnership which enters into a series of transactions intended to (i) accelerate income to a tax-exempt transitory partner (a foreign corporation) whose interest is promptly liquidated and (ii) generate an artificial built-in loss to shelter taxable income of the two remaining partners. The example concludes that the partnership was formed or availed of to substantially reduce the present value of the partners' aggregate tax liability in a manner inconsistent with the intent of Subchapter K. Because any purported business purpose for the overall transaction is "insignificant" in comparison to the tax benefits, the partnership is not respected. Id. See also ACM Partnership (1997).

§ 9. Depreciation Recapture

Under the recapture provisions, a portion of a partner's distributive share of gain from a sale of depreciable property may be characterized as ordinary income. See §§ 1245, 1250; see also § 1(h)(1), (6) (special capital gain rate for "unrecaptured" § 1250 gain). Allocations of depreciation recapture cannot have substantial economic effect, since classification as recapture affects only the character of income. To the extent possible, the § 1245 regulations attempt to match a partner's share of recapture gain with the depreciation deductions previously allocated to that partner. A partner's share of recapture gain is equal to the lesser of (i) the partner's share of total gain from disposition of the property (gain limitation rule) or (ii) the partner's share of prior depreciation deductions with respect to the property. Reg. § 1.1245–1(e)(2)(i), (ii)(A). Special rules apply to contributed or revalued property. Reg. § 1.1245–1(e)(2)(ii)(C).

Example (13): The AB general partnership sells depreciable equipment with an adjusted basis of $4,000 and a fair market value of $5,200, which it originally purchased for $5,000. Upon sale of the equipment, the partnership recognizes total gain of $1,200 (including $1,000 of § 1245 recapture gain). Assume that the depreciation attributable to the equipment was previously allocated $900 to A and $100 to B. Under the partnership agreement, gain from sale of the equipment is first allocated in proportion to the partners' prior depreciation deductions; any remaining gain is allocated equally to A and B. Thus, A and B are allocated total gain of $1,000 and $200, respectively. The recapture income must be allocated $900 to A and $100 to B, since each partner's share of the total gain exceeds his share of prior depreciation deductions.

If gain on sale of the equipment were instead allocated equally to A and B, A's share of the depreciation recapture would be limited to his share of the total gain ($600), even though A received $900 of depreciation deductions. The remaining depreciation recapture ($400) would be allocated entirely to B, since it does not exceed B's share of the total gain ($600). Thus, B would report ordinary income equal to his share of the prior depreciation deductions ($100) plus the "excess depreciation recapture" that cannot be allocated to A ($300) under the gain limitation rule. Accordingly, all $600 of A's gain would constitute ordinary income and $400 of B's $600 gain would constitute ordinary income.

§ 10. Family Partnerships

(a) General. Even though an allocation has substantial economic effect under the § 704(b) regulations, safeguards are necessary to prevent shifting of income between related partners. In a family partnership, for example, the owner of a partnership interest may seek to deflect income attributable to his capital or services to lower-bracket family members. The § 704(b) regulations are inadequate to prevent intrafamily shifting of income because they are premised on the assumption that the partners have adverse interests. See Reg. § 1.704–1(b)(1)(iii). Instead, § 704(e) essentially codifies assignment-of-income principles and provides special rules for (i) determining the status of a person as a partner and (ii) reallocating income between donors and donees.

(b) Partner Status. Prior to enactment of § 704(e), it was uncertain whether a family partnership would be respected for tax purposes. In *Culbertson*, the Supreme Court rejected the view that membership in a family partnership required a contribution of either "vital services" or "original capital" (i.e., the donee's own capital rather than capital acquired from the donor). Culbertson (1949). Contrary to assignment-of-income principles, the "original capital" doctrine would have prevented recognition of donees as partners even if they owned an interest in a partnership whose only income was derived from property. In *Culbertson*, the Court instead articulated a standard based on the parties' intent: "whether, considering all the facts ... the parties in good faith and acting with a business purpose intended to join together in the present conduct of the enterprise."

Section 704(e)(1) provides a nonexclusive safe harbor for determining when a person will be recognized as a partner for tax purposes. Thus, if a person owns a capital interest in a partnership in which capital is a material income-producing factor, the person will be recognized as a partner for tax purposes, regardless of whether the interest was acquired by gift or by purchase. By contrast, if a person acquires only a profits interest or an interest in a non-capital-intensive partnership, partner status is determined under the *Culbertson* intent test.

For purposes of § 704(e)(1), a person owns a capital interest if he would be entitled to a share of partnership assets upon liquidation of the partnership. Reg. § 1.704–1(e)(1)(v). The regulations provide guidelines for determining whether a purported partner is the true owner of a capital interest. Reg. § 1.704–1(e)(2). In general, a donee will be respected as the owner of a capital interest unless the facts and circumstances indicate that the gift was a sham or the donor retained excessive direct or indirect control over partnership income, distributions and management. Id.; Reg. § 1.704–

1(e)(1)(iii). The lack of management rights by a donee who is a limited partner, however, is immaterial. Reg. § 1.704–1(e)(2)(ix).

Whether capital is a material income-producing factor is determined based on all the facts. For example, the capital requirement is not met if income from the partnership's business consists principally of fees or other compensation for personal services. Reg. § 1.704–1(e)(1)(iv); see also Poggetto (1962) (service partnership). Courts have also considered whether capital is a material income-producing factor where the partnership's income is attributable to goodwill or activities financed predominantly with borrowed funds. See Bateman (1973); Carriage Square, Inc. (1977).

(c) Reallocation of Partnership Income. Section 704(e)(2) permits the Service to reallocate partnership income between a donor and a donee if the donor fails to receive adequate compensation for his services or the distributive share allocated to the donee's capital is proportionately greater than the distributive share allocated to the donor's capital. § 704(e)(2); Reg. § 1.704–1(b)(1)(iii). If the reallocation rules were restricted to donative transfers, the advantage of income-shifting could nevertheless be accomplished by structuring the transaction as a sale rather than a gift. In the case of intrafamily purchases, however, § 704(e)(3) treats the seller and purchaser as donor and donee, thereby triggering the reallocation rules. Reg. § 1.704–1(e)(3)(i).

(d) Method of Reallocation. Section 704(e)(2) reallocates income (in excess of a reasonable allowance for any services rendered by the donor or donee) between the donor and donee "in accordance with their respective interests in partnership capital." Reg. § 1.704–1(e)(3)(i)(b); Woodbury (1967). Although the determination of reasonable compensation is inherently factual, the regulations list certain factors that may be taken into account, e.g., differences in managerial responsibilities and exposure of the general partner's credit to the risks of the partnership's business. Reg. § 1.704–1(e)(3)(i)(c), (ii)(c).

CHAPTER 5

CONTRIBUTED PROPERTY: SECTION 704(c)

§ 1. Overview

Section 704(c)(1)(A) requires that income, gain, loss and deduction with respect to contributed property be "shared among the partners so as to take account of" any difference between basis and value at the time of contribution. The regulations provide detailed rules for allocations with respect to "§ 704(c) property," defined as property which has a book value different from its tax basis at the time of contribution. Reg. § 1.704–3(a)(3). Such allocations must be made "using a reasonable method that is consistent with the purpose of § 704(c)," namely, to prevent shifting of built-in gain or loss. Reg. § 1.704–3(a)(1). The regulations set forth three reasonable methods: the "traditional method," the "traditional method with curative allocations," and the "remedial allocation method." It is useful to examine first the traditional method and then consider the other two methods which build upon the traditional method. Finally, § 704(c)(1)(B) may require recognition of gain if § 704(c) property is distributed to another partner within seven years of contribution.

§ 2.   Traditional Method

(a) General. In its simplest terms, the traditional method requires that any built-in gain or loss attributable to contributed property be allocated to the contributing partner. If the contributed property is depreciable, depreciation deductions must be allocated in a manner that takes into account the variation between the adjusted tax basis and book value of the property. As a general rule, it is necessary to compute separately the partnership's tax and book items (gain, loss or depreciation) with respect to the contributed property and then apply the principle of the § 704(b) regulations that "tax follows book." With respect to the contributed property, the partnership's book gain, loss or depreciation is initially allocated among the partners in accordance with the partnership agreement, assuming that the allocations are valid under the § 704(b) regulations. The partnership's tax gain, loss or depreciation with respect to the contributed property is then allocated to the noncontributing partners to the extent of their share of the corresponding book items. Finally, the partnership's remaining tax gain, loss or depreciation with respect to the contributed property is allocated to the contributing partner. If the allocation of book items satisfies the substantial economic effect test, the allocation of the corresponding tax items under § 704(c) principles is deemed to be in accordance with the partners' interests in the partnership. Reg. § 1.704–1(b)(4)(i), (b)(5) (Ex. 17).

Example (1): A contributes land (basis $6,000, value $10,000) and B contributes $10,000 cash in exchange for equal partnership interests. If the partnership subsequently sells the land for $14,000, it will recognize a book gain of $4,000 ($14,000 less $10,000 book basis) and a tax gain of $8,000 ($14,-000 less $6,000 tax basis). The $4,000 book gain (i.e., the post-contribution appreciation) is allocated $2,000 each to A and B. B is allocated tax gain equal to his share of the book gain ($2,000), and the remaining tax gain of $6,000 (i.e., $4,000 of § 704(c) built-in gain plus $2,000 share of post-contribution appreciation) is allocated to A, eliminating the book/tax disparity:

| | A | | B | |
	Tax	Book	Tax	Book
Initial balance	$ 6,000	$10,000	$10,000	$10,000
Gain on sale	6,000	2,000	2,000	2,000
End balance	$12,000	$12,000	$12,000	$12,000

Example (2): The facts are the same as in Example (1), above, except that A contributes depreciable property instead of land. For simplicity, assume that the partnership will depreciate the property over a five-year period under the straight-line method, and that operating income will equal operating expenses in each year. The § 704(b) regulations provide that the amount of book depreciation bears the same ratio to the adjusted book value of the underlying property as the amount of tax depreciation bears to the adjusted tax basis of the property. Reg. § 1.704–1(b)(2)(iv)(g)(3). Thus, annual book depreciation is $2,000 (1/5 of $10,000 book basis), while annual tax depreciation is only $1,200 (1/5 of $6,000 tax basis). A and B are each allocated one half of the book depreciation ($1,000). B is allocated tax depreciation equal to his share of the book depreciation ($1,000), and the balance of the tax depreciation ($200) is allocated to A, reducing the book/tax disparity in A's capital account. In effect, the traditional method forces the contributing partner to recognize built-in gain attributable to depreciable property by allocating depreciation to the other partners. At the end of Year 5, the book/tax disparity will be eliminated:

	A		B	
	Tax	Book	Tax	Book
Initial balance	$6,000	$10,000	$10,000	$10,000
Year 1: depreciation	(200)	(1,000)	(1,000)	(1,000)
End Year 1	5,800	9,000	9,000	9,000
Years 2–5: depreciation	(800)	(4,000)	(4,000)	(4,000)
End balance	$5,000	$ 5,000	$ 5,000	$ 5,000

(b) Ceiling–Rule Limitation. Under the traditional method, noncontributing partners must be allocated tax items equal to their share of book items, to the extent possible. This goal may be frustrated, however, whenever the "ceiling rule" applies. Under the ceiling rule, the amount of income, gain, loss or deduction that can be allocated for tax purposes is limited to the amount taken into account by the partnership. Reg. § 1.704–3(b)(1). If the ceiling rule applies, built-in gain or loss may be shifted temporarily to the noncontributing partners. The ceiling rule may also limit the tax depreciation allocated to the noncontributing partners. Under the traditional method, ceiling-rule distortions will be remedied only upon sale or liquidation of the partners' partnership interests.

Example (3): The facts are the same as in Example (1), above, except that the contributed land declines in value and is sold for $8,000. Thus, the land is sold for a book loss of $2,000 ($10,000 book basis less $8,000) and a tax gain of $2,000 ($8,000 less $6,000 tax basis), triggering the ceiling rule. The amount of the partnership's realized tax gain ($2,000) is the maximum amount ("ceiling") that can be allocated to the partners. The entire tax gain of $2,000 must be allocated to A. Although B has sustained an economic loss of $1,000, he cannot claim a corresponding taxable loss until sale or liquidation of his partnership interest. The ceiling rule prevents an immediate allocation of additional taxable income of $1,000 to A; A will recognize an additional $1,000 of gain on sale or liquidation of his partnership interest. Immediately after the sale of the land, A and B have the following tax and book capital accounts:

| | A | | B | |
	Tax	Book	Tax	Book
Initial balance	$6,000	$10,000	$10,000	$10,000
Gain (loss)	2,000	(1,000)		(1,000)
End balance	$8,000	$ 9,000	$10,000	$ 9,000

Example (4): The facts are the same as in Example (2), above, except that the basis of the depreciable property is only $4,000. Since the basis of the contributed property ($4,000) is $1,000 less than

B's 50% share of its $10,000 value, the ceiling-rule limitation on depreciation applies. Annual book depreciation is $2,000 (1/5 of $10,000), and annual tax depreciation is $800 (1/5 of $4,000). At the end of Year 1, A and B have the following tax and book capital accounts:

| | A | | B | |
	Tax	Book	Tax	Book
Initial balance	$4,000	$10,000	$10,000	$10,000
Depreciation	0	(1,000)	(800)	(1,000)
End balance	$4,000	$ 9,000	$ 9,200	$ 9,000

The ceiling rule prevents allocation of a full $1,000 of tax loss to B (with an offsetting allocation of $200 of additional income to A). As a result, over the property's depreciable life $1,000 of taxable income ($200 annually) will be shifted from A to B. At the end of Year 5, A and B will each have book capital accounts of $5,000; their tax capital accounts will be $4,000 and $6,000, respectively.

§ 3. Traditional Method With Curative Allocations

(a) General. The regulations permit "reasonable curative allocations" to reduce or eliminate distortions attributable to the ceiling rule. A curative allocation is any allocation of tax items that differs from the allocation of the corresponding book items. Reg. § 1.704–3(c)(1). Generally, a curative allocation is considered reasonable only if it does not exceed the amount necessary to offset the effect of the ceiling rule and consists of tax items of the same type or character as the item limited by the ceiling rule. Reg. § 1.704–3(c)(3). Notwithstanding the character restriction, a curative allocation of gain from sale of § 704(c) property is generally considered reasonable to cure ceiling-rule limitations on depreciation. Id. If the partnership does not have sufficient tax items to cure the ceiling-rule disparity in the year it occurs, subsequent curative allocations to remedy the initial disparity are permitted only if made (i) over a reasonable period (such as the property's economic life) or (ii) on sale of the property. Id. A curative allocation affects only the partners' tax capital accounts (not book capital accounts).

(b) Operation. Curative allocations provide an effective remedy for ceiling-rule distortions whenever the partnership has sufficient other income (or loss) to allocate to the noncontributing partners. The partners may choose to wait until sale of contributed property to cure ceiling-rule limitations; they may also limit curative allocations to particular tax items (e.g., depreciation from specific property). Reg. § 1.704–3(c)(1). Because curative allocations depend on actual tax items, ceiling-rule distortions may not be entirely eliminated.

To illustrate the operation of the traditional method with curative allocations, assume that the contributed property in Example (4), above, is sold at the beginning of Year 2 for $10,000. Upon sale, the book gain of $2,000 ($10,000 less $8,000 book basis) would be allocated equally to A and B. Absent a curative allocation, the tax gain of $6,800 ($10,000 less $3,200 tax basis) would be allocated $1,000 to B and $5,800 to A; on a subsequent liquidation, B would recognize a tax loss of $200 ($10,200 basis less $10,000 cash) and A would recognize a tax gain of $200 ($10,000 cash less $9,800 basis). B's tax loss corresponds to the $200 shortfall in B's share of tax depreciation in Year 1. To counteract the prior ceiling-rule limitation, a curative allocation would require that the $6,800 tax gain on sale of the property be allocated $800 to B (rather than $1,000) and $6,000 to A (rather than $5,800). Taking into account the curative allocation, the partners would have the following tax and book capital accounts:

	A		B	
	Tax	Book	Tax	Book
End Year 1	$ 4,000	$ 9,000	$ 9,200	$ 9,000
Year 2: gain on sale	6,000	1,000	800	1,000
End balance	$10,000	$10,000	$10,000	$10,000

A curative allocation may consist of gain or loss from other property of a similar character. In Example (3), above, the contributed land is sold for a book loss of $2,000 and a tax gain of $2,000. Because of the ceiling rule, B is prevented from receiving a tax loss of $1,000 equal to his book loss of $1,000 upon sale of the land. Assume that the partnership also sells securities (basis $10,000, value $16,000) purchased with the cash B contributed. Absent a curative allocation, the $6,000 tax and book gain attributable to the securities would be allocated $3,000 each to A and B. Upon sale of the securities, the partnership may choose to make a curative allocation of $1,000 additional tax gain to A (and $1,000 less tax gain to B), eliminating the ceiling-rule distortion attributable to sale of the land. Immediately after sale of the land and securities, the partners would have the following tax and book capital accounts:

	A		B	
	Tax	Book	Tax	Book
Initial balance	$ 6,000	$10,000	$10,000	$10,000
Sale of land	2,000	(1,000)		(1,000)
Sale of securities	4,000	3,000	2,000	3,000
End balance	$12,000	$12,000	$12,000	$12,000

The curative allocation of gain from sale of the securities does not exceed the amount of the ceiling-limited loss on sale of the land. Because the character requirement is also satisfied, the curative allocation should be treated as reasonable.

In the case of depreciable § 704(c) property, the partnership does not have to wait until sale of the property to cure ceiling-rule limitations on depreciation. Instead, the partnership may choose to make offsetting curative allocations as ceiling-rule distortions arise. For example, the partnership may allocate additional tax depreciation from other property to the noncontributing partner (and away from the contributing partner). Alternatively, the partnership may shift additional taxable ordinary income to the contributing partner (or shift additional taxable ordinary deductions to the noncontributing partner).

In Example (4), above, assume that the partnership earns annual gross ordinary income of $400, which A and B share equally for book purposes.

Since B is deprived of $200 of tax depreciation from the property contributed by A, the partnership may make an offsetting curative allocation. If B's share of the gross income is reallocated entirely to A for tax purposes, A will be taxed on an additional $1,000 of ordinary income ($200 annually) over the five-year remaining useful life of the property (and B will be taxed on $1,000 less ordinary income), precisely offsetting the ceiling-rule distortion. At the end of Year 5, each partner will have a tax and book capital account of $6,000:

	A		B	
	Tax	Book	Tax	Book
Initial balance	$ 4,000	$10,000	$10,000	$10,000
Years 1-5: depreciation		(5,000)	(4,000)	(5,000)
Years 1-5: gross income	2,000	1,000		1,000
End balance	$ 6,000	$ 6,000	$ 6,000	$ 6,000

§ 4.   Remedial Allocation Method

(a) General. The remedial allocation method is a variation of a "deferred sale" approach. Under a deferred sale approach, the partnership would be treated as if it had purchased the contributed property for its fair market value on the date of contribution, but the contributing partner's built-in gain or loss would be deferred until subsequent events, e.g., disposition of the property. Because of timing and character differences, the deferred sale approach was considered too generous to the contributing partner. Instead of the deferred sale approach, the regulations provide for the remedial allocation method. While less susceptible to abuse than the deferred sale method, the remedial allocation method accomplishes a similar result with respect to the noncontributing partners. If the partnership adopts the remedial allocation method, the noncontributing partners receive, in effect, a cost basis in their share of the contributed property.

(b) Operation. The remedial allocation method eliminates ceiling-rule distortions by creating fictional tax items that offset exactly the ceiling-limited items in amount and character. Because the remedial items are purely notional and do not depend on the existence of actual tax items, noncontributing partners always receive identical tax and book allocations; the contributing partner receives an offsetting allocation of equal amount as the notional tax items allocated to noncontributing partners. Remedial allocations have no effect on computation of the partnership's taxable income or the adjusted basis of the partnership's property. Reg. § 1.704–3(d)(4). Since remedial allocations affect the partners' tax liability, however, the partners' outside bases and tax capital accounts (but not book capital accounts) are adjusted to reflect these items. Id.

In Example (3), above, assume that the partnership elects the remedial allocation method and has no items for the year other than the book loss of $2,000 and tax gain of $2,000 with respect to sale of the contributed land. Under the remedial allocation method, the partnership would allocate a notional tax loss of $1,000 to B equal to B's share of the book loss and an offsetting notional tax gain of $1,000 to A. Immediately after the sale, the partners would have the following tax and book capital accounts:

	A		B	
	Tax	Book	Tax	Book
Initial balance	$ 6,000	$10,000	$10,000	$10,000
Sale of land	2,000	(1,000)		(1,000)
Remedial allocation	1,000		(1,000)	
End balance	$ 9,000	$ 9,000	$ 9,000	$ 9,000

(c) Special Rule for Depreciable Property. In the case of depreciable § 704(c) property, a special rule applies for purposes of recovering book basis under the remedial allocation method. Consistent with the notion of a deferred sale, the remedial allocation method divides the book basis of depreciable § 704(c) property into two components: a "carryover" portion and "stepped-up" portion. To the extent that the book basis does not exceed the adjusted tax basis of the contributed property (the carryover portion), the partnership steps into the shoes of the contributing partner and recovers book basis in the same manner as the adjusted tax basis. The portion of the book basis in excess of the adjusted book basis of the contributed property (the stepped-up portion) is recovered using a depreciation method and recovery period available for newly-purchased property of the same kind as the contributed property. See Reg. § 1.704–3(d)(2), (d)(7) (Ex. 1).

Example (5): The facts are the same as in Example (4), above, except that the partnership elects the remedial allocation method. The carryover portion of the book basis ($4,000) is recovered in the same manner as the adjusted tax basis ($4,000) of the contributed property, yielding annual depreciation of $800 for tax and book purposes during Years 1–5 (using the straight-line method over the property's remaining useful life of five years). The stepped-up portion of the book basis ($6,000) is treated as newly-purchased property. Assume that the partnership recovers the stepped-up portion of the book basis using the straight-line method over 10 years (the recovery period for similar newly-purchased property). In Years 1–10, the partnership has annual depreciation of $600 for book purposes (and no corresponding tax depreciation) attributable to the stepped-up portion of the book basis. Accordingly, the partnership has the following tax and book depreciation in Years 1–10:

	Tax Basis	Carryover Book Basis	Stepped-Up Book Basis	Total Book Basis
Year 1	$ 800	$ 800	$ 600	$ 1,400
Years 2-5	3,200	3,200	2,400	5,600
Year 6			600	600
Years 7-10			2,400	2,400
Total	$ 4,000	$ 4,000	$ 6,000	$10,000

As under the traditional method, the partnership first determines the amount of book items for the taxable year and allocates them in accordance with the § 704(b) regulations. Remedial allocations are necessary only to the extent that, under the traditional method, the ceiling rule would give rise to a disparity between the tax and book allocations to the noncontributing partner. Reg. § 1.704–3(d)(1). In Years 1–5, the partnership's annual book depreciation of $1,400 ($800 carryover plus $600 stepped-up portions) is divided equally between A and B ($700 each); the annual tax depreciation ($800) is allocated $100 to A and $700 to B. No ceiling-rule distortions occur in Years 1–5, since B receives tax depreciation equal to his share of book depreciation. In Years 6–10, B is allocated $300 of book depreciation (50% of $600) annually and no tax depreciation; for tax purposes, the property has been fully depreciated. To cure the ceiling-rule limitation in Years 6–10, the partnership makes two offsetting annual remedial allocations for tax (but not book) purposes: $300 of depreciation to B and $300 of ordinary income to A. At the end of Year 10, the partners' have the following tax and book capital accounts:

	A Tax	A Book	B Tax	B Book
Initial balance	$ 4,000	$10,000	$10,000	$10,000
Year 1: depreciation	(100)	(700)	(700)	(700)
Years 2-5	(400)	(2,800)	(2,800)	(2,800)
End Year 5	3,500	6,500	6,500	6,500
Year 6: depreciation		(300)		(300)
remedial allocation	300		(300)	
Years 7-10: depreciation		(1,200)		(1,200)
remedial allocation	1,200		(1,200)	
End Year 10	$ 5,000	$ 5,000	$ 5,000	$ 5,000

By comparison to the traditional method (with or without curative allocations), the remedial allocation method has the effect of postponing ceiling-rule distortions until subsequent years because of the longer book-recovery period. Thus, the ceiling-rule limitation is not triggered until after Year 5 when the partnership's tax depreciation is fully exhausted. Because the partnership still has remaining book depreciation in Years 6–10, however, book/tax disparities are inevitable thereafter, triggering remedial allocations. The book/tax disparity is not fully eliminated until Year 10, when the stepped-up portion of the book basis is exhausted. Thus, the remedial allocation method may cure book/tax disparities more slowly than the traditional method with curative allocations.

§ 5. Limits on Flexibility

(a) Choice of Methods. Subject to the anti-abuse rules, the partners have considerable flexibility in choosing between different § 704(c) allocation methods. The particular method may vary from property to property, as long as the "overall method or combination of methods" is reasonable and consistent with the purpose of § 704(c). Reg. § 1.704–3(a)(2). Ignoring any character and timing differences, the net result under each allocation method is identical: tax items may be reallocated among the partners, but the reallocation does not affect the partnership's overall taxable income or loss. If the partners' effective tax rates are similar, the choice of allocation methods will generally not produce a significant net tax benefit. In other situations, however, the partners may be able to improve their overall tax position.

For example, a high-bracket contributing partner who desires to defer built-in gain as long as possible may wish to avoid curative allocations. Such a partner may also benefit from deferral under the remedial allocation method due to the longer period for eliminating book/tax disparities. The benefit to the contributing partner is generally offset, however, by the corresponding detriment to the noncontributing partner. In Example (5), above, the remedial allocation method defers $1,500 of B's tax depreciation deductions until Years 6–10; correspondingly, $1,500 of remedial tax gain allocable to A is deferred until Years 6–10. If the partners have different tax brackets, a noncontributing partner can expect to be compensated for agreeing to an allocation method that benefits the contributing partner.

(b) Anti–Abuse Rules. The regulations include an anti-abuse rule which imposes some constraints on the choice of allocation method. Under the regulations, an allocation is considered unreasonable if the contribution of property and corresponding tax allocations "are made with a view to shifting the tax consequences of built-in gain or loss among the partners in a manner that substantially reduces the present value of the partners' aggregate tax liability." Reg. § 1.704–3(a)(10). While potentially quite expansive, the anti-abuse rule is apparently aimed primarily at attempts to exploit the ceiling-rule limitation or manipulate curative allocations.

For example, assume that A (a high-bracket taxpayer) contributes depreciable property (basis $10,-000, value $100,000) and B (a low-bracket taxpayer) contributes $100,000 cash, in exchange for equal partnership interests. Using the traditional method, the partnership depreciates A's property over its remaining useful life of one year. A and B are each allocated half of the book depreciation ($50,000), and B is allocated the entire tax depreciation ($10,-000). When the § 704(c) gain has been reduced to zero (i.e., both the tax and book basis of the contributed property are zero), the partnership sells the contributed property for $100,000 and allocates the corresponding tax and book gain equally to A and B. Under these circumstances, the regulations conclude that the use of the traditional method is unreasonable. Reg. § 1.704–3(b)(2) (Ex. 2). It is assumed that the partners undertook the transaction with a view to shifting $40,000 of A's built-in gain to B ($50,000 tax gain allocated to B less $10,000 tax depreciation). A reasonable method of handling the book/tax disparity would be to require a curative allocation of gain upon sale of the contributed property. Id.

Use of the traditional method with curative allocations may also be unreasonable. The regulations illustrate this point with an example quite similar to the one above, except that the tax brackets of the contributing and noncontributing partners are reversed. Reg. § 1.704–3(c)(4) (Ex. 3). The partnership again depreciates the tax and book basis of the contributed property over its one-year remaining recovery period, allocating the tax and book depreciation equally among the partners. At the end of the first year, the partnership sells other property which generates $80,000 of ordinary income. Although the ordinary income is allocated equally to A and B for book purposes, the partnership elects to make a curative allocation of $40,000 of ordinary income to A. The curative allocation eliminates the book/tax disparity attributable to A's property, and simultaneously shifts $40,000 of ordinary income away from B. The example concludes that the curative allocation is unreasonable because the purpose of the transaction is to shift a significant amount of ordinary income from a high-bracket partner (B) to a low-bracket partner (A).

In both examples, the underlying abuse is apparently attributable to the partners' ability to recover the entire book value of the property over a one-year period, even though the property's remaining economic life is assumed to be significantly longer. Because of the unrealistically short recovery period for book purposes, the noncontributing partner is permitted, in effect, to "expense" her investment in the property. Thus, the noncontributing partner potentially receives more favorable treatment than would a purchaser of an undivided interest in the property who depreciated the cost basis over a longer useful life.

By contrast, the bifurcated book-recovery period under the remedial allocation method more closely approximates the overall useful life that would be available if the property were newly-purchased. Given this characteristic, the remedial allocation method might appear to represent a "baseline" for measuring when an impermissible shift in built-in gain has occurred. Nevertheless, the anti-abuse rules do not provide a safe harbor for the remedial allocation method. Thus, the Service may apparently challenge even use of the remedial allocation method if the partners have the requisite view to shifting built-in gain and the allocations improve the partners' overall tax situation in present-value terms. While adding some uncertainty, the § 704(c) anti-abuse rules may represent a useful prophylactic against overly aggressive planning. These specific rules should presumably take precedence over the general § 701 anti-abuse rules.

§ 6. Revaluation of Property

(a) General. Apart from in-kind contributions of property, book/tax disparities may arise whenever partnership property is revalued under the § 704(b) regulations. A revaluation is permitted (i) in connection with a contribution of money or other property to the partnership by a new or existing partner in exchange for a partnership interest; (ii) in connection with a liquidation of the partnership or a distribution of money or other property to a retiring or continuing partner in exchange for all or a portion of his partnership interest; or (iii) in accordance with generally accepted industry practices if substantially all of the partnership's assets consists of stock, securities or similar instruments that are readily tradeable on an established securities market. Reg. § 1.704–1(b)(2)(iv)(f)(5).

(b) Capital Account Adjustments. In the case of an optional revaluation, the capital account ad-

justments must be based on the fair market value of
the partnership's property (taking § 7701(g) into
account) and must reflect the manner in which any
unrealized income, gain, loss or deduction inherent
in the property (and not previously reflected in the
partners' capital accounts) would be allocated
among the partners on a taxable disposition. Once
partnership property has been revalued, capital accounts must subsequently be adjusted for the partners' distributive shares of book items (depreciation
and gain or loss) with respect to the revalued property, and § 704(c) principles must be applied in
determining the partners' distributive shares of tax
items with respect to such property to take account
of book/tax disparities arising from the revaluation.
Reg. §§ 1.704–1(b)(2)(iv)(f)(1)–(4); 1.704–3(a)(6).

A revaluation serves to "lock in" the existing
partners' shares of unrealized appreciation (or decline in value) upon admission of a new partner,
and thus to prevent an inadvertent capital shift.
For example, but for a revaluation (or special allocation), a new partner would become entitled to an
equal share of unrealized appreciation at the time
of admission, resulting in a capital shift from the
existing partners to the new partner. The regulations warn that such a capital shift may be treated
as compensation for services or a disguised gift,
depending on the circumstances. Reg. §§ 1.704–
1(b)(2)(iv)(f)(5), (b)(1)(iii)–(iv).

Example (6): In exchange for equal partnership
interests, A and B each contribute $100 cash to the
newly-formed AB partnership which purchases land

worth $200. When the land has appreciated to $400, C contributes $200 in exchange for a 1/3 partnership interest, and the partnership revalues its property. The partnership uses C's contribution to improve the land, and subsequently sells the improved land for $900. Immediately after the sale, the partners have the following tax and book capital accounts:

	A		B		C	
	Tax	Book	Tax	Book	Tax	Book
Initial balance	$100	$100	$100	$100	$200	$200
Bookup adjustment		100		100		
Revalued balance	100	200	100	200	200	200
Gain on sale	200	100	200	100	100	100
End balance	$300	$300	$300	$300	$300	$300

The revaluation at the time of C's admission produces a $100 upward adjustment to each existing partner's capital account, reflecting his share of unrealized appreciation in the unimproved land. After the improvements, the land has a book basis of $600 ($400 fair market value at the time of C's admission plus $200 subsequent improvements) and a tax basis of $400 ($200 original basis plus $200 improvements). Upon sale, the partnership recognizes a book gain of $300 ($900 less $600 book basis) and a tax gain of $500 ($900 less $400 tax basis). The book gain is allocated to the partners in equal shares. Tax gain is allocated to the partners in amounts equal to their shares of book gain (totalling $300), and the remaining $200 of tax gain is allocated to A and B in equal shares.

Without actually booking up capital accounts, the partners may accomplish a similar result by specially allocating to the existing partners any pre-admission built-in gain realized on a subsequent sale of the property. See Reg. § 1.704–1(b)(5) (Ex. (14)(iv)). Such a special allocation postpones the capital account adjustment for unrealized gain until the property is sold. If the gain realized on sale is less than the built-in gain (e.g., because of an intervening decline in value), the existing partners' capital accounts will be increased only by the realized gain, and they will thus bear the risk of any decline in value. By contrast, if the existing partners' capital accounts are booked up immediately, all of the partners will share the risk of decline in value.

§ 7. Distributions of § 704(c) Property

(a) General. Section 704(c)(1)(B) is intended to prevent circumvention of the § 704(c) allocation rules when property contributed by one partner is distributed to another partner within seven years after contribution. If § 704(c)(1)(B) applies, the contributor recognizes taxable gain or loss equal to the amount that would have been specially allocated to him under § 704(c) upon a deemed sale of the property for its fair market value at the time of distribution. Reg. § 1.704–4(a)(1). The remaining built-in gain or loss at the time of the distribution depends on the § 704(c) allocation method used by the partnership. See Reg. § 1.704–4(a)(5) (Ex. 2) (traditional method) and (Ex. 3) (remedial allocation method).

The character of the gain or loss is determined as if the partnership had sold the property to the distributee. Reg. § 1.704–4(b)(1). Both the contributor's outside basis and the partnership's basis in the distributed property are adjusted appropriately to reflect any gain or loss recognized. § 704(c)(1)(B)(iii); Reg. § 1.704–4(e). The adjustment to the basis of the distributed property occurs immediately before the distribution, and is taken into account for purposes of determining the distributee's basis under § 732 (and any optional basis adjustments under § 754). Reg. § 1.704–4(e)(2). Section 704(c)(1)(B) applies only if a transaction is not treated as a disguised sale under § 707(a)(2)(B). See Reg. § 1.704–4(a)(2); see also Chapter 7.

Example (7): A contributes land with a basis of zero and a fair market value of $100, and B and C each contribute $100 cash, to the ABC partnership in exchange for equal 1/3 partnership interests. The partnership uses the traditional method of making allocations under § 704(c). Three years later, when the land is still worth $100, the partnership distributes a 50% undivided interest in the land to B in a current distribution. Under § 704(c)(1)(B), A recognizes $50 of the built-in gain, increasing her outside basis to $50. B takes a basis of $50 in the distributed land (equal to the partnership's pre-distribution basis in the land of zero increased by A's recognized gain of $50). A's remaining built-in gain ($50) is deferred until the partnership disposes of the remaining land or A sells or liquidates her partnership interest. If the land instead declined in value to $40 at the time of the distribution, A's recognized gain (and increase in outside basis) would be limited to $20, while B would take a basis of $20 in her one-half of the land.

(b) Like–Kind Property. Section 704(c)(2) provides a special rule if the contributing partner (or his successor) receives a timely distribution of property of a like kind (within the meaning of § 1031) to the contributed property which is distributed to another partner. § 704(c)(2). In this situation, the amount of gain (or loss) that the contributing partner would otherwise recognize under § 704(c)(1)(B) is reduced by any built-in gain (or loss) inherent in the distributed like-kind property in the hands of the contributing partner immediately after the distribution. Reg. § 1.704–4(d)(3). The contributing partner's basis in the distributed property is determined under the normal distribution rules of § 732 as if such property were distributed separately (and without taking into account any increase in outside basis attributable to gain recognized under § 704(c)(1)(B)). Id. This provision gives the contributing partner the benefit of like-kind exchange treatment to the extent that the contributor's built-in gain (or loss) is preserved in the distributed property. See Reg. § 1.704–4(d)(4); see also Chapter 9.

(c) Special Rules. Under § 704(c)(3), a successor partner steps into the contributor's shoes when he acquires the contributor's partnership interest. Reg. § 1.704–4(d)(2). Thus, the built-in gain (or loss) recognized by the contributor on the sale of his partnership interest may be taxed again to the successor partner when the partnership subsequently sells or distributes the contributed property, unless a § 754 election is in effect. See Chapter 8. In addition to numerous exceptions and special rules, the regulations also contain an anti-abuse rule for transactions intended to circumvent the purpose of § 704(c)(1)(B). Reg. § 1.704–4(f).

§ 8. Accounts Receivable and Accounts Payable

Section 704(c) principles also apply to unrealized income and deductions when a cash-method partner contributes accounts receivable, accounts payable or other accrued but unpaid items. § 704(c)(3); Reg. § 1.704–3(a)(4). When the partnership collects zero-basis accounts receivable, the pre-contribution unrealized income must be allocated to the contributor. Similarly, when a partnership pays accounts payable or other accrued but unpaid items (e.g., unpaid interest expenses) contributed by a partner, the resulting partnership deductions must be allocated to the contributor or capitalized if he is no longer a partner.

For purposes of the liability-sharing rules of § 752, an obligation of a cash-method taxpayer that will generate a deduction when paid is not treated as a "liability." Rev. Rul. 88–77. Such obligations are excluded from the definition of liabilities because they have not yet generated a tax benefit for the contributor. Accordingly, the partnership is not treated as assuming accounts payable of a cash-method contributor, and the contribution does not cause a reduction in the contributor's outside basis (or immediate gain recognition). Cf. § 357(c)(3) (analogous treatment in the corporate context when a cash-method taxpayer contributes zero-basis receivables and accounts payable in a § 351 exchange).

If an accrual-method partner contributes accounts receivable, the basis of the receivables in the contributor's hands will reflect the prior inclusion in income. Moreover, accounts payable and other accrued but unpaid items of an accrual-method taxpayer are treated as liabilities for purposes of § 752, since such items have already generated a tax deduction.

Example (8): A contributes $50,000 cash and B (a cash-method taxpayer) contributes $60,000 worth of zero-basis receivables and $10,000 of payables to the AB partnership in exchange for equal partnership interests. Assuming that the payables are deductible items, B recognizes no gain on the contribution and takes an outside basis of zero equal to his basis in the receivables; A's outside basis is $50,000. When the partnership collects the receivables, B must be allocated $60,000 of taxable income, increasing his outside basis to $60,000. Finally, when the partnership pays the $10,000 of payables, the resulting deduction must be allocated entirely to B, reducing his outside basis to $50,000.

CHAPTER 6

PARTNERSHIP LIABILITIES

§ 1. Overview

Section 752 maintains parity between inside and outside basis by coordinating adjustments to the partners' outside bases with increases and decreases in partnership liabilities. The linkage between inside and outside basis is especially important in ensuring that items of deduction attributable to partnership liabilities flow through to the same partners who have outside basis reflecting the underlying liabilities. A partner who is allocated a deduction attributable to a partnership liability generally must be allocated a corresponding share of the liability. A partner's share of partnership liabilities is also important for purposes of determining gain or loss upon sale of his partnership interest under § 741 and the treatment of partnership distributions under § 731. See Chapters 8 and 9.

The former § 752 regulations (pre–1988) allocated partnership liabilities in a relatively straightforward manner. Recourse liabilities were generally shared by general partners in accordance with their loss-sharing ratios, while nonrecourse liabilities were shared by all partners, general and limited, in accordance with their profit-sharing ratios. Former

Reg. § 1.752–1(e). While the former liability-sharing rules were easily stated, they sometimes invited manipulation and gave rise to uncertainty in the case of complex commercial arrangements. In particular, the former regulations failed to resolve problems arising from side agreements requiring limited partners to satisfy partnership liabilities. See Raphan (1985). The current § 752 regulations reflect the Treasury's response to a 1984 congressional mandate to revise the liability-sharing rules "to ensure that the partner receiving basis with respect to a partnership liability ... bears the economic risk of loss with respect to such liabilities."

The § 752 regulations coordinate the liability-sharing rules with the economic effect analysis developed in the § 704(b) regulations. The sharing of recourse liabilities is determined by identifying which partners would bear the economic risk of loss based on the consequences of a "constructive liquidation"—a hypothetical event in which all partnership assets become worthless and the partnership liquidates. While the regulations are phrased in terms of "economic risk of loss" (a defined term), they focus primarily on the partners' sharing of the ultimate legal liability for the partnership's obligations. Generally, the allocation of economic risk of loss can be determined by answering the question: If the partnership defaulted on its obligations, to what extent (if any) would a partner be obligated to pay the liability from personal funds, without any right to reimbursement? If no partner would bear the economic risk of loss, the liability is classified as nonrecourse. Nonrecourse liabilities are allocated according to flexible rules based on the manner in which the partners share the profits that would presumably be used to repay such liabilities.

§ 2. Definition of Liability and Assumption

(a) Definition. Under § 752, a liability affects outside basis only to the extent that it creates or increases the basis of property (including cash) or gives rise to a current deduction or a nondeductible noncapital expenditure (e.g., a fine). See Rev. Rul. 88–77; Rev. Rul 95–26 (short sale of securities). This treatment generally preserves parity between aggregate inside and outside basis. For example, unpaid expenses and accounts payable of cash-basis taxpayers are not treated as liabilities for purposes of § 752, because these obligations are not deductible until paid. See Chapter 5. Contingent obligations may be ignored or taken into account only when the contingency is resolved. Reg. § 1.752–2(b)(4); see Estate of Baron (1986) (nonrecourse obligation too contingent to be included in basis). If the amount of a nonrecourse obligation unreasonably exceeds the fair market value of acquired property at the time of purchase, the transaction may lack economic substance. See Estate of Franklin (1976) (no bona fide debt); Bergstrom (1996) (following Estate of Franklin).

(b) Whose Liability. The § 752 regulations provide that a person is generally treated as "assuming" a liability only to the extent that he becomes subject to personal liability with respect to such

liability. The assumption will be respected only if
the assuming partner is directly liable to the creditor and no other partner (or related person) would
be treated as bearing the economic risk of loss
under the § 752 regulations. Reg. § 1.752–1(d). For
example, a limited partner is not treated as assuming a partnership liability if he is only indirectly
liable to a creditor. The general rules concerning
assumptions do not apply to contributions or distributions of property subject to liabilities. Under
§ 752(c), the transferee is treated as assuming such
liabilities, subject to the fair-market-value limitation, even though no personal liability exists.
§ 752(c); Reg. § 1.752–1(e).

§ 3. Recourse Liabilities

(a) **Economic Risk of Loss.** A partnership liability is recourse to the extent that any partner
bears the economic risk of loss with respect to such
liability. Reg. § 1.752–1(a)(1). If a liability is part
recourse and part nonrecourse, the regulations bifurcate the liability. Reg. § 1.752–1(i); see Reg.
§ 1.752–2(f) (Ex. 5). A partner's share of partnership recourse liabilities equals the portion of such
liabilities for which he bears the economic risk of
loss. Reg. § 1.752–2(a). In general, a partner bears
the economic risk of loss with respect to a partnership liability to the extent that the partner (or a
related person) would be obligated to make a net
payment or a net contribution with respect to such
liability if the partnership were constructively liquidated. Reg. § 1.752–2(b)(1).

In effect, a partner's economic risk of loss is measured by his ultimate responsibility to pay the creditor or to contribute additional funds to the partnership (after determining the consequences of the constructive liquidation). In sorting out the partners' obligations, the regulations first determine a partner's gross payment or contribution obligation and then reduce this amount by any reimbursement to which the partner (or a related person) would be entitled as a result of the payment or contribution. Reg. § 1.752–2(b)(5). Except in abusive situations, partners (or related persons) are generally assumed to discharge their obligations, regardless of net worth. Reg. § 1.752–2(b)(6) (deemed-satisfaction rule).

(b) Constructive Liquidation. The regulations trace the economic risk of loss by reference to a hypothetical liquidation in which the following events are deemed to occur: (i) the partnership's assets (including cash) become worthless, (ii) the partnership's liabilities become due and payable in full, (iii) the partnership disposes of its assets in a fully taxable exchange for no consideration (other than relief from limited liabilities), and (iv) the partnership allocates its items of income, gain, loss, deduction and credit among the partners and liquidates. Reg. § 1.752–2(b)(1).

In the constructive liquidation, the partnership is treated as realizing the amount of any liability for which "the creditor's right to repayment ... is limited solely to one or more assets of the partnership." Reg. § 1.752–2(b)(2)(i). This category of "limited liabilities" includes "true" nonrecourse debt which would be extinguished by the deemed transfer of the partnership's assets. See Reg. § 1.1001–1; Tufts (1983). The constructive liquidation is treated as a foreclosure of the property subject to such debt, giving rise to gain or loss equal to the difference between the amount of the debt extinguished and the tax basis (or book value, if different) of the securing property. If tax basis and book value differ, the consequences of the constructive liquidation are determined by reference to the book value of the partnership property. Such a book/tax disparity may arise whenever property is contributed to the partnership subject to § 704(c) or is subsequently revalued.

Example (1): A partnership purchases equipment for $250 cash and a nonrecourse purchase-money note of $750. Upon a constructive liquidation, the partnership would be treated as transferring the equipment (deemed to be worthless) for an amount equal to the nonrecourse liability, triggering a loss of $250 ($1,000 basis less $750 amount realized). If the basis of the equipment were less than the amount of the debt (e.g., because of depreciation deductions), the partnership would recognize *Tufts* gain on the constructive liquidation. For example, if the constructive liquidation occurred when the equipment had a basis of $300 and the debt remained $750, the partnership would recognize a gain of $450 ($750 amount realized less $300 basis).

With respect to its remaining property, the partnership recognizes a loss on the deemed disposition equal to the tax basis (or book value, if different) of such property, triggering a corresponding reduction in the partners' capital accounts. The aggregate deficit in the partners' book capital accounts immediately after the constructive liquidation will generally equal the amount of the partnership's recourse liabilities. The constructive liquidation is deemed to occur whenever it is necessary for tax purposes to determine the partners' shares of partnership liabilities and outside basis. Reg. § 1.752–4(d).

Example (2): A and B each contribute $5,000 to the AB general partnership in exchange for equal partnership interests. The partnership maintains capital accounts in accordance with the § 704(b) regulations, and each partner is obligated to restore any deficit in his capital account. The partnership purchases a building (worth $100,000) for $10,000 cash and a $90,000 recourse purchase-money note. Upon a constructive liquidation, the partnership would realize a loss of $100,000 (i.e., the amount realized would not include the $90,000 recourse liability because that liability is not discharged as a result of the transfer). The loss would be allocated $50,000 to A and $50,000 to B as equal partners, and each partner would have a capital account deficit of $45,000 ($5,000 contribution less $50,000 loss). Accordingly, each partner would have an obligation to contribute $45,000 to the partnership to pay the recourse liability.

Example (3): During its first year, the AB general partnership in the preceding example has operating income of $150,000, operating expenses of $110,000 and depreciation deductions of $20,000. The partnership uses its net cash flow of $40,000 to repay a portion of the $90,000 debt, reducing the principal amount to $50,000. Upon a constructive liquidation at the end of the year, the partnership would recognize a loss of $80,000 (i.e., the adjusted basis of the building). The partnership's total losses of $60,000 ($20,000 net taxable income decreased by $80,000 constructive loss) would produce a deficit of $25,000 in each partner's capital account ($5,000 contribution less $30,000 loss). Accordingly, each partner would have an obligation to contribute $25,000 to the partnership to pay the recourse liability. In the example, the partners' liability-sharing ratio remains 50/50 with respect to the outstanding debt, since the partners share all items of income, gain, loss and deduction equally. If the partners' sharing ratios are more complex, however, the allocation of the partnership liability may change over time.

(c) Direct Payment Obligations. A partner also bears the economic risk of loss to the extent of any obligation to make a direct payment to a creditor (or to reimburse another partner for such a payment). Payment obligations running directly to the creditor include guarantees, assumptions, indemnities and similar arrangements. Because the regulations focus on ultimate responsibility for a partnership liability rather than formal structure, it is important to take account of any collateral arrangement that affects a partner's economic risk of loss.

If a limited partner guarantees a recourse liability of the partnership, the guarantee normally does not shift the basis for the liability away from the general partner. See Reg. § 1.752–2(f) (Ex. 3) (deemed satisfaction by general partner). If the limited partner were required to pay the obligation, he would be subrogated to the lender's rights against the partnership and would accordingly be entitled to reimbursement from the general partner. Unless he waived his right of subrogation, the limited partner would not be obligated to make a net payment. See Reg. § 1.752–2(f) (Ex. 4).

By contrast, a limited partner who guarantees a nonrecourse debt should generally be allocated basis up to the amount of the guarantee. See Reg. § 1.752–2(f) (Ex. 5). In effect, the regulations classify a nonrecourse debt as a recourse liability (a defined term) if one of the partners bears the economic risk of loss, even though the partnership has no personal liability. The partner-guarantor is personally obligated to pay the creditor under the guarantee, and has no right to reimbursement from the partnership or the other partners. Reg. §§ 1.752–1(a)(1), 1.752–2(b)(1).

Under an indemnity agreement, one partner (the "indemnitor") may be obligated (i) to satisfy the liability of another partner (the "indemnitee") to a third-party creditor or (ii) to reimburse the indemnitee for payment of the underlying liability. An indemnity agreement may be enforceable directly by the creditor (e.g., as a third-party beneficiary under applicable state law). An indemnitor generally becomes ultimately liable for payment to the extent of the indemnity. For example, if a limited partner agrees to indemnify the general partner for 50% of any payment to the creditor, each partner is allocated 50% of the liability. The term "indemnity" may also be used to describe a partner's agreement to hold a creditor harmless (rather than to indemnify the obligor). If the creditor can proceed against the indemnitor only in the event that it cannot recover from the general partner, however, the indemnity may be ineffective to shift basis for the liability. On a constructive liquidation, the general partner is presumed to discharge his obligation to satisfy partnership liabilities. Reg. § 1.752–2(b)(6); but cf. Reg. § 1.752–2(j) (anti-abuse rules).

(d) Disproportionate Loss Sharing. Generally, the regulations seek to minimize the effect of the § 704(d) limitation on outside basis by coordinating the § 704(b) loss-sharing rules and the § 752 liability-sharing rules. The allocation of losses is first determined under § 704(b) and the corresponding liabilities are then assigned under § 752 to the partners who were allocated a share of losses. This treatment reflects a policy decision that § 704(d) should not impose additional hurdles for loss allocations that withstand scrutiny under § 704(b). If the partners share losses disproportionately to their capital contributions, however, a deficit restoration obligation may produce unexpected results. See Reg. § 1.752–2(f) (Ex. 1–2).

Example (4): A and B contribute $1,500 and $500, respectively, to a general partnership and agree to share profits and losses equally. The partnership maintains capital accounts in accordance with the § 704(b) regulations, and each partner is obligated to restore any deficit in her capital account. The partnership purchases land for $2,000 cash and a $1,000 recourse purchase-money note. Upon a constructive liquidation, the land would be presumed to be worthless and the partnership would realize a loss of $3,000. The loss would be allocated $1,500 to A and $1,500 to B, in accordance with the loss-sharing ratio under the partnership agreement. A's capital account would be reduced to zero ($1,500 contribution less $1,500 loss); B would have a capital account deficit of $1,000 ($500 contribution less $1,500 loss), and would be obligated to contribute $1,000 to the partnership. Because B bears the economic risk of loss, the $1,000 liability is allocated entirely to B, increasing B's initial outside basis from $500 to $1,500; A's outside basis remains $1,500.

In effect, the regulations allocate a disproportionate share of recourse liabilities to the partner with the lower capital account balance immediately before the constructive liquidation. As a result, in the above example each partner has sufficient outside basis to absorb her share of losses. If A and B had instead made equal capital contributions of $1,000, each partner would bear the economic risk of loss for $500 of the $1,000 liability, and would again have an outside basis of $1,500 ($1,000 contribution plus $500 of partnership liabilities) sufficient to absorb her share of losses.

Example (5): A and B each contribute $500 cash to a general partnership. Under the partnership agreement, profits and losses are allocated 40% to A and 60% to B. The partnership maintains capital accounts in accordance with the § 704(b) regulations, and each partner is obligated to restore any deficit in her capital account. The partnership purchases land for $1,000 cash and a $200 recourse purchase-money note. Upon a constructive liquidation, the $1,200 loss would be allocated 40% to A ($480) and 60% to B ($720), leaving A with a capital account balance of $20 ($500 contribution less $480 loss) and B with a capital account deficit of $220 ($500 contribution less $720 loss). B would accordingly be obligated to contribute $220 to the partnership, while A would be entitled to a liquidating distribution of $20. B's economic risk of loss for the liability would be limited to $200, determined by multiplying B's net contribution obligation ($220) by the partnership's recourse liability ($200), divided by the partners' total net contribution obligations ($220). B's initial outside basis would be $700 ($500 contribution plus $200 of partnership liabilities). B's obligation to contribute an additional $20 to repay A's positive capital account balance is not treated as a partnership liability in determining B's outside basis. As a result, the § 704(d) limitation on losses in excess of outside basis may suspend $20 of B's losses. In effect, B has "borrowed" $20 from A but does not receive a corresponding increase in her outside basis until she makes an additional contribution.

(e) Partner Loans. The regulations treat a recourse loan from a partner (or a related person) in the same manner as a loan from a third-party creditor. If, however, the loan would otherwise be nonrecourse (e.g., because no other partner has guaranteed or assumed the liability), the economic risk of loss is assigned to the partner who makes the loan (or is related to the lender). Reg. § 1.752–2(c)(1). The partner-loan rule is intended to prevent other partners from claiming basis for a nonrecourse liability owed to a partner (or related party). For purposes of the partner-loan rule, a partner and another person are related if they bear a relationship specified in § 267(b) or § 707(b)(1), with certain modifications. Reg. § 1.752–4(b)(1).

The partner-loan rule is subject to a de minimis exception if (i) the loan constitutes "qualified nonrecourse financing" within the meaning of § 465(b)(6) (but not limited to activities involving the holding of real property) and (ii) the lending partner (and related persons) possesses an interest of 10% or less in each item of partnership income, gain, loss deduction, or credit for each year in which the loan is outstanding. Reg. § 1.752–2(d)(1). The de minimis rule would apply, for example, to a loan from an institutional lender who is also a 10% partner. The lender's status as a partner would be ignored, and the basis for the loan would be allocated under the nonrecourse rules.

(f) Pledge of Property as Security. If a partner pledges his own separate property (other than his partnership interest) as security for a partnership liability, the partner is treated as bearing the economic risk of loss to the extent of the value of such property. Reg. § 1.752–2(h)(1). A similar rule applies if a partner contributes property ("contributed security") to a partnership which uses such property solely to secure a partnership liability. Reg. § 1.752–2(h)(2). Upon a constructive liquidation, contributed security is excluded from the general rule that all partnership assets are deemed to be worthless, and the contributed security is deemed to be transferred to the creditor, to the extent of its value, in full or partial satisfaction of the secured liability. Reg. § 1.752–2(b)(1)(ii). For purposes of § 752, the value of pledged property is limited to its fair market value determined at the time of the pledge or contribution. Reg. § 1.752–2(h)(3).

(g) Time Value of Money. The regulations apply time-value-of-money concepts to deferred obligations. Generally, a deferred obligation is taken into account at its outstanding principal amount only if the obligation bears adequate interest; otherwise, only the discounted present value of the obligation (determined under the rules of § 1274(b)) is taken into account. Reg. § 1.752–2(g)(2). If a partner contributes his own promissory note (other than a readily tradeable note) to a partnership, the contributed note is not reflected in his capital account upon contribution. Instead, the promissory note is treated as an additional contribution obligation and may increase the partner's outside basis under § 752 to the extent of the partner's economic risk of loss.

(h) Anti–Abuse Rules. The § 752 regulations contain anti-abuse rules intended to reinforce the allocation of recourse liabilities based on the economic risk of loss. Applying general substance-over-form principles, the Service can look behind illusory obligations intended to create the appearance of economic risk of loss and treat other arrangements in accordance with their economic effect. Reg. § 1.752–2(j)(1). It is not entirely clear how the general anti-abuse rules under § 701 should be coordinated with the § 752 rules for allocating partnership liabilities. Despite the artificiality of the economic risk concept, the partners' arrangement for sharing liabilities under § 752 presumably reflects the "intent of Subchapter K," as articulated by the § 701 regulations. Thus, transactions structured to take advantage of the liberal § 752 rules should generally not be considered abusive under § 701 even if comparable treatment would not be available outside Subchapter K. See Reg. § 1.701–2(d) (Ex. 4) (use of partnership to avoid gain recognition under § 351(c) for liabilities in excess of basis) and (Ex. 6) (valid allocation of nonrecourse liabilities).

§ 4. Nonrecourse Liabilities

(a) General. A partnership liability is nonrecourse to the extent that no partner bears the economic risk of loss for that liability. Reg. § 1.752–1(a)(2). Under the § 752 regulations, nonrecourse liabilities are allocated in three tiers. The first two "priority" tiers consist of (i) a partner's share of "partnership minimum gain" as determined under the § 704(b) regulations concerning allocation of nonrecourse deductions and (ii) the amount of taxable gain that would be allocated to a partner under § 704(c) principles ("§ 704(c) minimum gain") if the partnership disposed of all property subject to nonrecourse liabilities in a taxable transaction in full satisfaction of such liabilities and for no other consideration. Reg. § 1.752–3(a). The third tier consists of "excess" nonrecourse liabilities, i.e., the residual category left after initially allocating the partnership's nonrecourse liabilities to the two priority tiers. A partner's share of nonrecourse liabilities equals the sum of his shares of partnership minimum gain, § 704(c) minimum gain and excess nonrecourse liabilities.

In accordance with the *Crane* rule, the regulations include nonrecourse liabilities in the partnership's inside basis and the partners' outside bases. The underlying theory is that a partner who receives a disproportionate allocation of nonrecourse deductions should also receive a corresponding share of the *Crane* basis generated by the nonrecourse liability. In other words, the allocation of nonrecourse liabilities follows the allocation of nonrecourse deductions, i.e., "liabilities follow losses." The mechanism for accomplishing this result is relatively straightforward: whenever a partner is allocated a nonrecourse deduction, he is also allocated the *Crane* basis that generated the deduction.

The allocation of nonrecourse liabilities is equal to the increase in the partner's share of partnership minimum gain attributable to the corresponding allocation of nonrecourse deductions.

Nonrecourse liabilities up to the amount of the partnership's basis in the underlying property (i.e., the portion which has not yet generated nonrecourse deductions) constitute excess nonrecourse liabilities which are allocated in accordance with the partners' overall profit-sharing ratios. The underlying assumption is that partnership profits will be used to repay the liability. The regulations also permit the partners to allocate excess nonrecourse liabilities by agreement in any manner that is "reasonably consistent with allocations (which have substantial economic effect under the § 704(b) regulations) of some significant item of partnership income or gain." Reg. § 1.752–3(a)(3). Alternatively, excess nonrecourse liabilities may be allocated in the manner in which it is "reasonably expected" that the corresponding nonrecourse deductions will be allocated. The method of allocating excess nonrecourse liabilities may vary from year to year.

Example (6): A and B each contribute $50,000 cash to the AB general partnership which purchases a building (worth $1,000,000) for $100,000 cash and a $900,000 nonrecourse note. The partnership agreement complies with all of the requirements under the § 704(b) regulations. Under the partnership agreement, all items of income, gain, loss and deduction are allocated equally. Immediately after formation of the partnership, the partners share the excess nonrecourse liability equally because they have equal interests in partnership profits. See Reg. § 1.752–3(b) (Ex. 1). Accordingly, A and B each have an outside basis of $500,000 ($50,000 contribution plus $450,000 share of excess nonrecourse liabilities).

During Year 1, the partnership's operating income equals its operating expenses; the partnership also has $200,000 of depreciation deductions. At the end of Year 1, each partner has a $50,000 share of the partnership minimum gain of $100,000 (i.e., the excess of the $900,000 liability over the $800,000 basis of the building). Accordingly, A and B continue to share the nonrecourse liability equally; each partner is allocated $50,000 of the nonrecourse liability to match her share of partnership minimum gain, and the $800,000 residual nonrecourse liability is allocated $400,000 each to A and B. Each partner has an outside basis of $400,000 at the end of Year 1 ($50,000 contribution plus $450,000 share of liabilities less $100,000 share of loss).

Example (7): The facts are the same as in Example (6), above, except that A contributes no capital and B contributes $100,000; the partnership agreement validly allocates all depreciation deductions to B. If the partners share nonrecourse liabilities 50:50 (i.e., in accordance with their overall profit-sharing ratios), the partners' initial outside bases will be $450,000 (A) and $550,000 (B). When the building is fully depreciated, B's share of partnership minimum gain will be $900,000; the first priority tier (partnership minimum gain) will thus absorb the entire liability. Because A is allocated none of the nonrecourse deductions, her share of "excess" nonrecourse liabilities will shift to B as the property is depreciated, triggering annual recalculation of the partners' outside bases.

The regulations offer a much simpler alternative that makes it unnecessary to recalculate the partners' shares of liabilities each year. Under the regulations, the partners may agree to allocate excess nonrecourse liabilities in the manner in which it is reasonably expected that the corresponding nonrecourse deductions will be allocated. In Example (7), above, if the liability is allocated in accordance with expected nonrecourse deductions, B's share of the liability immediately after formation of the partnership is $900,000. Thus, A and B have initial outside bases of zero and $1,000,000, respectively. See Reg. § 1.752–3(b) (Ex. 2).

If a partner receives a distribution of nonrecourse liability proceeds, the distribution carries out a share of partnership minimum gain for purposes of § 704(b). See Chapter 4. Under the § 752 liability-sharing rules, the distributee is allocated a portion of the nonrecourse liability equal to his share of the increase in partnership minimum gain attributable to the distribution. Since the increase in outside basis is deemed to occur immediately before the distribution, the distributee should not recognize gain under § 731 as a result of the distribution.

(b) Coordinating §§ 704(c) and 752. If appreciated property is contributed to a partnership, the built-in gain must be allocated to the contributing partners under § 704(c) principles. See Chapter 5. As discussed in Chapter 2, a partner who contributes property subject to a nonrecourse liability is allocated an amount of the liability at least equal to the § 704(c) minimum gain (i.e., the excess of the nonrecourse liability over the tax basis of the property). This taxable gain is the minimum amount that would be allocated to the contributing partner if the encumbered property were sold for no consideration other than relief of the nonrecourse liability. The method of allocating § 704(c) gain may affect the amount of nonrecourse liabilities allocated to the contributing partner. See Rev. Rul. 95–41.

Example (8): A contributes depreciable property with a basis of $4,000 and a fair market value of $10,000, subject to a nonrecourse liability of $6,000, to the equal AB partnership; B contributes $4,000 cash. Immediately after the contribution, there is no partnership minimum gain because the book value of the contributed property ($10,000) exceeds the amount of the nonrecourse liability ($6,000). If the partnership uses the traditional method of allocation under § 704(c), A would be allocated $2,000 of taxable gain ($6,000 liability less $4,000 basis) upon a sale of the property for no consideration other than relief of the nonrecourse liability. Thus, A's share of the partnership's nonrecourse liability is $4,000, i.e., $2,000 § 704(c) minimum gain plus $2,000 (50% of the $4,000 excess liability). The traditional method with curative allocations would yield the same result, since the timing and amount of any curative allocation is uncertain.

Example (9): The facts are the same as in Example (8), above, except that the partnership uses the remedial allocation method. On a hypothetical sale of the property for the amount of the nonrecourse liability, the partnership would recognize a book loss of $4,000 ($10,000 book value less $6,000 liability), allocated equally to A and B. The $2,000 of taxable gain ($6,000 liability less $4,000 basis) would be allocated entirely to A. Under the remedial allocation method, the partnership would allocate a notional tax loss of $2,000 to B (equal to B's share of the book loss) and an offsetting notional tax gain of $2,000 to A. Following the hypothetical sale, the partners would have the following tax and book capital accounts:

| | A | | B | |
	Tax	Book	Tax	Book
Initial balance	$(2,000)	$ 4,000	$ 4,000	$ 4,000
Hypothetical sale	2,000	(2,000)		(2,000)
Remedial allocation	2,000		(2,000)	
End balance	$ 2,000	$ 2,000	$ 2,000	$ 2,000

A's share of the partnership's nonrecourse liability would be $5,000, i.e., $4,000 § 704(c) minimum gain ($2,000 actual tax gain plus $2,000 remedial tax gain) plus $1,000 (50% of $2,000 excess liability). The remedial allocation method generally minimizes the amount of excess nonrecourse liabilities shifted away from the contributing partner.

If partnership property is revalued, the § 752 regulations allocate a portion of the partnership's nonrecourse liabilities to the existing partners equal to the § 704(c)-type gain arising from the revaluation. For example, assume that the AB partnership has depreciable property with a basis of zero and a fair market value of $450, subject to a nonrecourse liability of $150. If the partnership property is revalued in connection with admission of a new partner, the revaluation will eliminate any partnership minimum gain since the book value of the property ($450) exceeds the nonrecourse liability ($150). See Reg. § 1.704–2(d)(3). The revaluation creates § 704(c)-type gain of $150 ($150 liability less zero basis) allocable to the existing partners, thereby preventing a shift in liabilities. Thus, A and B would each be allocated $75 of the partnership's nonrecourse liability (equal to their former share of the total partnership minimum gain of $150). See Reg. § 1.752–3(a)(2).

§ 5. Review Problem

A, B and C make the following contributions to the newly-formed ABC general partnership in exchange for their respective partnership interests. A contributes $90 cash, B contributes nonmarketable securities with a basis of $60 and a fair market value of $60, and C contributes land with a basis of $150 and a fair market value of $150. The partnership purchases equipment (worth $240) for $90 cash and a $150 purchase-money note. Under the partnership agreement, profits and losses are allocated 30% to A, 20% to B and 50% to C. The partnership agreement requires that capital accounts be maintained in accordance with the § 704(b) regulations and provides for restoration of deficit capital accounts; liquidating distributions will be in accordance with positive capital accounts. In each of the following situations, determine the proper allocation of the $150 liability immediately after formation of the partnership.

(a) The purchase-money note is a recourse obligation.

(b) Same as (a), above, except that the partners share profits and losses equally under the partnership agreement.

(c) Same as (a), above, except that the partnership is a limited partnership and B is the sole limited partner. B is not required to restore any deficit in her capital account, but the partnership agreement otherwise satisfies the requirements of the alternate economic effect test.

(d) Same as (c), above, except that B has a deficit restoration obligation of $30.

(e) Same as (c), above, except that B guarantees $30 of the purchase-money note.

(f) Same as (c), above, except that the purchase-money note is a nonrecourse obligation secured only by the equipment. The partnership agreement contains a minimum gain chargeback provision and otherwise satisfies the requirements of the § 704(b) regulations.

(g) Same as (f), above, except that B guarantees $50 of the purchase-money note.

Answers: (a) Upon a constructive liquidation, the ABC partnership would realize a loss of $450, allocated in the ratio 30:20:50 under the partnership agreement. Accordingly, A's capital account would show a deficit of $45 ($90 original balance less $135 share of loss); B's capital account would show a deficit of $30 ($60 original balance less $90 share of loss); and C's capital account would show a deficit of $75 ($150 original balance less $225 share of loss). Since each partner would be obligated to restore the deficit in her capital account, the $150 recourse liability would be allocated $45 to A (30%), $30 to B (20%) and $75 to C (50%).

(b) Since the partners' loss-sharing ratio is disproportionate to their capital contributions, the sharing of the recourse liability will change. Upon the constructive liquidation, A's capital account will show a deficit of $60 ($90 original balance less $150 share of loss) and B's a deficit of $90 ($60 original balance less $150 share of loss); C's capital account will be zero ($150 original balance less $150 share of loss). Accordingly, the $150 recourse liability will be allocated $60 to A and $90 to B.

(c) Since B is not obligated to restore any deficit in her capital account, an allocation of losses in excess of B's capital contribution would lack substantial economic effect under the § 704(b) regulations. Accordingly, the partnership agreement should provide that all taxable loss will be allocated to A and C once B's capital account is reduced to zero. In this event, the $150 recourse liability will be allocated $56.25 to A (3/8) and $93.75 to C (5/8); no portion of the liability will be allocated to B.

(d) Since B has a deficit restoration obligation of $30, the result will be the same as in (a), above.

(e) The result will generally be the same as in (c), above. Unless B waives the right of subrogation, B would be entitled to reimbursement if required to perform under the guarantee; thus, B would have no net payment obligation. See Reg. § 1.752–2(f) (Ex. 4). Alternatively, if the creditor must first exhaust its rights against the partnership before proceeding against B, no payment obligation would arise because A and C would be deemed to satisfy the partnership's obligations. See Reg. § 1.752–2(f) (Ex. 3). If B waives the right of subrogation, however, she may be deemed to have a $30 deficit restoration obligation. See Reg. § 1.704–1(b)(2)(ii)(h).

(f) Since the entire $150 liability is an excess nonrecourse liability, it will be allocated in accordance with the partners' overall profit-sharing ratio (30:20:50). Upon a constructive liquidation, the partnership would realize a loss of $300 ($450 basis less $150 amount realized), reducing the partners' capital accounts to zero but not giving rise to any deficit.

(g) The $150 liability is bifurcated into a nonrecourse liability ($100) and a recourse liability ($50). Reg. § 1.752–1(i). The nonrecourse liability of $100 is allocated in accordance with the partners' overall profit-sharing ratio (30:20:50). The $50 balance of the liability is a recourse liability allocated entirely to the partner-guarantor (B), assuming that such partner is not entitled to reimbursement from the partnership for any payments to the creditor. See Reg. § 1.752–2(f) (Ex. 5). If B has a right to reimbursement from the other partners, however, B's economic risk of loss is limited to her *net* payment obligation. A reimbursement obligation might arise, for example, if A and C were allocated a share of the losses attributable to the $50 recourse liability and were obligated to restore their capital account deficits. If A and C (rather than B) guaranteed $50 of the $150 purchase-money note, B would not bear any economic risk of loss since she would have no obligation to restore any deficit in her capital account. Thus, the § 752 regulations effectively prevent limited partners from sharing nonrecourse debt guaranteed by general partners. See Raphan (1985).

CHAPTER 7

PARTNER–PARTNERSHIP TRANSACTIONS

§ 1. Overview

In classifying transactions between a partner and a partnership, it is important to determine whether or not the partner is acting in his capacity as a partner. Section 707(a) provides that "[i]f a partner engages in a transaction with a partnership other than in his capacity as a member of such partnership, the transaction shall ... be considered as occurring between the partnership and one who is not a partner." For example, a bona fide sale or exchange of property between a partner and a partnership is treated as a transaction between unrelated parties, subject to certain statutory limitations. See §§ 707(b), 267.

Payments to a partner in his capacity as a partner constitute "guaranteed payments" under § 707(c) to the extent they are made for services or the use of capital and are determined without regard to partnership income. For purposes of §§ 61 (inclusion in partner's gross income) and 162 (deduction to the partnership, subject to capital-expenditure rules of § 263), guaranteed payments are treated as amounts paid to a nonpartner, but timing and other tax consequences are determined as if such payments were a distributive share of partnership income. Payments falling outside §§ 707(a) and 707(c) are treated as distributions relating to a partner's distributive share under the normal aggregate rules of Subchapter K. For example, a special allocation of partnership net income to a partner (in his capacity as a partner) as compensation for services is treated as a distributive share rather a § 707(a) or § 707(c) payment.

§ 2.   Scope of §§ 707(a) and 707(c)

(a) General. Prior to enactment of Subchapter K, courts generally considered that a partner could not act as an employee of his own partnership, and concluded that "salary" payments made by a partnership to a partner were taxable as distributions attributable to his distributive share of partnership income. See, e.g., Moran (1956). In enacting § 707(a), Congress recognized that a partner could deal with a partnership in a nonpartner capacity. See Heggestad (1988) (brokerage commissions paid to partnership included in payor partner's distributive share). Section 707(c) was intended to eliminate complex computations when fixed payments (e.g., salary or interest) to a partner in his capacity as a partner exceed partnership taxable income. Such fixed payments were considered difficult to reconcile with the concept of a distributive share which is contingent on partnership income. Although § 707(c) was intended to eliminate confusion, it is not always easy to distinguish between partner and nonpartner payments.

(b) Tax Consequences. If a payment is classified as a nonpartner payment under § 707(a), the character of the payment depends upon the underlying transaction, e.g., a loan, sale of property, or payment for services or the use of property. For example, a nonpartner payment for services is taxed as ordinary income to the recipient; the partnership deducts or capitalizes the amount of the payment depending on the nature of the services. If § 707(a) applies, the partnership's deduction is generally deferred until the taxable year in which the recipient includes the amount in income. See § 267(e)(1) (treating a partner and partnership as related parties for purposes of § 267(a)(2)).

The tax treatment of § 707(a) payments and § 707(c) payments is virtually identical, except for timing differences. If § 707(c) applies, the recipient includes the payment under the timing rule for distributive shares; thus, the partner must include such payments in "his taxable year within or with which ends the partnership taxable year in which the partnership deducted such payments" under its method of accounting. Reg. § 1.707–1(c). Section 707(c) payments for services or the use of capital are taxed to the recipient as ordinary income (i.e., as compensation or interest-type payments). Both § 707(a) payments and § 707(c) payments are subject to the capitalization requirements of § 263(a).

(c) Payments for Services. Salary-type payments to a partner may be governed by § 707(a) or § 707(c), depending on whether the underlying services are rendered in a nonpartner or partner capacity. Prior to the Deficit Reduction Act of 1984 (the "1984 Act"), the controlling provision was generally determined by the nature of the services rendered. A partner who performed services with respect to a single transaction "outside the scope of the partnership" was treated as acting in a nonpartner capacity under § 707(a). See Pratt (1975). By contrast, compensation to a partner for continuing services closely related to the partnership's activities was treated either as a § 707(c) payment (if fixed) or as a distributive share (if determined with regard to partnership income).

In classifying payments under § 707(a) or § 707(c), however, the courts reached inconsistent results. See, e.g., Pratt (1977). It was also unclear whether payments measured by a partnership's gross income could qualify as guaranteed payments under § 707(c). See Rev. Rul. 81–300 (real-estate management fee based on a percentage of gross income qualified as a guaranteed payment under § 707(c)); but cf. Rev. Rul. 81–301 (similar fee treated as § 707(a) payment). The problem of determining whether a partner's services are rendered in a partner or nonpartner capacity is further complicated by § 707(a)(2)(A), enacted in 1984. The primary purpose of this provision is to prevent parties from disguising § 707(a) payments as distributive shares of partnership income. See § 3 below.

Under § 707(a)(2)(A), the inquiry focuses on the compensation received rather than the services rendered: payments that are relatively fixed and certain are likely to be § 707(a) payments, while payments that are subject to significant entrepreneurial risk are likely to be treated as a partner's distributive share under § 702. Since § 707(c) payments are by definition fixed, all such payments might plausibly be treated as § 707(a) payments. Current proposals would eliminate the "intermediate" category of § 707(c) payments. The distinction between partner and nonpartner payments would focus exclusively on whether both the amount and fact of payment is contingent upon the entrepreneurial risks of the partnership's business. Payments not contingent on entrepreneurial risk would be classified as § 707(a) payments for tax purposes; all other payments would be classified as a distributive share of partnership income, taxed under the normal rules for distributive shares. See §§ 702(a), 704(b) and 731.

(d) Timing of Income and Deduction. Prior to the 1984 Act, § 707(a) offered a potential timing advantage when the partnership and the partner used different methods of accounting. For example, an accrual-method partnership could deduct a § 707(a) payment in the year of accrual, while a cash-method partner would not have to include the payment in gross income until the year of receipt. In the 1984 Act, however, Congress extended the matching rules of § 267(a)(2) to § 707(a) transactions. See § 267(e)(1), (3). Thus, the partnership's deduction is deferred until such payments are includible in the recipient's income.

If a payment is characterized as a § 707(c) payment, the recipient's inclusion is accelerated to match the partnership's deduction, thereby preserving symmetrical treatment. The existence of two different timing rules is potentially confusing. Current proposals would tax § 707(c) payments under the timing rules for § 707(a) payments and might eventually lead to the repeal of § 707(c).

Example (1): A (a cash-method taxpayer) is entitled to a $10,000 annual payment for ordinary and necessary services rendered to the equal ABCD partnership (an accrual-method taxpayer). Both A and the partnership use the calendar year. The partnership accrues the $10,000 payment in 2000 but defers payment until January 15, 2001. The partnership's taxable income for 2000 (determined without regard to the payment to A) is $70,000. If § 707(a) applies, § 267(a)(2) defers the partnership's deduction until 2001 when the payment is includible in A's gross income. As a result, each partner reports a $17,500 distributive share for 2000 and a $2,500 deduction for 2001.

If § 707(c) applies, the deductible § 707(c) payment reduces the partnership's taxable income to $60,000, and each partner reports a $15,000 distributive share; in addition, A must include the $10,000 as ordinary income. Thus, A reports a total of $25,000 ($10,000 payment and $15,000 distributive share) for 2000. A should not be taxed again on the $10,000 payment when actually received in 2001.

See Gaines (1982). The guaranteed payment could be treated as giving rise to a receivable in A's hands, with a basis equal to the amount previously included in gross income.

(e) Capital Expenditures. Regardless of whether § 707(a) or § 707(c) applies, the partnership must capitalize any payments which constitute capital expenditures. §§ 263, 707(c); see Cagle (1974). By contrast, the capital-expenditure rules have no effect on amounts properly characterized as a distributive share of partnership income. In the case of a distributive share, the other partners receive the equivalent of a deduction because their share of partnership income is reduced. Distributive share treatment is appropriate to the extent that the recipient is subject to entrepreneurial risk in his capacity as a partner. See § 3 below.

Example (2): In 2000, A receives a § 707(a) payment of $10,000 for nonpartner services related to improvements on property owned by the partnership. Both A and the partnership use the calendar year. A must include the entire $10,000 in income in 2000, even though the cost of the improvement is capitalized. The result would be similar if A (acting in a nonpartner capacity) leased property to the partnership for a four-year period for a lump sum payment of $10,000: A would include the § 707(a) payment in income when received, and the partnership would amortize the prepaid rent over the four-year period.

(f) Guaranteed Minimum. A guaranteed payment may take the form of a formula amount payable to a partner whose distributive share of partnership income falls below a stated level (a "guaranteed minimum"). For example, assume that the partners of the ABC partnership share profits and losses equally, and that only A (in his capacity as a partner) performs services for the partnership; the partnership agreement provides that A is to receive an amount equal to the greater of (i) one third of the partnership's income (determined before taking into account any guaranteed payments) or (ii) $10,000. If the partnership has income of $30,000, A's distributive share (without regard to any guaranteed payment) would be $10,000. As long as A's distributive share equals or exceeds the guaranteed minimum, the entire amount received by A is treated as a distributive share. See Reg. § 1.707–1(c) (Ex. 2).

If the partnership instead has only $21,000 of income (before the guaranteed payment), A's distributive share is $7,000. The additional $3,000 payable to A (i.e., the difference between A's $10,-000 guaranteed minimum and his $7,000 distributive share) is treated as a guaranteed payment. If the guaranteed payment is deductible, it reduces the partnership's income from $21,000 to $18,000; after A is allocated a $7,000 distributive share in accordance with the partnership agreement, the remaining $11,000 is allocated equally between B and C. Thus, A reports a total of $10,000 ($7,000 distributive share plus $3,000 guaranteed payment), while B and C each report $5,500. See Reg. § 1.707–

1(c) (Ex. 2). The result is the same as if the $3,000 deduction were specially allocated to B and C, reducing their distributive shares by $1,500 each.

If the guaranteed minimum exceeds the partnership's income (before the guaranteed payment), the computation is less clear. For example, if the partnership has only $3,000 of income (before the guaranteed payment), A's distributive share is $1,000 and the remaining $9,000 is a guaranteed payment. If the guaranteed payment is deductible, the partnership ends up with a loss of $6,000. In order to give effect to A's $1,000 distributive share of income, however, the taxable loss allocated to B and C must be increased to $7,000. The situation is similar to a special allocation of gross income which is sufficiently large to create an overall taxable loss, so that one partner has positive income while the other partners have losses.

If § 707(c) were repealed, it would be appropriate to treat the entire amount of any guaranteed minimum as a § 707(a) payment; no portion of such a payment is contingent on the entrepreneurial risks of the partnership's business. Under this approach, A would have a $10,000 payment under § 707(a) and the resulting $7,000 loss ($3,000 income less $10,000 deduction) would be allocated equally among all the partners.

§ 3. Disguised Payments for Services: § 707(a)(2)

(a) **General.** A partner may receive compensation for services in the form of a special allocation of partnership income under § 704(b). If respected, the special allocation is taxable to the service partner as a distributive share under §§ 702(a) and 704(b), and a corresponding distribution of cash equal to the amount of his special allocation is generally tax free under § 731. The allocation and distribution offset each other, with no net effect on the partner's outside basis or capital account. An allocation of gross income will have the same character (e.g., ordinary income or capital gain) as the items comprising the partnership's income. In some situations, it may be difficult to distinguish a special allocation from a § 707(a) payment. Section 707(a)(2) is intended, in part, to perform this function.

(b) Section 707(a)(2) Payments. Congress was aware that a special allocation and related distribution of partnership income could be used to avoid the capitalization requirements of § 263. By reducing the other partners' distributive shares, the net effect of a special allocation to a service partner for expenses of a capital nature is equivalent to a current deduction for a capital expenditure. Section 707(a)(2)(A) combats this technique by providing that allocations and distributions in connection with performance of services may be recharacterized as § 707(a) payments for nonpartner services, if necessary to reflect properly their economic substance. Depending on the character of the services, the partnership must capitalize the payment to the nonpartner, thereby increasing the other partners' shares of partnership taxable income.

Example (3): A, an architect, designs a commercial office building which the ABC partnership constructs and net leases for $100,000 annually. In lieu of his normal fee of $40,000 for architectural services, A receives a special allocation of the first $20,000 of the partnership's rental income for each of the first two years. If the $20,000 special allocation is respected, A will receive approximately the same amount during the first two years as if he charged the normal fee for his architectural services. From the other partners' perspective, however, the special allocation reduces their distributive shares of partnership income for each year from $100,000 to $80,000, just as if the partnership had paid a deductible fee to A. If the special allocation is disregarded under § 707(a)(2)(A), the partnership must capitalize the $40,000 fee for A's services, restoring the partnership's taxable income to $100,-000. The principal effect of the disguised payment rules is thus to increase the remaining partners' distributive shares of taxable income. The tax consequences to A will generally be the same whether he reports the $40,000 as a distributive share of ordinary income or as a § 707(a) payment.

The legislative history lists six factors for determining whether a putative partner is receiving an allocation and distribution in a nonpartner capacity. The most important factor is whether the service partner is subject to a "significant entrepreneurial risk" as to both the amount and fact of payment. An arrangement most closely resembles a § 707(a) payment if the service partner is reasonably certain to receive an amount approximating his normal fee. Other indicia of a disguised payment for services include (i) transitory partner status, (ii) closeness in time between the performance of services and the allocation/distribution, (iii) tax motivation for the arrangement, and (iv) disproportionately low value of the service partner's overall partnership interest compared to the purported allocation.

Section 707(a)(2)(A) applies primarily to disguised payments for services rather than property. See § 4 below. Since contributed property must be booked at fair market value under the § 704(b) capital-account rules, an allocation and related distribution as a disguised payment for property is generally economically unfeasible. In effect, an allocation of additional income as a disguised payment to the contributing partner would cause the partnership to pay twice for the property.

In enacting § 707(a)(2)(A), Congress was concerned principally with avoidance of the capital-expenditure rules. The provision is not intended to affect nonabusive transactions that properly reflect the partners' economic arrangements. Typically, allocations and distributions that are contingent in amount are not treated as disguised § 707(a) payments because the service partner bears a significant entrepreneurial risk. Even contingent arrangements may be recharacterized as § 707(a) payments, however, if the service partner performs similar services for others and the method of compensation resembles the manner in which third parties would be compensated. Payments linked to the level of the service provider's own performance more closely resemble fees than a distributive share based on the entrepreneurial risks of the partnership's business. See Rev. Rul. 81–301 (treating gross income allocation to adviser general partner of investment partnership as § 707(a) payment).

It would be possible to eliminate both §§ 707(a)(2)(A) and 707(c) if the distinction between partner and nonpartner payments were based strictly on entrepreneurial risk. A payment devoid of entrepreneurial risk would automatically be classified as a § 707(a) payment. Distributive share treatment would be reserved exclusively for allocations contingent upon the entrepreneurial risks of the partnership's business.

§ 4. Disguised Sales Between Partners and Partnerships

(a) General. Congress enacted § 707(a)(2)(B) to deal with "disguised sales" between partners and partnerships. The problem of disguised sales was highlighted by several cases permitting tax-free treatment of contributions and distributions that closely resembled sales of property or partnership interests. See, e.g., Otey (1978). The courts generally refused to recharacterize these transactions as disguised sales under the step-transaction doctrine. But see Jacobson (1991). The regulations under § 707 contain several safe harbors and presumptions intended to clarify when a contribution and distribution are sufficiently related to be treated as a disguised sale. Reg. §§ 1.707–3 through 1.707–9.

(b) Entrepreneurial Risk. Section 707(a)(2)(B) applies only to the extent that the purported contribution and distribution, when viewed together, are "properly characterized" as a sale or exchange. Characterization of a transaction depends on whether the partner who contributes property acquires a genuine entrepreneurial interest in partnership capital. If he does, the form of the transaction will be respected. On the other hand, disguised-sale treatment applies if the contributing partner "cashes out" his investment instead of exposing it to the entrepreneurial risks of the partnership's business. The concept of entrepreneurial risk focuses on the likelihood that a partner who contributes property to a partnership will receive a related distribution from the partnership without regard to the success of the partnership's business. It may be difficult, however, to distinguish between distributions which should be recharacterized as part of a disguised sale and those which merely represent a return of the partner's investment in the partnership.

(c) Presumptions. Under the regulations, a disguised sale occurs if, based on all the facts and circumstances, (i) a transfer of money or other consideration by the partnership to a partner would not have been made but for the partner's transfer of property (other than money) to the partnership and (ii) in the case of nonsimultaneous transfers, the subsequent transfer is not dependent on the entrepreneurial risks of the partnership's operations. Reg. § 1.707–3(b)(1). A contribution and distribution occurring within a two-year period are presumed to constitute a disguised sale; conversely, such transfers occurring more than two years apart are presumed not to constitute a disguised sale. Reg. § 1.707–3(c)(1), (d). Both presumptions may be rebutted by a showing of facts and circumstances to the contrary. Reg. § 1.707–3(f) (Ex. 3–8). The regulations list certain facts and circumstances that tend to indicate the existence of a disguised sale. Reg. § 1.707–3(b)(2).

Some types of payments are presumed not to be part of a disguised sale even if made within a two-year period. These "favored" payments include (i) reasonable guaranteed payments and "preferred returns" with respect to contributed capital, (ii) distributions not in excess of the partner's interest in net cash flow from operations, and (iii) reimbursements for qualifying capital expenditures incurred during the two-year period preceding the related transfer by the partner to the partnership. Reg. § 1.707–4. The safe harbor for these types of payments is intended to prevent most routine distributions from violating the disguised-sale rules.

(d) Tax Consequences. If § 707(a)(2)(B) applies, the transfer of property by the partner to the partnership is treated as a sale occurring on the date the partnership becomes the owner of the property (determined under general income tax principles). Reg. § 1.707–3(a)(2). When payments are deferred, the contributing partner is treating as having exchanged the contributed property for the partnership's debt obligation, subject to the installment-sale rules. See §§ 453, 483 and 1274. In the case of a part-sale, part-contribution, the transferor's basis in the transferred property is allocated between the sale portion and the contribution portion; only the latter is reflected in the transferor's capital account. In appropriate circumstances, § 707(a)(2)(B) may trigger a deemed sale by the partnership to a partner. See Reg. § 1.707–6.

Example (4): In exchange for equal interests in the newly-formed AB partnership, A contributes $100 cash and B contributes land with a fair market value of $200 and a basis of $120 in B's hands; simultaneously, the partnership distributes $100 cash to B. B is treated as selling one half of the land to the partnership and recognizes gain of $40 ($100 amount realized less $60 allocable basis). See Reg. § 1.707–3(f) (Ex. 1). The partnership takes a cost basis ($100) in the purchased portion of the land and a substituted basis ($60) in the contributed portion of the land, preserving B's remaining built-in gain of $40. Immediately after formation, the partnership has the following balance sheet:

	Basis	Value		Basis	Value
Assets			Capital		
Land (½)	$100	$100	A	$100	$100
Land (½)	60	100	B	60	100
Total	$160	$200	Total	$160	$200

Assume that B instead receives a distribution of $121 two years after formation of the partnership.

Section 707(a)(2)(B) would treat B as exchanging the contributed property for an installment obligation with an imputed principal amount of $100 (assuming a discount rate of 10%) and interest of $21 ($121 stated principal amount less $100 imputed principal amount). See § 1274. B could avoid disguised-sale treatment by showing that the distribution was subject to substantial risk.

(e) Liabilities. Disguised-sale treatment may also apply if encumbered property is transferred to a partnership and the liability is shifted from the contributing partner to the other partners. The regulations focus primarily on liabilities incurred by the contributing partner "in anticipation of the transfer" of property to a partnership ("nonqualified liabilities"). In this situation, the contributing partner has, in effect, cashed out a portion of his investment. If the partnership assumes or takes subject to nonqualified liabilities, the accompanying reduction in the contributing partner's share of liabilities is treated as consideration received in a part-sale. Reg. § 1.707–5(a)(1). Any liability incurred by a partner within two years of a transfer to the partnership is generally presumed to be incurred in anticipation of the transfer. Reg. § 1.707–5(a)(7).

By contrast, the partnership's assumption of (or taking subject to) a "qualified liability" is generally viewed as nonabusive and thus not a disguised sale. See Reg. § 1.707–5(a)(1), (5). Qualified liabilities (not in excess of the fair market value of the property) include (i) all liabilities incurred more than two years before the transfer, (ii) liabilities incurred within the two-year period but not in anticipation of the transfer, (iii) liabilities incurred to acquire or improve the contributed property (subject to certain caps), and (iv) trade payables if substantially all of the assets used in the underlying business are transferred to the partnership. Reg. § 1.707–5(a)(6).

Example (5): In exchange for a 25% general partnership interest, A contributes property with a basis of $100,000 and a fair market value of $200,000, subject to a $160,000 recourse liability. The partnership assumes the recourse liability which was incurred more than two years before the contribution. Even though A remains liable for only $40,000 of the liability (25%), the disguised-sale rules are inapplicable because the liability is a qualified liability. See Reg. § 1.707–5(f) (Ex. 5).

Example (6): The facts are the same as in Example (5), above, except that the liability is a nonqualified liability incurred within two years of the contribution. A is treated as receiving consideration of $120,000, i.e., the excess of the liability assumed by the partnership ($160,000) over A's share of the liability immediately after the assumption ($40,-000). See Reg. § 1.707–5(f) (Ex. 2). Thus, A is treated as selling three fifths of the property, triggering recognized gain of $60,000 ($120,000 less $60,000 allocable basis).

The § 707 regulations follow the § 752 rules for sharing recourse liabilities, but apply a special rule to determine a partner's share of nonrecourse liabilities. Reg. § 1.707–5(a)(2). Under the normal rules of § 752, "excess" nonrecourse liabilities are allocated according to the partners' share of profits (or expected deductions); only liabilities in excess of the two priority categories (partnership minimum gain and § 704(c) minimum gain) are considered excess liabilities. See Chapter 6. The § 707 regulations ignore the two priority categories and instead determine a partner's share of nonrecourse liabilities based on his percentage share of excess liabilities. Evidently, the Treasury considered the § 704(c) minimum gain concept under the § 752 regulations too generous for purposes of § 707, since it would minimize the reduction in the contributing partner's share of liabilities.

Example (7): The facts are the same as in Example (6), above, except that the partnership liability is a nonrecourse liability incurred within two years of the contribution. Under the general § 752 rules, A's share of the nonrecourse liability would be $85,000, i.e., $60,000 § 704(c) minimum gain ($160,000 liability less $100,000 basis) plus $25,000 (25% of $100,000 excess liability); only $75,000 of the nonrecourse liability would be treated as shifted to the other partners. Because A has only a 25% share of the excess liability, however, § 707 treats $120,000 of the nonrecourse liability as shifted to the other partners (75% of $160,000). Accordingly, A is treated as selling three fifths of the property, resulting in recognized gain of $60,000 ($120,000 less $60,000 allocable basis). See Reg. § 1.707–5(f) (Ex. 1).

(f) Special Rule for Qualified Liabilities. If the disguised-sale rules would not otherwise apply, no portion of a qualified liability is treated as sales proceeds. To the extent that the contributing partner receives other consideration (in addition to the partnership's assumption of qualified liabilities), however, a portion of a qualified liability is treated as sales proceeds. Reg. § 1.707–5(a)(5). The amount of the qualified liability treated as sales proceeds cannot exceed the lesser of (i) the portion of the qualified liability shifted to the other partners or (ii) the amount of the qualified liability multiplied by the contributing partner's "net equity percentage." The net equity percentage is determined by dividing the total consideration received (other than qualified liabilities) by the fair market value of the contributed property net of qualified liabilities. Id. This rule is intended to ensure that a qualified liability is never treated less favorably than a nonqualified liability. A partner's net equity percentage is the percentage of the property that would be treated as sold if the property were not encumbered by the qualified liability; the same percentage of the qualified liability is treated as sales proceeds.

Example (8): The facts are the same as in Example (5), above, except that A simultaneously receives $20,000 cash from the partnership (in addition to assumption of the $160,000 qualified liability). The amount of the qualified liability treated as sales proceeds is limited to the lesser of (i) $120,000 (the portion of the liability shifted to the other partners) or (ii) $80,000 (the $160,000 liability multiplied by

A's net equity percentage of 50%). A's net equity percentage is equal to the amount of other consideration ($20,000 cash) divided by the fair market value of the contributed property net of qualified liabilities ($40,000). Accordingly, A is treated as realizing total consideration of $100,000 ($80,000 of the qualified liability in addition to $20,000 actual cash received), resulting in a sale of one half of the property. See Reg. § 1.707–5(f) (Ex. 6).

(g) Debt–Financed Distributions. The legislative history indicates that § 707(a)(2)(B) was intended to overrule the holding in *Otey* (1978). In *Otey*, the taxpayer contributed unencumbered property to a partnership and shortly thereafter received a distribution from partnership borrowings equal to the value of the contributed property. The court treated the pre-arranged contribution and distribution as tax free under §§ 721 and 731.

Under the § 707 regulations, the amount of disguised-sale proceeds does not include the portion of a debt-financed distribution attributable to the partner's "allocable share" of the partnership liability incurred to finance the distribution. A partner's allocable share of such a liability is determined by multiplying the partner's share of the liability by a fraction having a numerator equal to the portion of the liability traceable to the distribution and a denominator equal to the total amount of the liability. Reg. §§ 1.707–5(b) (90–day rule), 1.707–5(f) (Ex. 10). For example, if the taxpayer in *Otey* remained liable for 25% of the borrowing used to finance the distribution, he would be treated as selling 75% of the property. The result is the same as if the contributing partner had borrowed an amount equal to the fair market value of the property immediately before the contribution and then shifted responsibility for 75% of the liability to the other partners.

(h) Disguised Sales of Partnership Interests. In amending § 707(a)(2)(B), Congress sought, in part, to reverse the result in cases where taxpayers had successfully avoided treatment of related contributions and distributions as disguised sales of partnership interests. See Communications Satellite Corp. (1980); Jupiter Corp. (1983). In *Colonnade*, however, the Tax Court recharacterized a contribution and distribution as a taxable § 741 sale of a partnership interest, even though the only consideration was an assumption by new partners of a proportionate share of the partnership liabilities allocable to the existing partner whose interest was reduced. Colonnade Condominium, Inc. (1988). The court noted that "there was no new or additional capital transferred" to the partnership and the interests of the other partners were not affected by the transaction. The § 707 regulations reserve the treatment of disguised sales of partnership interests. Reg. § 1.707–7.

(i) Avoidance of General Utilities Repeal. The Service has also issued proposed regulations to curb the use of partnerships to avoid repeal of the General Utilities doctrine. Prop. Reg. § 1.337(d)–3. The proposed regulations are aimed at transactions in which a corporation transfers appreciated property to a partnership which owns or acquires the corporation's stock; a subsequent distribution of the stock to the corporate partner may be treated as a deemed redemption of its stock in exchange for appreciated property (triggering corporate-level gain under § 311(b)).

§ 5. Sales or Exchanges With Respect to Controlled Partnerships

(a) Loss Disallowance. Section 707(b)(1)(A) disallows losses with respect to direct or indirect sales or exchanges between a partnership and any person owning (directly or indirectly) more than 50% of the capital or profits interests in such partnership. Similarly, § 707(b)(1)(B) disallows losses with respect to sales or exchanges between commonly-controlled partnerships. If § 707(b)(1) applies, the transferor's entire loss with respect to the sale or exchange is disallowed; the disallowed loss, however, may be allowed as an offset against gain realized by the transferee on a subsequent disposition. §§ 707(b)(1) (flush language), 267(d). In determining ownership of capital or profits interests, the constructive ownership rules of § 267(c) (other than § 267(c)(3)) apply. § 707(b)(3). Section 707(b) includes transactions between a partnership and a related nonpartner who constructively owns more than 50% of the capital or profits interests in the partnership. See also Reg. § 1.267(b)–1(b)(1).

If § 707(b)(1) applies, each partner's outside basis is reduced by his share of the disallowed loss. Rev. Rul. 96–10. The downward adjustment to basis prevents recognition of the disallowed loss if the partners subsequently sell their partnership interests. Similarly, each partner's outside basis is increased by his share of gain not recognized as a result of §§ 707(b)(1) and 267(d). Id. The upward adjustment to basis ensures that the partners will not recognize artificial gain on a subsequent disposition of their interests. Accordingly, the basis adjustments preserve the intended benefit or detriment of §§ 707(b)(1) and 267(d).

Example (9): A and B own 60% and 40%, respectively, of the capital and profits interests in the AB partnership; A and C own 80% and 20%, respectively, of the capital and profits interests in the AC partnership. A, B and C are unrelated individuals. The AB partnership sells land (with a basis of $15,000) to the AC partnership for its fair market value of $10,000. The AC partnership subsequently sells the land to an unrelated party for $15,000. Under § 707(b)(1)(B), the two partnerships are treated as commonly-controlled because A owns more than 50% of each partnership. Therefore, the AB partnership's $5,000 realized loss on the sale to the AC partnership is disallowed. The disallowed loss is allocated $3,000 to A (60%) and $2,000 to B (40%), decreasing each partner's outside basis. Under § 267(d), the AC partnership recognizes no gain or loss on the subsequent sale ($5,000 realized gain offset by $5,000 previously disallowed loss). The tax-exempt income of $5,000 is allocated $4,000 to A (80%) and $1,000 to C (20%), increasing each partner's outside basis.

(b) Ordinary Income Treatment. Section 707(b)(2) treats gain on a sale of property between a partnership and a controlling person (or between commonly-controlled partnerships) as ordinary income if the property is a non-capital asset in the transferee's hands. This provision is intended to prevent related parties from taking advantage of preferential capital gains treatment to obtain a stepped-up basis, thereby reducing future ordinary income. Section 707(b)(2) overlaps with § 1239, which serves a similar function with respect to property that is depreciable in the transferee's hands. Section 707(b)(2) is broader, however, because it also applies to sales of nondepreciable assets such as inventory and land used in the taxpayer's trade or business. See § 1221(1)-(2). Finally, § 453(g) denies installment-sale treatment with respect to sales of depreciable property between related parties, unless the taxpayer demonstrates the absence of a tax-avoidance purpose.

CHAPTER 8

TRANSFERS OF PARTNERSHIP INTERESTS

§ 1. Overview

Under the entity approach of § 741, a sale or exchange of a partnership interest is treated as a disposition of a unitary capital asset. The transferor generally recognizes capital gain or loss equal to the difference between his amount realized and his outside basis. The amount realized includes cash and the fair market value of any other property received by the transferor, as well as his share of partnership liabilities. If the partnership holds "unrealized receivables" or inventory, however, the so-called collapsible partnership provisions of § 751 treat all or a portion of the amount realized as ordinary income. The collapsible partnership provisions were originally intended to prevent partners from converting ordinary income into capital gain. Their practical significance depends on the degree of preferential treatment afforded to capital gains and limitations on deductibility of capital losses.

Upon a transfer of a partnership interest, the transferee's outside basis is determined under § 742. If the transferee acquires a partnership interest in a taxable sale or exchange, he takes a cost basis which includes his share of partnership liabilities. If he acquires a partnership interest from a decedent or by gift, his basis is determined under § 1014 or § 1015. Under § 743, the transfer of a partnership interest generally does not trigger an adjustment in the basis of partnership assets, unless the partnership has a § 754 election in effect. A sale or exchange of a partnership interest may also trigger a constructive termination of the partnership under § 708.

§ 2. Treatment of the Transferor Partner

(a) **Amount Realized.** The amount realized by a partner who transfers his partnership interest includes not only cash and the fair market value of any other property received but also the transferor's share of partnership liabilities assumed (or taken subject to) by the transferee. § 752(d); Reg. § 1.1001–2(a). For example, a partner who is allocated $250 of partnership liabilities and sells his partnership interest for $750 realizes $1,000 on the sale. Reg. § 1.752–1(h). In *Tufts*, the Supreme Court held that the fair-market-value limitation of § 752(c) does not apply to a sale of a partnership interest. Instead, § 752(d) requires that the full amount of nonrecourse liabilities be included in the selling partner's amount realized even if such liabilities exceed the fair market value of the underlying property. See § 7701(g).

A sale or other disposition of a partnership interest triggers a deemed discharge of the transferor's share of partnership liabilities. Reg. § 1.1001–

2(a)(4)(v). Thus, the transferor may recognize gain attributable to discharge of partnership liabilities in an otherwise nontaxable disposition, e.g., under the charitable "bargain sale" or part-gift, part-sale rules. See Reg. § 1.1001–2(c) (Ex. 4), (e)(1); Rev. Rul. 75–194. If a partnership interest encumbered by liabilities is abandoned or becomes worthless, any realized loss will generally be characterized as a capital loss resulting from a deemed sale or exchange. See Rev. Rul. 93–80. By contrast, if no liabilities are relieved, an ordinary loss may be allowed under § 165. Id.; Citron (1991) (no deemed sale or exchange).

(b) Basis Allocation. If a partner transfers less than his entire partnership interest, his basis must be allocated between the retained and transferred portions based on their respective fair market values. For example, if a partner's entire interest has a basis of $1,000 and the value of the transferred portion is 1/4 of the total value, the basis allocable to the transferred portion is $250. If a partner has only one type of interest (i.e., general or limited), the percentage of the interest transferred will generally determine the allocation of the transferor's basis and share of liabilities discharged under § 752(d). The Service has held that a partner has a unitary basis in his partnership interest, even if he holds both general and limited partnership interests. Rev. Rul. 84–52. Special adjustments may be necessary, however, in allocating liabilities among different types of interests. Rev. Rul. 84–53.

(c) Interim Adjustments. Under § 706(c)(2)(A), the partnership's taxable year closes with respect to a partner who sells or exchanges his entire partnership interest. Thus, the selling partner must report his distributive share of partnership items of income, gain, loss and deduction through the date of sale, triggering corresponding adjustments to his outside basis. Reg. § 1.705–1(a). These interim adjustments prevent the selling partner from converting his distributive share of ordinary income or loss into capital gain or loss. For example, assume that a partner sells his entire partnership interest for $20,000 on June 30, when his outside basis is $5,000, before adjustment for his $15,000 distributive share of partnership ordinary income for the first six months. The selling partner recognizes $15,000 of ordinary income as his distributive share, and his outside basis is accordingly increased by $15,000, with the result that he recognizes no gain or loss on the sale. Reg. § 1.706–1(c)(2)(ii). If a partner sells less than his entire interest, the "varying interest" rule determines his distributive share of partnership items through the date of sale. § 706(c)(2)(B), (d)(1); see § 5 below.

(d) Operation of § 751(a). The collapsible partnership provisions bifurcate a sale or exchange of a partnership interest into separate dispositions of (i) the transferor's undivided interest in the partnership's § 751 assets (unrealized receivables and inventory as defined in § 751(c) and (d)) and (ii) his remaining partnership interest. A "hypothetical sale" approach is used to determine the amount of ordinary income (or loss) recognized by the selling partner. Prop. Reg. § 1.751–1(a)(2). Thus, the partnership is deemed to sell all of its assets in a fully taxable transaction for fair market value immediately before the transfer. The selling partner recognizes ordinary income (or loss) on the transfer equal to his allocable share of the partnership's total ordinary income (or loss) on the hypothetical sale of the partnership's § 751 assets. For purposes of the hypothetical sale, any § 704(c) allocations are taken into account. The selling partner then determines the amount of capital gain (or loss) attributable to the transferred interest. This amount is equal to the difference between the selling partner's recognized ordinary income (or loss) and the capital gain (or loss) that would have been realized in the absence of § 751.

Example (1): A sells her partnership interest to D for $15,000 when the partnership has the following balance sheet:

	Basis	Value		Basis	Value
Assets			Capital		
Cash	$15,000	$15,000	A	$15,000	$15,000
Unrealized			B	15,000	15,000
Receivables	0	15,000	C	15,000	15,000
Capital Asset	30,000	15,000	Total	$45,000	$45,000
Total	$45,000	$45,000			

Overall, A has no net economic gain or loss, since the appreciation in her share of ordinary income assets exactly offsets the decline in value of her share of capital assets. If § 751 did not apply, A would recognize no gain or loss on sale of her partnership interest. Section 751, however, requires that A recognize $5,000 of ordinary income that would be allocated to her upon sale of the partnership's unrealized receivables for $15,000. Under § 741, A also recognizes a capital loss of $5,000, the difference between the capital gain that she would have realized in the absence of § 751 (zero) and the ordinary income recognized under § 751 ($5,000). Under § 1211(b), A may be allowed to deduct only $3,000 of her capital loss, subject to a $2,000 carryover.

(e) **Unrealized Receivables.** Under § 751(c), the term "unrealized receivables" includes any right to payment for delivery of non-capital goods or rendition of services, to the extent not previously includible in income under the taxpayer's method of accounting. This definition excludes any right to payment in connection with the sale of § 1221 capital assets (whether long-term or short-term); it may also exclude obligations received on sale of § 1231 quasi-capital assets, subject to the netting requirements of § 1231. Unrealized receivables include zero-basis accounts receivable of a cash-method taxpayer but not unpaid amounts previously taken into income by an accrual-method taxpayer. Courts have interpreted the term unrealized receivables broadly to include the right to payment under a management contract to perform future services. See Ledoux (1981). Such payments may be difficult to distinguish, however, from payments for goodwill or going concern value.

Congress has expanded the category of unrealized receivables to include potential depreciation recapture from § 1245 property or § 1250 property. § 751(c) (flush language, first sentence); Reg. § 1.751–1(c)(4). For example, assume that a partnership owns depreciable equipment with an adjusted basis of $100 and a fair market value of $700, which it originally purchased for $500. If the equipment were sold for fair market value, the partnership would have $400 of § 1245 depreciation recapture, i.e., the amount by which the lesser of the "recomputed basis" of the property ($500) or the amount realized ($700) exceeds the adjusted basis of the property ($100). See Reg. § 1.1245–1(a). Section 751(c) bifurcates such property into (i) an unrealized receivable with a zero basis and a fair market value equal to the amount of the potential recapture and (ii) the rest of the property. For instance, in the example above, the partnership would be treated as owning a § 751 asset (basis $0, value $400) and a non–§ 751 asset (basis $100, value $300). See Reg. § 1.751–1(c)(5).

(f) Inventory. Under § 751(d), the term "inventory" includes § 1221(1) property (i.e., stock-in-trade and property held primarily for sale) and "any other property" that would not be treated as a capital asset (or § 1231 quasi-capital asset) in the partnership's hands. § 751(d)(1), (2). This expansive definition includes accounts receivable (whether or not realized) for services rendered or for sale of § 1221(1) property. Reg. § 1.751–1(d)(2)(ii). Indeed, the regulations state further that inventory items include "any unrealized receivables." Id.

The treatment of all unrealized receivables as inventory under § 751(d)(2), however, seems questionable. For example, potential depreciation recapture is an unrealized receivable but should arguably not be treated as an inventory item. Section 751(d)(2) literally applies only to "property" which would not be treated as a capital asset (or quasi-capital asset) upon sale. Thus, the application of § 751(d)(2) apparently depends upon the character of the underlying asset rather than the character of the gain generated from the sale. Moreover, potential depreciation recapture was added to the category of § 751(c) unrealized receivables only after the regulations were first issued.

Under current law, the inclusion of unrealized receivables under § 751(d)(2) has no operative effect when a partnership interest is sold. Unrealized receivables are taxed only once under § 751(a), and the selling partner's recognized ordinary income is the amount determined under the hypothetical sale approach. The 1997 Act amended § 751(a) by repealing the "substantial appreciation" test for inventory with respect to sale of a partnership interest, but left § 751(b) (disproportionate distributions of § 751 assets) virtually intact. Since unrealized receivables (whether or not appreciated) are treated as inventory items under § 751(d)(2), they may affect whether the partnership's inventory is substantially appreciated for purposes of § 751(b). See Chapter 9.

Example (2): A sells her 1/3 partnership interest in the ABC general partnership to D for $22,000 cash when the partnership has the following balance sheet:

	Basis	Value		Basis	Value
Assets			Liabilities	$36,000	$ 36,000
Cash	$18,000	$ 18,000	Capital		
Securities	27,000	21,000	A	20,000	22,000
Equipment*	0	6,000	B	20,000	22,000
Accounts			C	20,000	22,000
Receivable	21,000	21,000	Total	$96,000	$102,000
Inventory	30,000	36,000			
Total	$96,000	$102,000			

*Includes $6,000 of § 1245 recapture.

A realizes $34,000 on the sale of her interest ($22,000 cash plus $12,000 share of partnership liabilities). If § 751 did not apply, A would recognize $2,000 of capital gain on sale of her partnership interest ($34,000 amount realized less $32,000 outside basis). Section 751 requires, however, that A recognize her allocable share of the total ordinary income from a hypothetical sale of all of the partnership's § 751 assets, consisting of potential § 1245 recapture (basis $0, value $6,000), accounts receivable (basis $21,000, value $21,000) and inventory (basis $30,000, value $36,000). § 751(c), (d). Thus, A must recognize ordinary income of $4,000 (1/3 of $12,000 total ordinary income) on transfer of her partnership interest. Under § 741, A also recognizes a capital loss of $2,000, i.e., the capital gain that she would otherwise have realized on the sale of her interest ($2,000) less the ordinary income recognized under § 751 ($4,000). A's overall gain

($4,000 ordinary income and $2,000 capital loss) is equal to her net economic gain ($2,000).

The character of inventory items may also depend on the selling partner's situation. Under § 751(d)(4), inventory includes any partnership assets that would be treated as inventory "if held by the selling ... partner." This provision is intended to prevent a selling partner who is a "dealer" in property from obtaining capital gain treatment when he would have recognized ordinary income on a sale of the underlying partnership property.

Example (3): A, a dealer in real property, sells his 1/3 partnership interest in the ABC general partnership to D for $4,300, when the partnership has the following balance sheet:

	Basis	Value		Basis	Value
Assets			Capital		
Cash	$3,000	$ 3,000	A	$2,200	$ 4,300
Land	3,000	9,000	B	2,200	4,300
Inventory	600	900	C	2,200	4,300
Total	$6,600	$12,900	Total	$6,600	$12,900

Since A is a dealer in real property, the partnership's land is classified as an inventory item with respect to A. § 751(d)(4). A's entire gain of $2,100 (A's 1/3 share of the unrealized appreciation in the land and other inventory items) is treated as ordinary income under § 751(a). By contrast, if B or C is an investor (rather than a dealer in real estate), he would recognize ordinary income of $100 (⅓ of the unrealized appreciation in the inventory) and capital gain of $2,000 (⅓ of the unrealized appreciation in the land).

(g) Tiered Partnerships. If an upper-tier partnership owns an interest in a lower-tier partnership, § 751(f) treats the upper-tier partnership as owning a proportionate share of the lower-tier partnership's assets. This "look-through" provision is intended primarily to prevent circumvention of the collapsible partnership rules where an upper-tier partnership owns a partnership interest in a lower-tier partnership with § 751 assets. An upper-tier partner who sells his partnership interest may be forced to recognize ordinary income even though the upper-tier partnership does not own any § 751 assets directly.

(h) Installment Sales. Generally, a partner may report gain from sale of his partnership interest on the installment method under § 453. If § 751 does not apply (i.e., because the partnership has no unrealized receivables or inventory), all of the selling partner's gain apparently qualifies for installment treatment under an entity approach. See Rev. Rul. 89–108. If the partnership owns § 751 assets that, if sold directly, would be ineligible for installment treatment, however, the selling partner is required to recognize a portion of his gain immediately. Under § 453(i)(2), a selling partner cannot defer recognition of § 751 ordinary income attributable to §§ 1245/1250 recapture. Moreover, § 453A authorizes regulations that would treat a sale of a partnership interest as a sale of a proportionate share of the partnership's assets. See § 453A(e)(2); see also § 453(k)(2) (denying installment treatment for marketable securities and certain other property).

(i) Exchange of Partnership Interests. Under § 1031(a)(2)(D), an exchange of partnership interests is ineligible for § 1031 nonrecognition treatment and thus is treated as a fully taxable disposition. An interest in a partnership which has a valid § 761(a) election in effect is treated as an interest in the underlying assets rather than a partnership interest. § 1031(a)(2) (last sentence). It is unclear whether the underlying policy of § 1031(a)(2)(D) denies nonrecognition treatment to an exchange of like-kind property immediately followed by a partnership contribution (or preceded by a partnership distribution), or whether such a transaction represents a mere continuation of the original investment in modified form. See Magneson (1985). The Service may argue that § 1031 nonrecognition treatment should be denied under the step-transaction doctrine. See, e.g., Crenshaw (1971).

Section 1031(a)(2)(D) is not intended to deny tax-free treatment to a partner who converts a general partnership interest into a limited partnership interest in the same partnership, or vice versa: the Service generally views such a transaction as a tax-free § 721 contribution of the old interest to the partnership followed by a tax-free § 731 distribution of the new partnership interest. See Rev. Rul. 84–52; see also Rev. Rul. 95–37 (conversion of general partnership into limited liability company);

Rev. Rul. 95–55 (conversion of general partnership into limited liability partnership).

(j) Incorporation of Partnership. In Revenue Ruling 84–111, the Service ruled that the form of the transaction controls the tax consequences of incorporating a partnership under § 351. This ruling permits the parties to select the most favorable tax treatment (i.e., basis, holding period and recognized gain) by casting the transaction in any of the following three forms: (i) a partnership transfer of assets in exchange for stock and assumption of liabilities, followed by a liquidating distribution of stock to partners, (ii) a liquidating distribution by the partnership followed by a transfer of assets by the former partners in exchange for stock and assumption of liabilities, or (iii) a transfer of partnership interests in exchange for stock followed by a termination of the partnership.

§ 3.   Treatment of the Transferee Partner

(a) Optional Basis Adjustment. If a partner acquires his partnership interest by purchase, he takes a cost basis which includes his share of partnership liabilities. §§ 742, 752(d) and 1012. Similarly, a partner who acquires his partnership interest from a decedent generally takes a fair-market-value basis under § 1014(a). See Chapter 10. Section 743(b) provides for an adjustment to the basis of partnership assets upon transfer of a partnership interest by sale or exchange or at the death of a partner, if the partnership has a § 754 election in effect. The § 743(b) adjustment is intended to put the transferee partner in roughly the same position as if he had acquired a portion of the partnership's assets directly. The § 743(b) adjustment is personal to the transferee partner. The amount of the adjustment is equal to the difference between the transferee's outside basis and his share of the common basis of partnership assets. Although the § 743(b) adjustment affects only the transferee's special basis in partnership assets, the § 754 election is made at the partnership level.

Once a § 754 election takes effect, it applies automatically to all subsequent transfers of partnership interests. The election is advantageous if the partnership property has a net built-in gain: a positive § 743(b) adjustment increases the transferee's special basis in partnership assets, thereby reducing or eliminating his share of the partnership's gain on a subsequent sale of such assets. Conversely, the election may be disadvantageous if the partnership property has a net built-in loss: a negative § 743(b) adjustment reduces the transferee's special basis in partnership assets, thereby reducing or eliminating his share of the partnership's loss on a subsequent sale of such assets. A transferee's special basis adjustment under § 743 is also taken into account in determining his share of depreciation deductions and the basis of property distributed to him. Prop. Reg. § 1.743–1(g), (j)(4). For depreciation purposes, the rules for newly-purchased property (cost-recovery period and method) apply to any basis increase under § 743(b). Prop. Reg. § 1.743–1(j)(4)(B). Thus, a § 754 election may affect both the timing and the character of the transferee's gain or loss.

Under § 703, the partnership determines its income, deduction, gain or loss without regard to any § 743(b) adjustments. Each partner's capital account is then adjusted to reflect his distributive share of these items in accordance with the § 704(b) regulations. The partnership reports to the transferee his distributive share of partnership items increased or decreased to reflect any positive or negative § 743(b) adjustments. Prop. Reg. § 1.743–1(j)(2). Thus, the transferee includes only his adjusted share of partnership items, net of any § 743 basis adjustments. In determining any § 743(b) adjustments, the partnership may generally rely on information furnished by the transferee concerning the cost or § 1014 basis of the acquired interest. Prop. Reg. § 1.743–1(k)(2), (3).

Example (4): A sells her 1/3 partnership interest in the ABC general partnership to D for $9,000 cash when the partnership has the following balance sheet:

	Basis	Value		Basis	Value
Assets			Capital		
Cash	$3,000	$ 3,000	A	$3,000	$ 9,000
Land	6,000	24,000	B	3,000	9,000
Total	$9,000	$27,000	C	3,000	9,000
			Total	$9,000	$27,000

A recognizes $6,000 capital gain ($9,000 amount realized less $3,000 outside basis). D takes a $9,000 cost basis in her partnership interest. If no § 754 election is in effect, the basis of the partnership assets cannot be adjusted to reflect D's cost basis in her partnership interest. As a result, the sum of the partners' outside bases ($15,000) will exceed the partnership's aggregate inside basis ($9,000) by an amount equal to the unrealized appreciation in D's share of the partnership assets ($6,000). If the partnership subsequently sells the land for $24,000, D will be taxed on her share of partnership gain ($6,000) and her outside basis will be correspondingly increased; a subsequent sale or liquidation of D's interest will generate a capital loss of $6,000.

By contrast, if a § 754 election is in effect, D receives a special basis adjustment in the land (the only appreciated asset) of $6,000, i.e., the excess of D's $9,000 cost basis over her $3,000 share of the partnership's common basis (1/3 of $9,000). If the partnership subsequently sells the land for $24,000, D's special basis adjustment offsets her 1/3 share of the partnership's built-in gain, eliminating her share of taxable gain.

Example (5): A sells his 1/3 interest in the ABC general partnership to D for $4,000 cash when a § 754 election is in effect and the partnership has the following balance sheet:

	Basis	Value		Basis	Value
Assets			Liabilities	$6,000	$6,000
Land	$18,000	$ 9,000	Capital		
Securities	6,000	3,000	A	8,000	4,000
Inventory	6,000	6,000	B	8,000	4,000
Total	$30,000	$18,000	C	8,000	4,000
			Total	$30,000	$18,000

D's outside basis is $6,000 ($4,000 cash plus $2,000 share of partnership liabilities), which is $4,000 less than his 1/3 share of the common basis of the partnership assets ($10,000). The negative § 743(b) adjustment of $4,000 is allocated $3,000 to the land and $1,000 to the securities (D's share of the unrealized loss inherent in each asset). § 755. If the partnership subsequently sold the land and securities for $9,000 and $3,000, respectively, D would report no gain or loss ($4,000 allocable share of loss offset by $4,000 negative basis adjustment). The remaining partners would each recognize $4,000 of loss on the sale.

(b) Share of Common Basis. The amount of the § 743(b) adjustment is the difference between the transferee's outside basis and his share of the partnership's common basis in its assets. A transferee's share of the partnership's common basis is equal to "the sum of [his interest] in the partnership's previously taxed capital, plus [his] share of partnership liabilities." Prop. Reg. § 1.743–1(d)(1). The proposed regulations determine a transferee's share of previously taxed capital by reference to a "hypothetical transaction" in which, immediately after the transfer, the partnership is deemed to sell all of its assets for fair market value in a fully taxable transaction. Prop. Reg. § 1.743–1(d)(2). The transferee's share of previously taxed capital is equal to: (i) the amount of cash he would receive on liquidation of the partnership immediately following the hypothetical sale, (ii) increased by his share of tax loss on the hypothetical sale and (iii) decreased by his share of tax gain on the hypothetical sale. Id.

If the partnership maintains capital accounts in accordance with the § 704(b) regulations, a transferee's share of previously taxed capital will generally be equal to the transferor's tax capital account immediately before the transfer. Under the § 704(b) regulations, the transferor's capital account (or the portion attributable to the transferred interest) carries over to the transferee, who steps into the transferor's shoes for capital account purposes. Reg. § 1.704–1(b)(2)(iv)(l). The transferee inherits any § 704(c) gain or loss allocable to the transferor. Reg. § 1.704–3(a)(7). Partnership liabilities are reflected in the partnership's common basis and the partners' outside bases (but not capital accounts). Thus, the transferee's share of the partnership's common basis is generally equal to his tax capital account (carried over from the transferor) plus his share of partnership liabilities.

Example (6): A contributes land with a basis of $400 and a fair market value of $1,000 and B and C each contribute $1,000 cash to the ABC general partnership in exchange for equal 1/3 partnership interests. The partnership borrows $600 recourse which it uses to purchase securities; each partner has a 1/3 share of the partnership's recourse liability under § 752. D purchases A's 1/3 partnership interest for $1,100 cash when a § 754 election is in effect and the partnership has the following balance sheet:

	Basis	Value		Basis	Value
Assets			Liabilities	$600	$600
Cash	$2,000	$2,000	Capital		
Land	400	1,300	A	400	1,100
Securities	600	600	B	1,000	1,100
Total	$3,000	$3,900	C	1,000	1,100
			Total	$3,000	$3,900

Under § 742, D's outside basis is $1,300 ($1,100 cash plus $200 share of liabilities). D's share of the partnership's common basis is $600 (tax capital account of $400 carried over from A plus $200 share of liabilities). Accordingly, D receives a positive § 743(b) adjustment of $700 ($1,300 outside basis less $600 share of common basis) allocated entirely to the land. If the partnership immediately sold the land, D (as A's successor) would be allocated gain of $700 ($600 § 704(c) gain plus $100 share of post-contribution appreciation), offset by D's special basis adjustment. If D purchased B's (rather than A's) partnership interest, D's share of the partnership's common basis would be $1,200 (tax capital account of $1,000 carried over from B plus $200 share of liabilities). Accordingly, D would receive a positive § 743(b) adjustment of $100 ($1,300 outside basis less $1,200 share of common basis). On sale of the land, D would be allocated $100 of gain, offset by D's § 743(b) adjustment.

(c) **Basis Allocation.** If a § 754 election is in effect, the § 743(b) adjustment is assigned to individual partnership assets under § 755. First, the partnership assets are divided into two classes of property, viz. "capital assets" (capital assets and § 1231 quasi-capital assets) and "ordinary assets" (all other assets). § 755(b). The § 743(b) adjustment is then allocated (i) between the two classes and (ii) among the assets within each class based on the amount of tax gain (or loss) that would be allocated to the transferee if, immediately after the transfer, the partnership sold all of its assets for fair market value. Prop. Reg. § 1.755–1(b)(1). The § 743(b) adjustment is treated as a "net" adjustment which may comprise a positive adjustment for one class and a negative adjustment for the other class. Within each class of assets, adjustments may increase the basis of some assets and decrease the basis of others. By contrast, the former basis allocation rules under § 755 generally prohibited "two-way" allocations, and thus often produced a mismatch between the tax and economic consequences to the transferee.

Under the proposed § 755 regulations, the first step is to determine the amount of the § 743(b) adjustment allocated to the class of ordinary assets. This amount is generally equal to the total ordinary income (or loss) that would be allocated to the transferee if all the partnership's assets were sold for fair market value. Prop. Reg. § 1.755–1(b)(2). The remaining portion of the transferee's § 743(b) adjustment is allocated to the class of capital assets. Id. Within each class of assets, positive (or negative) basis adjustments are then allocated among particular assets based on the amount of income (or loss) that the transferee would recognize with respect to the particular asset. Prop. Reg. § 1.755–1(b)(3). Generally, the transferee will wind up with a basis adjustment in each asset (ordinary or capital) equal to his share of the built-in gain (or loss) attributable to the asset. Thus, the transferee's share of common basis plus his special basis adjustment in each asset will generally be equal to his share of the fair market value of each asset.

Example (7): D purchases A's partnership interest for $2,000 when a § 754 election is in effect and the partnership has the following balance sheet:

	Basis	Value		Basis	Value
Assets			Capital		
Inventory	$0	$3,000	A	$2,000	$2,000
Land	6,000	3,000	B	2,000	2,000
Total	$6,000	$6,000	C	2,000	2,000
			Total	$6,000	$6,000

Since D's outside basis equals her $2,000 share of the partnership's common basis (1/3 of $6,000), the amount of D's net § 743(b) adjustment is zero. Upon a hypothetical sale of the partnership's assets for fair market value, D would be allocated $1,000 of ordinary income and $1,000 of capital loss. Thus, D receives a positive basis adjustment of $1,000 with respect to the inventory and a negative basis adjustment of $1,000 with respect to the land.

Example (8): A, B and C form the equal ABC partnership. A contributes nondepreciable Asset #1 with a fair market value of $18,000 and a basis of $15,000 in A's hands. B and C each contribute $18,000 cash which the partnership uses to purchase nondepreciable Assets ##2, 3 and 4. A sells her partnership interest to D for $20,500, when A's share of the partnership's common basis is still

$15,000. At the time of D's purchase, a § 754 election is in effect and the partnership has the following balance sheet:

	Basis	Value
Capital Assets		
Asset #1	$15,000	$21,000
Asset #2	12,000	18,000
Ordinary Assets		
Asset #3	$16,000	$17,500
Asset #4	8,000	5,000
Total	$51,000	$61,500

D receives a § 743(b) adjustment of $5,500 ($20,500 outside basis less $15,000 share of common basis carried over from A). If the partnership sold all of its assets for fair market value, D would be allocated $4,000 of capital gain from Asset #1 ($3,000 § 704(c) built-in gain plus $1,000 share of post-contribution gain) and $2,000 of capital gain from Asset #2. D would also be allocated total ordinary loss of $500, consisting of $500 of ordinary income from Asset #3 and $1,000 of ordinary loss from Asset #4.

A negative basis adjustment of $500 is allocated to the class of ordinary assets, and a positive basis adjustment of $6,000 ($5,500 § 743(b) adjustment increased by $500 negative adjustment allocable to ordinary assets) is allocated to the class of capital assets. The $6,000 positive basis adjustment to capital assets is allocated $4,000 to Asset #1 and $2,000 to Asset #2 (D's share of the gain inherent in each asset). The class of ordinary assets has both unrealized appreciation and depreciation. Accordingly, appreciated Asset #3 receives a positive basis adjustment of $500 and depreciated Asset #4 receives a negative basis adjustment of $1,000. Thus, D's share of common basis plus her special basis adjustment in each asset will be equal to her share of the fair market value of each asset.

In some situations, the transferee will not obtain exactly a fair-market-value basis in each asset. For example, discrepancies may arise when the transferee acquires his interest in a "bargain" purchase, i.e., the purchase price is less than the fair market value of the transferee's share of the partnership's assets (including goodwill). Since the § 743(b) adjustment is allocated first to the class of ordinary assets, any "shortfall" in the basis adjustment must generally be spread among assets within the capital class (in proportion to their relative fair market value). See Prop. Reg. § 1.755–1(b)(3)(iii) (Ex. 2). Any "excess" purchase price is allocated to goodwill (or going concern value), as discussed below.

Example (9): The facts are the same as in Example (8), above, except that A sells her interest to D for $19,200 (rather than $20,500). D receives a § 743(b) adjustment of $4,200 ($19,200 outside basis less $15,000 share of common basis carried over from A). A negative basis adjustment of $500 is allocated to the class of ordinary assets, and a positive basis adjustment of $4,700 ($4,200 § 743(b) adjustment increased by $500 negative adjustment allocable to ordinary assets) is allocated to the class of capital assets. Each ordinary asset receives a fair-market-value basis adjustment ($500 positive adjustment to appreciated Asset #3 and $1,000 negative adjustment to depreciated Asset #4).

The total capital gain allocable to D ($6,000) exceeds the remaining § 743(b) adjustment to capital assets ($4,700). Accordingly, the shortfall ($1,300) must be allocated between the two capital assets in proportion to their relative fair market values. Of the basis shortfall, $700 is allocated to Asset #1 ($1,300 × $21,000/$39,000) and $600 is allocated to Asset #2 ($1,300 × $18,000/$39,000). Thus, Asset #1 receives a basis adjustment of $3,300 ($4,000 allocable gain less $700 basis shortfall) and Asset #2 receives a basis adjustment of $1,400 ($2,000 allocable gain less $600 basis shortfall). If both capital assets were sold for their respective fair market values, D would report capital gain equal to the basis shortfall ($700 gain on Asset #1 and $600 gain on Asset #2), increasing her outside basis from $19,200 to $20,500.

(d) Goodwill. If the assets of the partnership constitute a trade or business, the "residual method" of valuing goodwill (or going concern value) applies for purposes of allocating any § 743(b) adjustment under § 755. § 1060(d); Temp. Reg. § 1.755–2T. If the purchase price exceeds the total fair market value of all identifiable tangible and intangible assets (other than goodwill and going concern), the "excess" purchase price is allocated to goodwill and going concern value. Temp. Reg. § 1.755–2T(b), (e) (Ex. 1). As a result, the residual method generally produces a higher basis for goodwill than if the total purchase price were simply allocated among all assets in proportion to their respective fair market values.

In 1993, Congress created a new category of "§ 197 intangibles" (including goodwill and going concern value) which must generally be amortized over a 15–year period using the straight-line method. § 197; Prop. Reg. § 1.197–2. The enactment of § 197 represents a compromise intended to eliminate disputes between taxpayers and the Service over amortization of particular intangibles purchased as part of a business. For purposes of the § 1060 purchase-price allocation rules, all § 197 intangibles (whether or not amortizable) are allocated to two "junior" classes (Class IV and Class V). See Temp. Reg. § 1.1060–1T(d)(2). Class IV includes all § 197 intangibles except those assigned to Class V, which consists of goodwill and going concern value. See id.

(e) Effect on Capital Accounts. Regardless of whether a partnership has a § 754 election in effect, a transfer of a partnership interest generally does not give rise to an adjustment to the partners' capital accounts. Reg. § 1.704–1(b)(2)(iv)(m)(2). Although the no-adjustment rule may seem surprising, it normally does not affect the transferee's final capital account or his share of liquidating distributions. The no-adjustment rule also applies if a transfer of a partnership interest triggers a deemed termination of the partnership under § 708(b)(1)(B). See § 4 below.

(f) Coordinating §§ 704(c) and 743(b). If a partnership interest is purchased from a partner who contributed § 704(c) property, a portion of a transferee's § 743(b) adjustment may reflect § 704(c) built-in gain. Even though a portion of the basis adjustment is attributable to § 704(c) built-in gain, §§ 704(c) and 743(b) generally operate independently. Because the § 743(b) adjustment is personal to the transferee, it cannot serve to eliminate book/tax disparities resulting from the ceiling rule. Thus, the noncontributing partners cannot be allocated deductions attributable to the transferee's § 743(b) adjustment in order to cure ceiling-rule distortions. Instead, the partnership must use curative or remedial allocations to remedy such problems.

Example (10): A contributes land with a basis of $20 and a fair market value of $50 and B contributes $50 cash in exchange for equal interests in the AB partnership; when the land has appreciated in value to $150 and the partnership has a § 754 election in effect, C purchases A's partnership interest for $100. C receives a § 743(b) adjustment of $80 ($100 outside basis less $20 share of common basis inherited from A); the adjustment reflects C's § 704(c) built-in gain ($30) and his 50% share of the post-contribution appreciation in the land ($50). The BC partnership uses the traditional method of allocating § 704(c) gain and subsequently sells the land for $40. On the sale, the partnership has a book loss of $10 ($50 book basis less $40 amount realized) allocable equally to B and C and a tax gain of $20 ($40 amount realized less $20 tax basis) allocable entirely to C. Accordingly, the partners would have the following tax and book capital accounts immediately after the sale:

	B		C	
	Tax	Book	Tax	Book
Initial	$50	$50	$20	$50
Gain (loss) on sale		(5)	20	(5)
Ending balance	$50	$45	$40	$45

C reports a loss of $60 ($20 gain less $80 § 743(b) adjustment), reducing C's outside basis to $40. Although B has sustained an economic loss of $5, he cannot be allocated a corresponding tax loss until sale or liquidation of his partnership interest. See Prop. Reg. § 1.743–1(j)(3)(ii) (Ex. 2).

Example (11): The facts are the same as in Example (10), above, except that the partnership uses the remedial allocation method. Thus, B would be allocated $5 of remedial tax loss to match his $5 of book loss, and C would be allocated an offsetting $5 of remedial tax gain. Accordingly, the partners would have the following tax and book capital accounts immediately after the sale:

	B		C	
	Tax	Book	Tax	Book
Initial	$50	$50	$20	$50
Gain (loss) on sale		(5)	20	(5)
Remedial allocation	(5)		5	
Ending balance	$45	$45	$45	$45

C reports a loss of $55 ($25 gain less $80 positive basis adjustment), reducing C's outside basis to $45. See Prop. Reg. § 1.743–1(j)(3)(ii) (Ex. 3).

(g) Subsequent Transfers. On successive transfers of partnership interests, the last transferee's special basis adjustment is normally determined by reference to the common basis without regard to the prior transferee's special basis adjustment. Prop. Reg. § 1.743–1(f). In the case of a gift of a partnership interest, however, the donee is treated as stepping into the donor's shoes with respect to any special basis adjustment. See id.

(h) Subsequent Distributions. If a transfer of a partnership interest triggers a § 743(b) adjustment with respect to property which is subsequently distributed to the transferee partner, the transferee partner's basis in the distributed property generally includes the amount of the § 743(b) adjustment. Prop. Reg. § 1.743–1(g)(1). Under § 732, a distributee partner's basis in the distributed property is equal to the partnership's common basis in such property increased (or decreased) by the partner's positive (or negative) § 743(b) adjustment with respect to such property. See Reg. § 1.732–2(b). If the partnership distributes such property to another partner, the § 743(b) adjustment is not taken into account in determining the distributee partner's basis in the distributed property; instead, the § 743(b) adjustment is reallocated under the rules of § 755 to partnership property of the same class (or to any such property simultaneously distributed to the transferee partner). Prop. Reg. § 1.743–1(g)(2)-(3).

(i) Effect of § 732(d) Election. Section 732(d) provides relief for a transferee partner who acquires his partnership interest when no § 754 election is in effect and then receives a distribution of partnership property within two years after the transfer. Under § 732(d), the transferee partner may elect to treat the distributed property as having a pre-distribution basis in the partnership's hands equal to the basis such property would have had if a § 743(b) adjustment had been made when he acquired his partnership interest.

Example (12): D purchases A's partnership interest when A's share of the partnership's inventory has a basis of zero and a fair market value of $10,000; the partnership's only other asset consists of cash, and no § 754 election is in effect. Within two years after the transfer, the partnership distributes the inventory to D. If D makes a § 732(d) election, she will be treated as if a § 743(b) adjustment of $10,000 had been made with respect to her share of the partnership's inventory. Accordingly, D will receive a $10,000 cost basis in the distributed inventory ($0 share of common basis plus $10,000 § 743(b) adjustment) and will recognize no gain or loss on an immediate sale of the inventory. If the inventory were not distributed, D might otherwise recognize ordinary income of $10,000 upon a subsequent sale of her partnership interest (or the partnership's sale of the inventory). See § 751(a); Prop. Reg. § 1.751–1(a)(2).

(j) Tiered Partnerships. In the case of tiered partnerships, a § 743(b) adjustment to the basis of the upper-tier partnership's assets triggers a corresponding adjustment to the basis of the lower-tier partnership's assets only if both partnerships have § 754 elections in effect. Rev. Rul. 87–115; see also Rev. Rul. 92–15 (§§ 734(b)/754 adjustments).

§ 4. Termination of Partnership

(a) General. Under the general rule of § 708(a), a partnership is treated as continuing to exist until a termination occurs. Under § 708(b), a termination occurs only if (i) no part of the partnership's business continues to be conducted in partnership form or (ii) upon a sale or exchange of 50% or more of the total interests in partnership capital and profits within a 12–month period. § 708(b)(1). For example, a voluntary termination of a partnership occurs if the partners agree to discontinue business in partnership form and distribute all of the partnership's assets in complete liquidation. Retention of even a nominal amount of partnership assets may be sufficient, however, to prevent termination of a partnership until final winding up of the partnership's business. See Foxman (1965).

With proper planning, a partnership may generally avoid an unwanted termination as a result of a sale or exchange of partnership interests. Under § 708(b)(1)(B), all sales of partnership interests within any 12–month period are aggregated for purposes of the 50%-or-more rule, but successive sales of the same interest are not counted twice. Reg. § 1.708–1(b)(1)(ii). For example, if A sells a 30% interest in capital and profits in the ABC partnership to D in May, and B sells another 30% interest in capital and profits to E the following

March, the partnership terminates as a result of the March sale. If, however, D (rather than B) sold her 30% interest to E, the partnership would not terminate because a sale of the same partnership interest is counted only once. The deemed termination rules of § 708(b)(1)(B) do not apply to electing large partnerships. § 774(c); see Chapter 1.

Certain dispositions of partnership interests (e.g., by gift, bequest, inheritance or liquidation) are not treated as sales or exchanges for purposes of the termination rules. Reg. § 1.708–1(b)(1)(ii). Various other dispositions are generally treated as sales or exchanges, for example, a contribution of a partnership interest to a corporation (or to another partnership) and a distribution of a partnership interest from a corporation (or another partnership). See § 761(e); Rev. Rul. 81–38 (§ 351 transfer); see also Rev. Rul. 90–17 (merger of partnerships; § 761(e) inapplicable).

In a tiered partnership structure, a sale or exchange of interests in the upper-tier partnership that results in termination of the upper-tier partnership is treated as a sale or exchange of the upper-tier partnership's entire interest in the lower-tier partnership under § 761(e), which may in turn cause a constructive termination of the lower-tier partnership. See Reg. § 1.708–1(b)(1)(ii). A non-terminating sale or exchange of interests in an upper-tier partnership is not treated as proportionate sale or exchange of the lower-tier partnership's interests. See id. For example, assume that the equal AB partnership owns a 60% interest in the

CD partnership, and that B sells a 50% interest in AB to E. The AB partnership terminates as a result of B's sale, and the AB partnership is treated as exchanging its entire interest in the CD partnership, triggering a termination of the CD partnership under § 708(b)(1)(B).

(b) Consequences of Termination. If a partnership terminates under § 708(b)(1)(B), the terminated partnership is deemed to contribute all of its assets and liabilities to a new partnership in exchange for an interest in the new partnership; the terminated partnership is then deemed to distribute interests in the new partnership to the purchasing partner and the continuing partners in complete liquidation. See Reg. § 1.708–1(b)(1)(iv). The treatment of a technical termination as a deemed § 721 contribution of assets followed by a deemed § 731 distribution of partnership interests is intended to coordinate the tax consequences of a technical termination with the rules of §§ 704(c), 731(c) and 737. See Chapters 5 and 9.

Under the § 704(b) regulations, the tax and book capital accounts of the partners in the terminated partnership carry over to the new partnership; thus, the deemed contribution and liquidating distribution are disregarded. See Reg. §§ 1.704–1(b)(2)(iv)(*l*), 1.708–1(b)(1)(iv). The technical termination does not trigger a new seven-year period for purposes of §§ 704(c)(1)(B) and 737; instead, any § 704(c) built-in gain (or loss) at the time of the termination is preserved in the hands of the new partnership and may be triggered upon a subsequent distribution of such property. See Reg. §§ 1.704–3(a)(3)(i), 1.704–4(a)(4)(ii), 1.704–4(c)(3), 1.737–2(a); see also Reg. § 1.731–2(g)(2) (termination does not trigger § 731(c)). The new partnership is not required to use the same § 704(c) allocation method as the terminated partnership. See Reg. § 1.704–3(a)(2).

In the absence of a § 754 election, the bases of the assets deemed contributed to the new partnership will not be adjusted to reflect the purchasing and continuing partners' aggregate outside bases. If the terminated partnership has a § 754 election in effect, the purchasing partner will be entitled to a § 743(b) adjustment with respect to his proportionate share of the assets deemed contributed to the new partnership. See Reg. § 1.708–1(b)(1)(v). For purposes of § 743 (but not § 708), the terminated partnership's deemed distribution of interests in the new partnership is treated as a sale or exchange of interests in the new partnership under § 761(e). See Reg. § 1.761–1(e). Thus, if the new partnership has a § 754 election in effect, all of the partners in the new partnership will be entitled to a § 743(b) adjustment with respect to the assets deemed contributed. Any § 743(b) adjustments are allocated under the rules of § 755. If the partnership has a § 754 election in effect, the deemed termination may also affect the basis of § 197 intangibles deemed contributed to the new partnership. See Prop. Reg. § 1.197–2(g)(2)(iv).

§ 5.   Distributive Share Allocations When Interests Shift

(a) General. When a partner transfers his partnership interest or a partnership admits a new partner by a contribution of capital, the resulting shift in the partners' interests raises issues concerning (i) closing of the partnership's taxable year, (ii) allocation of partnership items between the transferor and transferee and (iii) retroactive allocations to the incoming partner. Section 706(c) governs the closing of the partnership's taxable year, and §§ 706(d) and 704(b) control allocation of the partners' distributive shares.

(b) Closing of Taxable Year. The partnership's taxable year closes prematurely (i) with respect to all partners if there is a termination of the partnership under § 708, or (ii) with respect to any partner "whose entire interest in the partnership terminates (whether by reason of death, liquidation, or otherwise)." § 706(c)(1), (2)(A). A closing of the partnership's taxable year may give rise to "bunching" of income if the partnership and affected partners have different taxable years. A partnership's taxable year generally does not close with respect to a partner who sells less than his entire interest or "whose interest is reduced (whether by entry of a new partner, partial liquidation of a partner's interest, gift or otherwise)." § 706(c)(2)(B).

(c) Distributive Share Allocations. If any partner's interest in the partnership changes during the taxable year, the partners' distributive shares of partnership income, gain, loss or deduction are determined by taking into account "the varying interests of the partners in the partnership during such taxable year." § 706(d)(1). The varying interest rule literally applies to any change in the partners' interests, including partial sales, gifts and reductions of a partner's interest. The regulations provide that the partners may agree to allocate their distributive shares by prorating partnership items in proportion to the number of days in the pre-and post-shift periods or by "any other reasonable method." Reg. § 1.706–1(c)(2)(ii). Otherwise, the partners' distributive shares must be determined by an interim closing of the partnership books as of the date of each shift. See id.

Example (13): A has a 40% interest, and B and C each have 30% interests in ABC, a calendar-year partnership. On May 1, C sells half of his 30% interest to D. The partnership incurs a net taxable loss of $1,200 for the entire year. Although the partnership's taxable year does not close, the partners' distributive shares are determined under the varying interest rule. Under the proration method, the partnership's taxable loss is allocated 40% to A, 30% to B, 20% to C (4/12 x 30% and 8/12 x 15%), and 10% to D (8/12 x 15%). Accordingly, the partnership's taxable loss is allocated $480 to A, $360 to B, $240 to C and $120 to D. If the partnership's $1,200 loss is incurred evenly throughout the year ($100 monthly), the interim-closing method would yield the same result. If the partnership instead incurred a $200 loss before the sale and a $1,000 loss after the sale, the partners may prefer to use the interim-closing method, since C would be allocated $210 of loss (30% x $200 and 15% x $1,000) and D would be allocated $150 of loss (15% x $1,000).

(d) Allocable Cash Basis Items. Section 706(d)(2) contains special rules for determining the partners' distributive shares of "allocable cash basis items." These rules are intended generally to prevent cash-basis partnerships from circumventing the varying interest rule by deferring payment of previously-accrued expenses until after admission of a new partner. For example, a calendar-year partnership might elect to close its books immediately before admitting a new 1/3 partner on December 30; if the partnership then made a year-end payment of interest that had become due on July 1, the new partner would arguably be entitled to a full 1/3 share of the deductible interest expense.

To curb such abuses, § 706(d)(2) in effect puts a cash-basis partnership on the accrual method for purposes of determining the partners' distributive shares of certain items. The partnership must assign a portion of such items to each day of the period to which it is attributable and then allocate each daily portion among the partners in proportion to their interests in the partnership at the close of the day. § 706(c)(2)(A). Allocable cash basis items include interest, taxes, payments for services or for the use of property and any other items (to be specified in regulations) necessary to prevent "significant misstatements" of the partners' income. § 706(d)(2)(B). In addition, depreciation deductions are deemed to occur ratably over the year. See Hawkins (1983). Since most partnerships are now required to use the accrual method, § 706(d)(2) is of limited practical significance.

Example (14): The equal ABCD partnership (a calendar-year, cash-method partnership) incurs a $1,200 rental expense for the year. On December 1, E purchases D's 25% interest in the partnership and, a few days later, the partnership pays the $1,200 rent. Even if the partnership uses the interim-closing method, E cannot be allocated a full $300 (25%) of the deductible rental expense because § 706(d)(2) treats rent as if it were paid ratably over the partnership's entire taxable year. Accordingly, the $300 rental expense allocable to the transferred interest is allocated $275 to D (11/12 x $300) and $25 to E (1/12 x $300).

When a cash-method partnership pays an allocable cash basis item that accrued economically in a prior year, § 706(d)(2)(C)(i) assigns the item to the first day of the year in which it is paid. Any deduction for the item, however, must be allocated among those persons who were partners in the partnership during the period when the item accrued economically, according to their varying interests during that period. § 706(d)(2)(D)(i). If an otherwise deductible amount is assigned to a person who was not a partner on the first day of the year, the partnership must capitalize the amount and allocate it among partnership assets under the rules of § 755. In the example above, for instance, if the partnership deferred payment of the $1,200 of rent until January 31 of the following year, D's share of the deduction ($275) would be capitalized.

A cash-method partnership may sometimes deduct an expense in a taxable year prior to the year in which it accrues economically. Under § 706(d)(2)(C)(ii), the prepaid expense is assigned to the last day of the year in which it is paid. For example, assume that a calendar-year partnership pays real property taxes of $1,200 on December 31, 2000, of which $600 is properly allocable to the first six months of 2001. The prepaid portion ($600) is allocated among the partners in accordance with their partnership interests on December 31, 2000.

(e) Tiered Partnerships. Section 706(d)(3) curbs the use of tiered partnerships to allocate partnership items retroactively to an incoming partner. Under prior law, if an upper-tier partnership used the interim-closing method, a proportionate share of the entire year's losses from a lower-tier partnership might be allocable to upper-tier partners admitted near the end of the year. Section 706(d)(3), however, generally prorates the upper-tier partnership's distributive share of all lower-tier partnership items (including allocable cash basis items) over the period of economic accrual by the lower-tier partnership, in accordance with the principles of § 706(d)(2).

(f) Relationship of §§ 704 and 706. Despite the anti-abuse provisions of § 706, some types of ''retroactive'' allocations remain viable. For example, the partners' distributive shares may be adjusted by modifying the terms of the partnership agreement at any time before the due date of the partnership's return for the taxable year. §§ 761(c), 704(a). The legislative history indicates that the varying interest rule was not intended to prevent such modifications, as long as the adjustments involve only current partners and no additional capital contributions are made during the year. See, e.g., Lipke (1983); Rodman (1976). Moreover, it may be possible to achieve the effect of a retroactive allocation by making a special allocation to an incoming partner of post-admission losses under § 704(b). See Ogden (1985).

CHAPTER 9

PARTNERSHIP DISTRIBUTIONS

§ 1. Overview

The rules governing current and liquidating distributions are intended generally to defer recognition of as much gain or loss as possible, both to the partnership and to the distributee partner. Section 731(b) provides that the partnership recognizes no gain or loss on a distribution of property (including cash) to a partner. The distributee, in turn, recognizes gain only to the extent that he receives a distribution of cash in excess of his basis in his partnership interest, and recognizes loss only on certain liquidating distributions. Any recognized gain or loss is treated as arising from the sale or exchange of the distributee's partnership interest. § 731(a). Finally, certain distributed property retains its ordinary income character in the distributee's hands. § 735.

The mechanism for preserving pre-distribution unrealized gain or loss in the distributed property depends upon whether the distributee's interest in the partnership continues or is completely liquidated. In a current distribution, the distributee generally takes a transferred basis in the distributed property equal to its pre-distribution basis in the partnership's hands. § 732(a). Any unrealized gain or loss is preserved through appropriate adjustments to the basis of the distributee's partnership interest. § 733. By contrast, in a liquidating distribution the distributee takes an exchanged basis in the distributed property determined by reference to his pre-distribution basis in his partnership interest. Regardless of the tax consequences to the distributee, a distribution generally produces no adjustments in the basis of undistributed partnership property, unless the partnership files an election under § 754 (relating to optional basis adjustments). § 734.

Congress has added several provisions recently that limit the broad nonrecognition policy of § 731. For example, a distribution of § 704(c) property within seven years of the contribution triggers recognition of gain (or loss) under § 704(c)(1)(B). See Chapter 5. Furthermore, under § 737, a partner who receives a distribution of partnership property must generally recognize any remaining § 704(c) gain attributable to property contributed by him within seven years of the distribution. § 737. Section 737 serves as a backstop to § 704(c)(1)(B) and the disguised sale rules of § 707(a)(2)(B). Finally, distributions of marketable securities (and similar items) may be treated as distributions of money for certain purposes, thereby triggering potential recognition of gain (but not loss). § 731(c). Any gain triggered under these provisions will result in appropriate basis adjustments.

This Chapter focuses initially on the application of §§ 731–737 to distributions that do not trigger § 751. Under § 751(b), a distribution that alters the distributee's proportionate share of unrealized receivables or substantially-appreciated inventory is treated in part as a sale or exchange of partnership property. Thus, § 751(b) may override nonrecognition treatment to prevent potential shifting of unrealized ordinary income among the partners. Finally, payments in liquidation of a retiring or deceased partner's interest in the partnership are subject to § 736, as discussed in Chapter 10.

§ 2. Current Distributions

(a) General. The regulations define a current distribution as any distribution which is not in liquidation of a partner's entire interest in the partnership. Reg. § 1.761–1(d). A current distribution may represent a partner's distributive share of the partnership's current earnings, a return of capital or a constructive distribution of cash under § 752 triggered by a decrease in his share of partnership liabilities. In certain cases, however, other statutory provisions may modify or preempt the normal distribution rules. For example, § 707 may treat a purported distribution as a disguised sale. See Chapter 7. Also, a transaction may be structured as a loan or a drawing against a partner's distributive share to avoid triggering gain on a distribution of cash in excess of outside basis. See Chapter 3. Characterization as a loan (rather than a current distribution) is generally respected only if there is "an unconditional and legally enforceable obligation to repay a sum certain at a determinable date." Rev. Rul. 73–301.

(b) Gain Recognition and Basis. A current distribution triggers recognition of gain to the distributee partner to the extent that he receives cash in excess of his outside basis immediately before the distribution. § 731(a)(1). Under § 733, the distributee's outside basis is reduced (but not below zero) by the amount of cash distributed. Thus, gain is recognized only to the extent that the distributee's pre-distribution basis is insufficient to absorb the full amount of a cash distribution. Unless one of the statutory exceptions applies, current distributions of property other than cash never trigger recognition of gain or loss. To preserve any unrealized gain or loss when property is distributed in kind, the distributee generally takes the same basis in the distributed property (other than cash) as its adjusted basis in the partnership's hands immediately before the distribution. § 732(a)(1). Moreover, the distributee's outside basis is further reduced (after taking account of any cash distributed) by the basis in the distributee's hands of the property distributed in kind. § 733.

If the distributee's outside basis (after taking account of any cash distributed) is insufficient to absorb the full amount of the partnership's basis in the distributed property, only the remaining outside basis is assigned to the property distributed in kind. § 732(a)(2). The distributee's outside basis is reduced to zero and the property distributed in kind takes a basis in the distributee's hands which, together with any cash distributed, does not exceed his pre-distribution basis in his partnership interest. Section 732(a)(2) ensures that the proper amount of gain (or loss) is preserved by limiting the basis of distributed property in the distributee's hands, and thus functions in a manner analogous to the recognition of gain upon a distribution of excess cash.

Example (1): Partner A has an outside basis of $50 in her partnership interest which has a fair market value of $100 (equal to A's share of the partnership assets). In exchange for 50% of her partnership interest, A receives a current distribution consisting of $15 cash and property having a basis of $25 in the partnership's hands and a fair market value of $35. Under § 732(a)(1), A takes a transferred basis of $25 in the distributed property, leaving A with a basis of $10 in her partnership. § 733. The $50 of unrealized gain inherent in A's former partnership interest ($100 fair market value less $50 basis) equals the aggregate unrealized appreciation in the distributed property ($35 fair market value less $25 basis) and in A's remaining partnership interest ($50 fair market value less $10 basis). See Reg. § 1.732–1(a) (Ex. 1).

If A's pre-distribution outside basis were instead $20, the basis of the distributed property in A's hands would be limited to $5 (pre-distribution outside basis of $20 less $15 cash distributed) under § 732(a)(2), and the basis of A's partnership interest would be reduced to zero under § 733. Immediately after the distribution, A would have a potential gain of $30 in the distributed property ($35 fair market value less $5 basis) and $50 in her remaining partnership interest ($50 fair market value less zero basis). Thus, the unrealized gain of $80 inherent in A's partnership interest immediately before the distribution ($100 fair market value less $20 basis) would be preserved. See Reg. § 1.732–1(a) (Ex. 2).

If A's pre-distribution outside basis were only $10, A would recognize a gain of $5 ($15 cash distribution less $10 outside basis), leaving A with a basis of zero both in the distributed property and in her remaining partnership interest. §§ 731(a)(1), 732(a)(2) and 733. The unrealized gain of $85 in these assets ($85 fair market value less zero basis) would equal the $90 of unrealized gain inherent in A's former partnership interest ($100 fair market value less $10 basis) less A's recognized gain of $5 on the distribution.

(c) Allocation of Basis. If the general transferred basis rule does not apply (i.e., because the distributee's outside basis, after reduction for any cash distributed, is less than the partnership's aggregate basis in the other distributed property), § 732(c) governs the allocation of basis among the properties distributed in kind. Prior to 1997, § 732(c) allocated any basis adjustments in proportion to the relative bases of the distributed assets. The 1997 Act amended § 732(c) to require basis adjustments to conform more closely to the fair market value of distributed assets. Current law preserves the priority allocation to "hot assets" under § 732(c), in order to maximize the distributee's basis in such assets and thereby minimize the ordinary income that they will generate. For this purpose, hot assets include unrealized receivables and inventory (whether or not substantially appreciated). See § 751(c), (d).

Under § 732(c), the distributee's remaining basis in his partnership interest (after reduction for any cash distributed) is allocated first to hot assets (up to their bases in the partnership's hands). § 732(c)(1)(A)(i). If the distributee's remaining basis is less than the partnership's total basis in distributed hot assets, the basis of these assets must be reduced to match the distributee's remaining basis. § 732(c)(1)(A)(ii). Any decrease is allocated first to distributed hot assets with unrealized depreciation in proportion to their unrealized depreciation (but not in excess of such amount) before the basis decrease; any remaining decrease is allocated to distributed hot assets in proportion to their adjusted bases (after taking into account any prior basis decrease). § 732(c)(3).

If the distributee partner has any remaining basis after the allocation to hot assets, such basis is allocated to other distributed assets (up to their bases in the partnership's hands). § 732(c)(1)(B). If the distributee's remaining basis is less than the partnership's total basis in other distributed property, the basis of such assets is decreased; the decrease is allocated first to non-hot assets in proportion to their unrealized depreciation (but not in excess of such amount) and then in proportion to their adjusted bases (after taking into account any prior basis decrease). § 732(c)(3).

Example (2): Partner A, whose outside basis is $15,000, receives a current distribution consisting of $4,000 cash, inventory worth $10,000 (basis of $8,000), capital asset X worth $1,000 (basis of $1,000), and capital asset Y worth $4,000 (basis of $5,000). A's outside basis ($15,000) is reduced by the amount of cash distributed ($4,000) and A's transferred basis in the inventory ($8,000). Assets X and Y are initially assigned a basis of $1,000 and $5,000, respectively. Since their aggregate basis to the partnership ($6,000) exceeds A's remaining outside basis ($3,000), the basis of X and Y must be decreased by $3,000. The basis decrease is allocated first to Y to the extent of Y's unrealized depreciation ($1,000), reducing Y's basis to $4,000; the remaining decrease ($2,000) is allocated $400 to X ($2,000 × $1,000/$5,000) and $1,600 to Y ($2,000 × $4,000/$5,000) in proportion to their bases (after taking into account the prior decrease in Y's basis). Accordingly, A takes a basis of $600 in X ($1,000 less $400 decrease) and $2,400 in Y ($5,000 less $2,600 decrease). See Prop. Reg. § 1.732–1(c)(4) (Ex. 2).

§ 3. Liquidating Distributions

(a) General. The regulations define a "liquidation of a partner's interest" as the "termination of a partner's entire interest in a partnership by means of a distribution, or a series of distributions, to the partner by the partnership." Reg. § 1.761–

1(d). When a partner's interest is liquidated by a series of distributions, the liquidation is held open until the time of the final distribution. Id. The rules governing liquidating distributions apply to distributions in connection with a liquidation or termination of the partnership itself as well as the liquidation of a single partner's interest.

Despite their apparent similarities, liquidating distributions are treated differently from current distributions in several important respects. First, while § 731(a) generally prescribes nonrecognition treatment, it provides for recognition of loss as well as gain on certain liquidating distributions. § 731(a)(2). Second, the distributee takes an exchanged basis in the distributed assets (determined by reference to his basis in his partnership interest) which may be higher or lower than the pre-distribution basis of the assets in the hands of the partnership. § 732(b). The treatment of liquidating distributions generally reflects an entity approach, as contrasted with the aggregate approach applicable to current distributions.

(b) Gain or Loss Recognition. In a liquidating distribution, the distributee recognizes gain to the extent that any cash distributed exceeds his pre-distribution basis in his partnership interest. § 731(a)(1). No loss is recognized unless the distributee receives solely cash, "hot assets" (defined for this purpose as unrealized receivables and inventory regardless of whether the inventory is substantially appreciated), or a combination thereof. § 731(a)(2). The recognized loss, if any, is equal to the excess of the distributee's outside basis immediately before the distribution over the sum of any cash distributed and the basis in his hands of the distributed hot assets. Loss recognition is a corollary of § 732(c), which limits the basis of hot assets in the distributee's hands to their pre-distribution basis and thereby preserves any ordinary gain or loss inherent in those assets. On the other hand, a retiring partner may receive hot assets with a reduced basis and ultimately recognize a larger ordinary gain than if the partnership had sold the hot assets.

Example (3): Partnership AB has $200 cash and inventory with a basis of $100 and a fair market value of $200. Upon liquidation of AB, the partnership distributes equal shares of each asset to A and B, who have bases in their partnership interests of $100 and $200, respectively. B takes a basis of $50 in her share of the inventory and recognizes a capital loss of $50 ($200 outside basis less $100 cash and $50 basis assigned to the inventory). §§ 731(a)(2), 732(c) and 741. If B sells her share of the inventory for $100 within five years after the distribution, she will recognize $50 of ordinary income. § 735(a)(2). Even though B has no economic gain or loss on the transaction, she recognizes $50 of capital loss on the distribution and has $50 of ordinary income on the subsequent sale. Under § 732(b), A takes a basis of zero in the inventory, and will realize $100 of ordinary income if she sells the inventory within five years after the distribution. The distribution of the inventory to A and B, followed by a sale within five years, thus triggers $50 more total ordinary income (and $50 more capital loss) than if the partnership had sold the inventory before liquidating.

(c) Basis Allocation. The basis allocation rules of § 732(c) apply to liquidating distributions in the same manner as to current distributions. In the case of liquidating distributions, however, the total basis to be allocated is independent of the partnership's pre-distribution basis in the distributed property; thus, the property may take a lower or (except in the case of hot assets) higher basis in the distributee's hands than it had in the partnership's hands. Any increase is allocated first to non-hot assets with unrealized appreciation in proportion to their unrealized appreciation (but not in excess of such amount); any remaining increase is allocated to non-hot assets in proportion to their relative fair market values.

Example (4): Partner A, whose outside basis is $110, receives a distribution of two capital assets (X and Y) in liquidation of her partnership interest. In the partnership's hands, X has a fair market value of $25 and a basis of $30, and Y has a fair market value of $50 and a basis of $10. A's outside basis is first allocated $30 to X and $10 to Y, equal to their bases in the partnership's hands. A's remaining outside basis ($70) is allocated $40 to Y (the only appreciated asset) to the extent of its unrealized appreciation; the remainder ($30) is allocated $10 to X ($30 × $25/$75) and $20 to Y ($30 × $50/$75) in proportion to their relative fair market values.

Thus, A takes a basis of $40 in X and $70 in Y. See Prop. Reg. § 1.732–1(c)(4) (Ex. 1).

(d) Anti–Abuse Rules. The § 701 anti-abuse rules recognize that § 732(c) is intended to provide simplifying administrative rules and may thus produce basis distortions. If the ultimate tax consequences are clearly contemplated under § 732(c), however, the transaction will be respected for purposes of § 701. See Reg. § 1.701–2(d) (Ex. 10, 11) (reflecting the pre–1997 version of § 732(c)). In one example, a liquidating distribution shifts a portion of the distributee's outside basis from nondepreciable to depreciable assets, thereby producing a timing advantage; because the ultimate tax consequences are clearly contemplated, the transaction is deemed to satisfy the "proper-reflection-of-income" test. Id. (Ex. 10). In another example, the withdrawing partner takes an artificially high basis in an "insignificant" asset that she plans to sell and an artificially low basis in land that she plans to retain; thus, the § 732(c) allocation allows the distributee, in effect, to recover a portion of the cost of the land. Id. (Ex. 11). Upon formation of the partnership, the distributee's acquisition of the land and use of § 732(c) to produce basis distortions were part of an underlying plan. Accordingly, the § 732(c) allocation fails the "proper-reflection-of-income" test and the transaction may be recast to achieve results consistent with the intent of Subchapter K. Id.

§ 4.   Treatment of Liabilities

A decrease in a partner's share of partnership liabilities is treated as a deemed distribution of cash under § 752(b), which may trigger recognition of gain to the distributee under § 731(a)(1). The deemed distribution is treated as an advance or draw up to the amount of the partner's distributive share of income for the taxable year. Rev. Rul. 94–4. Thus, the distributee's outside basis is increased by his distributive share of partnership income for the year before determining the consequences of the deemed distribution. See Reg. § 1.731–1(a)(1)(ii).

Example (5): The AB partnership has excess non-recourse liabilities of $10,000, which are allocated equally to partners A and B. A, whose outside basis is $50,000, receives a cash distribution of $50,000 which reduces his interest in the partnership (and his share of partnership liabilities) from 50% to 20%. The reduction in A's share of partnership liabilities from $5,000 (50%) to $2,000 (20%) is treated as a deemed distribution of $3,000 cash to A. If A's distributive share of income for the year is at least $3,000, A will recognize no gain as a result of the § 752(b) deemed distribution. B's share of the partnership's liabilities increases from $5,000 (50%) to $8,000 (80%), triggering a corresponding increase in B's outside basis.

The rules for distributions of encumbered property mirror the rules for contributions of encumbered property discussed in Chapter 2. The distributee partner's basis in his partnership interest is (i) increased by the amount of liabilities to which the distributed property is subject, (ii) decreased by his share of the reduction in partnership liabilities, and (iii) decreased by the basis of the distributed property in his hands. §§ 705, 722, 733 and 752. Under § 752, any increases and decreases in the distributee's share of partnership liabilities are netted against each other. Reg. § 1.752–1(f). The distributee's basis in his partnership interest is first adjusted to reflect the net increase or decrease in liabilities before determining the basis of the distributed property. Rev. Rul. 79–205. These ordering rules are intended to defer recognition of gain or loss, especially if a distribution results in a net increase in a partner's share of partnership liabilities.

§ 5. Distribution of Marketable Securities

(a) **General.** Section 731(c) generally treats a distribution of marketable securities (defined broadly) as a distribution of cash for purposes of §§ 731(a)(1) and 737. Thus, a distribution of marketable securities may trigger recognition of gain (but not loss) under § 731(a)(1). The purpose of § 731(c) is to limit deferral of gain when the distributee receives liquid assets equivalent to cash. For example, assume a partnership purchases marketable securities worth $100 and distributes such securities to a partner with an outside basis of $40. If the partner received solely cash, he would recognize gain of $60 under § 731(a)(1). Section 731(c) achieves the same result by treating the distribution of securities as a distribution of cash, reduced by the distributee's share of any net appreciation in such securities. See § 731(c)(3)(B). Under the anti-abuse rules, the Service may recast a transaction as appropriate to achieve results consistent with the purpose of § 731(c). Reg. § 1.731–2(h).

(b) Basis Consequences. The distributee's basis in the distributed securities is determined under the normal distribution rules of § 732 and increased by any gain recognized under § 731(c). § 731(c)(4)(A); Reg. § 1.731–2(f)(1). Any basis increase is allocated among the distributed securities in proportion to their unrealized appreciation in the distributee's hands before such basis increase. § 731(c)(4)(B). Under § 733, the distributee's remaining outside basis is reduced by the basis assigned to the securities under § 732, determined as if no gain were recognized under § 731(c). § 731(c)(5). The special treatment of marketable securities affects only the tax treatment of the distributee partner, and is not taken into account in determining optional basis adjustments under § 734(b). See Reg. § 1.731–2(f)(2).

Example (6): When A's 1/3 interest in the equal ABC partnership has a basis of $40 and a fair market value of $90, A receives a liquidating distribution of the partnership's only marketable security (X). X has a fair market value of $90 and a basis of $30 to the partnership. A is treated as receiving a cash distribution of $70 ($90 fair market value of X less $20 share of X's unrealized appreciation), triggering $30 of gain to A under § 731(a)(1). A takes a basis of $70 in X ($40 basis under § 732(b) increased by $30 gain recognized), preserving A's $20 share of unrealized appreciation in X and reducing A's outside basis to zero. If A instead received a current distribution, A would take a basis of $60 in X ($30 basis under § 732(a)(1) increased by $30 gain recognized); A's outside basis would be reduced to $10 ($40 less $30 basis allocated to X under § 732(a)(1)). See Reg. § 1.731–2(j) (Ex. 5).

(c) Reduction for Net Unrealized Appreciation. Under § 731 (c)(3)(B), the amount treated as cash under § 731(c) is limited to the fair market value of the distributed securities, reduced by the distributee's share of the net appreciation in such securities. The distributee's share of net appreciation is equal to the excess of (i) the distributee's share of the net gain if all of the partnership's marketable securities were sold for fair market value immediately before the distribution, over (ii) the distributee's share of the net gain if all of the partnership's marketable securities were sold for fair market value immediately after the distribution. § 731(c)(3)(B); Reg. § 1.731–2(b)(1), (2). The reduction in the amount treated as cash is intended to permit the distributee to continue to defer his share of the net appreciation inherent in the partnership's marketable securities.

Example (7): The facts are the same as in Example (6), above, except that the partnership also owns two other marketable securities (Y and Z) with an unrealized loss of $15 (Y) and an unrealized gain of $30 (Z). Accordingly, A would be allocated net gain of $25 if, immediately before the distribution, the partnership's securities were sold for their fair market value ($20 gain in X, $5 loss in Y, and $10 gain in Z). Following the liquidating distribution, A's share of the net gain inherent in the securities held by the partnership (Y and Z) is zero. The distribution results in a $25 decrease in A's share of the net gain inherent in the partnership's securities ($25 net gain before distribution less zero net gain after distribution). Thus, A is treated as receiving a cash distribution of $65 ($90 fair market value of X less $25 decrease in share of net gain). A recognizes $25 of gain ($65 less $40 outside basis) and takes a basis of $65 in X ($40 basis under § 732(b) increased by $25 gain recognized). See Reg. § 1.731–2(j) (Ex. 2).

(d) Special Rules. Section 731(c) does not apply to distributions of marketable securities by an investment partnership to an "eligible" partner. § 731(c)(3)(A)(iii). Section 731(c) also provides exceptions for marketable securities distributed to a partner who previously contributed such securities and for securities that were not marketable when acquired. § 731(c)(3)(A)(i)-(ii). Finally, § 731(c) applies only after giving effect to § 704(c)(1)(B); both §§ 704(c)(1)(B) and 731(c) take precedence over § 737. Reg. § 1.731–2(g); see § 10 below.

§ 6. Section 732(d) Election

Under certain circumstances, § 732(d) permits a distributee who acquired his partnership interest by purchase or bequest to treat assets distributed to him as having a pre-distribution basis in the partnership's hands equal to the basis such assets would have if a § 754 election had been in effect when the distributee acquired his partnership interest. The purpose of the § 732(d) election is to make available to the distributee, as nearly as possible, the same tax treatment as if he had been entitled to a § 743(b) adjustment when he acquired his interest. The § 732(d) election is available only if (i) the distributee acquired all or part of his partnership interest by "transfer," i.e., by sale or exchange or upon the death of a partner, (ii) the partnership did not have a § 754 election in effect at the time of the transfer, and (iii) the distribution occurs within two years after the original transfer. The election must accompany the transferee's tax return for (i) the year of the distribution if the distribution includes any depreciable property or (ii) in all other cases, the first taxable year in which the basis of the distributed property affects the distributee's income tax. Reg. § 1.732–1(d)(2). Unlike the § 754 election, the § 732(d) election has no effect on subsequent transfers of a partnership interest and does not require the partnership's consent.

Example (8): D inherits the partnership interest of deceased partner C, at a time when the ABC partnership has the following balance sheet and no § 754 election in effect:

Assets	Basis	Value	Capital	Basis	Value
Cash	$3,000	$ 3,000	A	$2,000	$ 4,000
Inventory	3,000	9,000	B	2,000	4,000
Total	$6,000	$12,000	C	2,000	4,000
			Total	$6,000	$12,000

D takes her 1/3 partnership interest with an outside basis equal to fair market value ($4,000) under § 1014, and within two years D receives a liquidating distribution of her pro rata share of the partnership's cash and inventory. In the absence of a § 732(d) election, D would take a $1,000 basis in the inventory and recognize a $2,000 capital loss on the liquidating distribution ($4,000 outside basis less $1,000 cash less $1,000 basis allocated to the inventory). See §§ 731(a)(2), 732(c) and 741. If D then sold the inventory, she would recognize $2,000 of ordinary income under § 735, offsetting her $2,000 capital loss. If D instead makes the § 732(d) election, she will take a basis of $3,000 in her share of the inventory (D's $1,000 share of the common basis of the inventory plus the $2,000 upward adjustment to which D would have been entitled under § 743(b)). Thus, the § 732(d) election eliminates D's artificial loss on the liquidating distribution as well as the overstated gain on the subsequent sale. If D had received any property other than cash and hot assets in liquidation of her interest, she would have reported no loss and any remaining basis in her partnership interest would have been allocated to such other property under § 732(c).

The application of § 732(d) may be mandatory (whether or not the distribution occurs within two years) if the fair market value of partnership property (other than money) exceeds 110% of its basis in the partnership's hands at the time the distributee acquires his partnership interest. § 732(d) (last sentence); see Reg. § 1.732–1(d)(4) (additional requirements). As indicated by the additional requirements in the regulations, mandatory application of

§ 732(d) is intended to prevent a shifting of basis from nondepreciable property to depreciable property in connection with a distribution. The 1997 changes in § 732(c) may lessen the need for mandatory § 732(d) basis allocations.

§ 7. Subsequent Dispositions of Distributed Property

Section 735 generally preserves the ordinary income character of distributed "hot assets" upon a subsequent disposition by the distributee. For this purpose, hot assets include unrealized receivables and inventory (whether or not substantially appreciated) but do not include § 1231 property (regardless of its holding period). The "taint" of ordinary gain or loss treatment is permanent for unrealized receivables, but lasts only five years for inventory if the inventory becomes a capital asset in the distributee's hands. § 735(a). For purposes of the five-year rule, the distributee is not permitted to tack the partnership's holding period for distributed inventory. § 735(b). There is no need for unrealized receivables to include depreciation recapture for purposes of § 735(a)(1), because the potential ordinary income inherent in depreciated property is generally preserved through the recapture provisions themselves. §§ 751(c), 1245 and 1250. If the distributee disposes of property subject to § 735(a) in a nonrecognition transaction, the taint of ordinary income treatment generally applies to any "substituted basis property" resulting from the transaction. §§ 735(c)(2), 7701(a)(42)-(44).

Example (9): Partnership ABC distributes to partner A a parcel of land which constitutes inventory in the partnership's hands having a basis of $1,000 and a fair market value of $900. A takes a basis of $1,000 in the land, holds the land for investment purposes and then sells the land three years later when its value has increased to $1,200. Even though all of the appreciation occurred while A held the land, the entire gain of $200 is ordinary income to A under § 735(a)(2). Conversely, any loss realized by A on a sale of the land within five years would be treated as ordinary.

§ 8. Optional Basis Adjustments

(a) General. Section 734(a) provides that a distribution of property to a partner does not trigger an adjustment to the basis of any property remaining in the partnership's hands after the distribution, unless an election under § 754 is in effect with respect to the partnership. Thus, the basis of the remaining partnership property is generally unchanged as a result of a distribution, in accordance with an entity approach. If a § 754 election is in effect, however, § 734(b) requires that the basis of retained partnership property be adjusted if, as a result of a distribution, the distributee recognizes gain or loss or takes a basis different from the partnership's basis in the distributed property. The correlation of tax consequences to the partnership and the distributee under § 734(b) reflects a quasi-aggregate approach to current and liquidating distributions.

While § 734(b) determines the amount of any increase or decrease in the basis of partnership property, the allocation of the basis adjustment is governed by § 755. § 734(c). Unlike the § 743(b) adjustment (which affects only the transferee-partner's share of the partnership's basis in its property, as discussed in Chapter 8), the § 734(b) adjustment increases or decreases the common basis of partnership property and thus affects all of the continuing partners (including the distributee, in the case of a current distribution). Where the § 734(b) adjustment would result in a net decrease in the partnership's inside basis, the partnership may be reluctant to make a § 754 election. See below.

(b) Recognized Gain or Loss. The § 734(b) adjustment avoids distortions of gain or loss that would otherwise arise under the general rule of § 734(a) if the basis of partnership property were not adjusted. If the partnership has a § 754 election in effect, the basis of partnership property is increased by the amount of any gain, and decreased by the amount of any loss, recognized by the distributee as the result of a current or liquidating distribution. § 734(b)(1)(A), (b)(2)(A).

Example (10): Partnership ABC distributes $200 cash to partner A in liquidation of his entire partnership interest. Immediately before the distribution, A had a basis of $100 in his partnership interest and the partnership's balance sheet was as follows:

	Basis	Value		Basis	Value
Assets			Capital		
Cash	$200	$200	A	$100	$200
Land	100	400	B	100	200
Total	$300	$600	C	100	200
			Total	$300	$600

As a result of the distribution, A recognizes gain of $100 ($200 cash distribution less $100 outside basis), equal to his 1/3 share of the unrealized appreciation in the land. If the partnership's basis in the land is not adjusted and the land is sold for $400, the partnership will realize $300 of gain which will all flow through to the continuing partners (B and C). In effect, A's 1/3 share of the unrealized appreciation ($100) will be taxed twice, once to A on liquidation and again to the continuing partners (B and C) on sale of the land. The overstatement of gain should be only temporary, however, since the continuing partners will increase their outside bases to reflect the full amount of gain from sale of the land. If the § 754 election is in effect, however, § 734(b)(1)(A) increases the partnership's basis in the land by the amount of A's recognized gain ($100), thus reducing the partnership's gain on sale of the land to $200 and eliminating the temporary double taxation to B and C. See Reg. § 1.734–1(b)(1) (Ex. 1). The post-distribution unrealized appreciation in the partnership's assets ($200) plus the gain recognized by A ($100) equals the pre-distribution unrealized appreciation in the partnership's assets ($300).

Example (11): Partnership DEF distributes $100 cash to partner D in liquidation of his entire partnership interest. Immediately before the distribution, D had a basis of $200 in his partnership interest, and the partnership's balance sheet was as follows:

Assets	Basis	Value	Capital	Basis	Value
Cash	$200	$200	D	$200	$100
Land	400	100	E	200	100
Total	$600	$300	F	200	100
			Total	$600	$300

As a result of the distribution, D recognizes a loss of $100 ($200 outside basis less $100 cash distribution) under § 731(a)(2). If the § 754 election is in effect, the partnership must decrease its basis in the land by $100 to reflect D's recognized loss, reducing the partnership's potential loss on sale of the land to $200 ($300 basis less $100 fair market value) in the partnership's hands. See Reg. § 1.734–1(b)(2) (Ex. 1). The post-distribution unrealized loss in the partnership's assets ($200) plus D's recognized loss ($100) is equal to the pre-distribution unrealized loss in the partnership's assets ($300). By reducing the partnership's basis in its remaining property, the § 734(b) adjustment eliminates the potential double-counting of D's share of pre-distribution unrealized loss.

(c) Shifts in the Basis of Distributed Property. The basis adjustment rules of § 734(b) also apply when a distributee receives distributed property and takes a basis different from the partnership's pre-distribution basis. To the extent that the basis of the distributed property in the distributee's hands is reduced under § 732(a)(2) or § 732(b), the partnership must increase its basis in the remaining partnership property; conversely, to the extent that the basis of the distributed property is increased under § 732(b), the partnership must reduce its basis in the remaining partnership property. § 734(b)(1)(B), (b)(2)(B). These adjustments are intended to preserve the aggregate unrealized gain or loss inherent in the partnership assets (both distributed and retained).

Example (12): Partnership GHI distributes Land #1 to partner G in liquidation of her entire partnership interest. Immediately before the distribution, G had a basis of $500 in her partnership interest, and the partnership's balance sheet was as follows:

	Basis	Value		Basis	Value
Assets			Capital		
Cash	$ 600	$ 600	G	$ 500	$ 600
Land #1	600	600	H	500	600
Land #2	300	600	I	500	600
Total	$1,500	$1,800	Total	$1,500	$1,800

Under § 732(b), G takes a basis in Land #1 equal to her pre-distribution basis in her partnership interest ($500), which is less than the partnership's pre-distribution basis ($600). If the partnership has a § 754 election in effect, the $100 difference is added to the partnership's basis in its remaining property, increasing the basis of Land #2 to $400. See Reg. § 1.734–1(b)(1) (Ex. 2). Giving effect to the § 734(b) adjustment, the partnership would realize a gain of $200 on a sale of Land #2 ($600 fair market value less $400 basis), while G would realize a gain of $100 ($600 fair market value less $500 basis) on a sale of Land #1. The aggregate unrealized appreciation in the partnership's assets (both distributed and retained) is thus $300 both before and after the distribution.

In the preceding example, assume instead that G receives Land #2 in liquidation of her partnership interest. Under § 732(b), G's basis in Land #2 would be $500, or $200 more than the partnership's pre-distribution basis. If G sold Land #2, she would recognize only $100 of gain ($600 fair market value less $500 basis). Moreover, in the absence of a downward adjustment of $200 to the partnership's basis in Land #1, that asset could be sold with no realized gain, thereby deferring the continuing partners' share of the partnership's pre-distribution unrealized appreciation ($200) until sale or liquidation of their partnership interests. In order to eliminate these distortions, the basis of Land #1 must be adjusted downward to $400. See Prop. Reg. § 1.755–1(c)(2)(ii).

(d) Basis Allocation. The regulations under § 755, which also govern § 743(b) adjustments, generally allocate § 734(b) adjustments in a manner that preserves the character and proportionate amount of unrealized appreciation (or depreciation) within separate classes of partnership property. Under § 755, partnership property is first divided into two classes of property, consisting of capital assets, including § 1231(b) property ("capital assets"), and any other partnership property ("ordinary assets"). Second, the § 734(b) adjustment is allocated (i) to property of the same class as the distributed property if the adjustment results from an increase or decrease in the basis of distributed property or (ii) entirely to capital assets if the adjustment results from recognition of gain or loss by the distributee. Prop. Reg. § 1.755–1(c)(1). Third, the § 734(b) adjustment is allocated to specific assets within the appropriate class based generally on the difference between the basis and fair market value of such property. § 755(a)(1). Adjustments may also be required that increase the disparity between the basis and fair market value of particular assets.

Any increase is allocated first among assets of the required character in proportion to their unrealized appreciation (but not in excess of such amount); any remaining increase is allocated among assets of the required character in proportion to their relative fair market values. Prop. Reg. § 1.755–1(c)(2)(i). Any decrease is allocated first among assets of the required character in proportion to their unrealized depreciation (but not in excess of such amount); any remaining decrease is allocated among assets of the required character in proportion to their relative bases. Prop. Reg. § 1.755–1(c)(2)(ii). If the § 734(b) adjustment cannot be allocated to specific assets within a class (e.g., because the partnership has no retained property of that class or such property has insufficient basis to absorb the adjustment), it is held in abeyance until it can be allocated to subsequently-acquired property of the same class. § 755(b) (flush language); Prop. Reg. § 1.755–1(c)(4). If goodwill exists and is reflected in the value of the distributed property, a portion of the basis adjustment must be allocated to the partnership's goodwill. Prop. Reg. § 1.755–1(c)(5).

Example (13): Immediately before partner A receives a liquidating distribution consisting of $100 cash, ordinary asset O and capital asset R, partnership ABC has the following balance sheet:

Assets	Basis	Value	Unrealized Appreciation/ (Depreciation)
Cash	$ 300	$ 300	$ 0
Ordinary Assets			
M	50	200	150
N	100	200	100
O	150	200	50
Total	$ 300	$ 600	$300
Capital Assets			
P	$ 100	$ 400	$300
Q	200	400	200
R	300	400	100
Total	$ 600	$1,200	$600
Capital			
A	$ 400	$700	$300
B	400	700	300
C	400	700	300
Total	$1,200	$2,100	$900

Under § 732(b) and (c), A takes a basis of $150 in capital asset R ($400 outside basis less $100 cash less $150 basis in ordinary asset O), which is $150 less than the partnership's basis ($300). Under §§ 734(b) and 755, the basis of the partnership's remaining capital assets is increased by $150. Prop. Reg. § 1.755–1(c)(1)(i). The basis increase is allocated $90 to capital asset P ($150 x $300/$500) and $60 to capital asset Q ($150 x $200/$500), in proportion to the relative unrealized appreciation of those assets in the partnership's hands. Prop. Reg. § 1.755–1(c)(2)(i). Immediately after the distribution, the partnership's balance sheet is as follows:

Assets	Basis	Value	Unrealized Appreciation/ (Depreciation)
Cash	$ 200	$ 200	$ 0
Ordinary Assets			
M	$ 50	$ 200	$ 150
N	100	200	100
Total	$ 150	$ 400	$ 250
Capital Assets			
P	$ 190	$ 400	$ 210
Q	260	400	140
Total	$450	$ 800	$350
Capital			
B	$400	$700	$300
C	400	700	300
Total	$800	$1,400	$600

The general effect of the § 734(b) allocation is thus to reallocate basis among the capital assets (the class of assets which received a different basis in A's hands), while leaving the basis of the ordinary income assets unchanged. After the § 734(b) adjustment, the partnership's total inside basis ($800) is equal to the total outside basis of the continuing partners (B and C), preserving their share of pre-distribution unrealized appreciation.

If a partner's outside basis differs from his share of the partnership's common basis, § 734(b) does not work well. For instance, in Example (13), assume that A purchased his partnership interest several years ago for $700 when the partnership did not have a § 754 election in effect. Upon a liquidating distribution, the basis of capital asset R would be stepped up to $450 in A's hands ($700 outside basis less $100 cash less $150 basis in ordinary asset O). Under §§ 734(b) and 755, the adjustment to the partnership's retained capital assets would be a $150 *decrease* (rather than a $150 increase), which would be allocated $50 to capital asset P ($150 × $100/$300) and $100 to capital asset Q ($150 × $200/$300) in proportion to their relative bases. The result is particularly harsh to the continuing partners (B and C) because it leaves them with too little inside basis ($500) in comparison to their outside bases ($800). This defect could be remedied if the § 734(b) adjustment were determined by reference to the distributee's share of inside basis rather than his actual outside basis, in a manner similar to the § 743(b) adjustment.

(e) Anti–Abuse Rule. While the elective feature of § 754 can be defended on grounds of administrative convenience, Congress clearly recognized that the absence of mandatory basis adjustments might give rise to distortions between the partnership's inside basis and the partners' outside bases. The § 701 anti-abuse regulations apply a facts-and-circumstances test to determine whether the tax consequences flowing from the failure to make a § 754 election run afoul of the "proper-reflection-of-income" test. Reg. § 1.701–2(d) (Ex. 8, 9). In one example, a withdrawing partner receives a distribution of assets with a higher basis in the partner's hands than in the partnership's hands; by failing to make a § 754 election, the partnership retains an artificially high basis in its remaining assets. Id. (Ex. 9). Nevertheless, the § 701 regulations conclude that the transaction should be respected, since the partnership was formed for a bona fide purpose and the ultimate tax consequences are clearly contemplated by § 754. Id. In another example, a partnership is formed for the purpose of duplicating a built-in loss inherent in contributed land; the absence of a § 754 election preserves the built-in loss in the partnership's hands upon a subsequent liquidation of the contributing partner's interest. Id. (Ex 8). The § 701 regulations conclude that the transaction lacks a substantial business purpose and that Congress did not contemplate the elective feature of § 754 with respect to partnerships formed for a tax-avoidance purpose. Id.

§ 9. Effect on Capital Accounts

(a) General. Distributions reduce the distributee partner's book capital account by the amount of money and the fair market value of property (net of liabilities which the distributee assumes or takes subject to). Reg. § 1.704–1(b)(2)(iv)(b)(4)–(5). Prior to the distribution, the partners' book capital accounts must first be adjusted to reflect the manner in which any unrealized income, gain, loss or deduction inherent in the property (and not previously reflected in the capital accounts) would be shared by the partners if the partnership sold the property for its fair market value on the date of the distribution (the "deemed sale adjustment"). Reg. § 1.704–1(b)(2)(iv)(e)(1). Although an in-kind distribution of property is generally nontaxable to the partnership, the capital account adjustments are necessary to balance the partnership's books and prevent economic distortions. The effect of a distribution on the partnership's balance sheet is to reduce both the left-hand side (showing assets) and the right-hand side (showing liabilities above and partners' capital below) by an amount equal to the gross fair market value of the distributed property.

Example (14): A and B each contribute $9,000 cash to the equal AB partnership, which uses the cash to purchase nonmarketable securities for $18,-000. When the securities have appreciated in value to $48,000, C is admitted as a 1/3 partner in exchange for a cash contribution of $24,000. In accordance with § 704(c) principles, the partnership agreement allocates the $30,000 of pre-admission unrealized appreciation in the securities entirely to A and B ($15,000 each), with any post-admission gain or loss to be shared equally by A, B and C. Subsequently, when the securities are worth $75,-000, the partnership distributes them pro rata to the partners. Immediately before the distribution, the partners' capital accounts must be adjusted to reflect the allocation of taxable gain ($57,000) that would have occurred if the securities had been sold for $75,000. After the deemed sale adjustment, the book value of the securities is equal to their fair market value. Each partner's capital account is then reduced by his share of the fair market value of the securities ($25,000):

	Capital Accounts		
	A	B	C
Initial balance	$ 9,000	$ 9,000	$24,000
Deemed sale adjustment	24,000	24,000	9,000
Less: distribution	(25,000)	(25,000)	(25,000)
Balance after distribution	$ 8,000	$ 8,000	$ 8,000

After the distribution, the partnership's books remain in balance. See Reg. § 1.704–1(b)(5) (Ex. 14(v)).

(b) Optional Revaluation. In lieu of a deemed sale adjustment, the partnership may elect to revalue the partners' capital accounts in connection with a distribution of money or other property. Reg. § 1.704–1(b)(2)(iv)(f)(5)(ii). An optional revaluation may appear more burdensome than a deemed sale adjustment because it requires an appraisal of all the partnership's assets (rather than only the distributed asset). This burden is often more than offset, however, by the usefulness of an optional revaluation in preventing inadvertent capital shifts and other distortions in the partners' economic arrangements. In order to comply with the § 704(b) regulations, the rules governing restatement of capital accounts must be followed. See Chapter 4. If partnership property is booked up, the partners' capital accounts are not adjusted separately for any § 734(b) adjustment, since the basis adjustment is already reflected in the fair market value of the partnership property. In the absence of an optional revaluation, the § 704(b) regulations provide guidance in allocating the § 734(b) adjustment among the partners' capital accounts. Reg. § 1.704–1(b)(2)(iv)(m)(4).

Example (15): A, B and C each contribute $300 cash to the equal ABC general partnership, which retains $300 cash and purchases two parcels of land (Parcel #1 and Parcel #2) for $360 and $240, respectively. When Parcel #2 has increased in value to $540, the partnership distributes Parcel #1 (still worth $360) to A in a current distribution. If the partnership elects to revalue its property in connection with the distribution, the partners' capital accounts immediately after the distribution will be as follows:

	A		B		C	
	Tax	Book	Tax	Book	Tax	Book
Initial balance	$300	$300	$300	$300	$300	$300
Bookup adjustment		100		100		100
Less: distribution	(300)	(360)				
Balance after distribution	$ 0	$ 40	$300	$400	$300	$400

The bookup adjustment reflects the $300 of unrealized appreciation in Parcel #2 (which the partnership continues to hold). The distribution reduces A's book capital account by the fair market value of Parcel #1 ($360) and her tax capital account by the tax basis of Parcel #1 in A's hands ($300). Because the basis of Parcel #1 is stepped down in A's hands, the partnership is entitled to a positive § 734(b) adjustment of $60 to the basis of Parcel #2 (assuming a § 754 election is in effect). Accordingly, the partnership's common basis in Parcel #2 is increased to $300 ($240 cost basis plus $60 § 734(b) adjustment).

On a subsequent sale of Parcel #2 for $540, the partnership would have no book gain but would recognize a tax gain of $240 ($540 less $300 tax basis). Without a special allocation, the partners would share the tax gain equally ($80 each) in proportion to their pre-distribution 1/3 interests. Thus, B and C would be taxed on only $160 of their total pre-distribution share of appreciation ($200 built-in gain less $40 share of § 734(b) adjustment), shifting a portion of the built-in gain to A. By analogy to § 704(c), however, the partnership should be permitted to specially allocate the benefit of the $60 § 734(b) adjustment entirely to A, who has a $60 potential gain outside the partnership. Accordingly, the taxable gain should be allocated $40 to A and $100 to each of B and C, restoring book/tax parity to their capital accounts:

	A		B		C	
	Tax	Book	Tax	Book	Tax	Book
Initial balance	$ 0	$40	$300	$400	$300	$400
Gain on sale	40	0	100	0	100	0
Ending balance	$40	$40	$400	$400	$400	$400

On liquidation of the partnership, A would receive $40 and B and C would each receive $400. The economic result is appropriate since A receives property (Parcel #1 worth $360 and $40 cash) equal in value to her 1/3 share of partnership assets before the distribution. A's pre-distribution share of appreciation ($100) is also recognized or preserved ($40 gain on sale of Parcel #2 and $60 potential gain on Parcel #1).

§ 10. Distributions to Contributing Partners: § 737

(a) **General.** Section 737(a) may require recognition of gain (but not loss) to a contributing partner who receives a distribution of property (other than money) within seven years after contributing § 704(c) property. The recognized gain is limited to the lesser of (i) the contributing partner's remaining § 704(c) gain in the contributed property ("net precontribution gain") or (ii) the excess of the fair market value of the distributed property (other than cash) over the distributee's outside basis reduced (but not below zero) by any cash distributed ("excess distribution"). Net precontribution gain is defined as the net gain that the contributing partner would have recognized under § 704(c)(1)(B) if, at the time of the distribution, all of the § 704(c) property contributed by that partner within the preceding seven years (and still held by the partnership) had been distributed to another partner. § 737(b). The character of the distributee's gain is determined by reference to the character of the net precontribution gain. See Reg. § 1.737–1(d) (deemed sale to unrelated party). The distributee's outside basis is increased by the amount of any gain recognized under § 737 before determining the basis of the distributed property. § 737(c)(1); Reg. § 1.737–3(b)(1). The partnership's basis in "eligible" § 704(c) property contributed by the distributee is also increased to reflect any gain recognized under § 737. § 737(c)(2); Reg. § 1.737–3(c).

Example (16): Partner A, whose outside basis is $60,000, receives a current distribution of $10,000 cash and property worth $75,000 (with a basis of $75,000 in the partnership's hands). Immediately before the distribution, A's net precontribution gain is $40,000, consisting of $5,000 remaining built-in loss from Asset #1 and $45,000 of remaining built-in gain from Asset #2 (both contributed by A within seven years). The cash distribution of $10,000 first reduces A's outside basis to $50,000. § 733(a)(1). Under § 737, A recognizes gain of $25,-000, i.e., the lesser of (i) the net precontribution gain of $40,000 or (ii) the excess distribution of $25,000 ($75,000 fair market value of distributed property less $50,000 remaining outside basis). Since A's outside basis is increased to reflect the gain recognized under § 737, A takes a basis of $75,000 in the distributed property. § 732(a)(1). Following the distribution, A's outside basis is zero. The partnership also increases the basis of Asset #2 (the only appreciated § 704(c) asset contributed by A) to reflect A's recognized gain under § 737. See Reg. § 1.737–3(c)(3).

(b) Distributions Triggering Both §§ 704(c)(1)(B) and 737. If § 704(c) property is distributed to another partner as part of a § 737 distribution, both §§ 704(c)(1)(B) and 737 may apply. See Chapter 5. Before determining the tax consequences under § 737, the distributee's net precontribution gain and outside basis are adjusted to reflect any gain (or loss) recognized under § 704(c)(1)(B). See Reg. § 1.737–1(c)(2)(iv). In connection with a § 737 distribution, the like-kind exception of § 704(c)(2) applies only if contributed property is actually distributed to another partner. See id. These ordering rules minimize any gain recognition under § 737.

Example (17): X, Y and Z contribute the following nondepreciable capital assets to the equal XYZ partnership:

Partner	Assets	Basis	Value
X	Asset #1	$7,000	$15,000
Y	Asset #2	$12,000	$15,000
Z	Asset #3	$15,000	$15,000

Three years later, when each asset is still worth $15,000, the partnership distributes Asset #2 to X in liquidation of his partnership interest, and one half of Asset #1 to Y in a current distribution. Assume that the assets are not of like kind and that § 707(a)(2)(B) does not apply.

Under § 704(c)(1)(B), X recognizes $4,000 of built-in gain attributable to Asset #1 as a result of the distribution to Y, increasing X's outside basis to $11,000 and reducing X's remaining net precontribution gain to $4,000. Under § 737, X recognizes additional gain of $4,000 upon receipt of Asset #2, the lesser of (i) X's remaining net precontribution gain of $4,000 or (ii) the excess distribution of $4,000 ($15,000 fair market value of Asset #2 less $11,000 outside basis). Under § 704(c)(1)(B), Y recognizes $3,000 of built-in gain attributable to Asset #2 as a result of the distribution to X, increasing Y's outside basis to $15,000 and reducing Y's remaining net precontribution gain to zero. Since Y's entire built-in gain has been recognized under § 704(c)(1)(B), Y recognizes no gain under § 737. The partnership increases the basis of Asset #1 to $15,000 ($7,000 plus $8,000 gain recognized by X) and the basis of Asset #2 to $15,000 ($12,000 plus $3,000 gain recognized by Y); the basis increase is deemed to occur immediately before the distribution. X takes a basis of $15,000 in Asset #2, and Y takes a basis of $7,500 in one half of Asset #1. § 732(a)(1), (b); Reg. § 1.737–1(e) (Ex. 3).

Example (18): The facts are the same as in Example (17), above, except that X receives like-kind Asset #2 and Y receives like-kind Asset #1 in liquidation of their respective interests. Under § 704(c)(1)(B), X and Y would normally recognize built-in gain of $8,000 and $3,000, respectively, when the contributed property is distributed to another partner within seven years after the contribution. Under the like-kind exception, however, no gain is triggered to the extent that the distributee's remaining built-in gain is preserved in the basis of the distributed property (determined under the normal distribution rules before applying § 704(c)(1)(B)). § 704(c)(2); see Chapter 5. Under § 732(b), X takes a basis of $7,000 in Asset #2

As a result of the deemed exchange, A recognizes $25 of ordinary income ($50 fair market value less $25 basis) and the partnership recognizes $30 of capital gain ($50 fair market value less $20 basis) allocated equally between the continuing partners (B and C). The portions of the capital asset and inventory included in the deemed exchange take a cost basis in the hands of A and the partnership, respectively. Finally, the partnership is treated as distributing to A the remaining 1/3 of the capital asset in liquidation of the rest of her partnership interest. Under § 732(b), A takes a basis of $10 (A's remaining basis in her partnership interest) in this portion of the capital asset.

A's share of the partnership's ordinary income and capital gain is recognized or preserved as follows: $25 of ordinary income recognized on the deemed exchange, and $15 of capital gain to be realized on sale of the capital asset which has a fair market value of $75 and a basis in A's hands of $60 ($50 cost basis of the purchased portion and $10 basis in the distributed portion). If the partnership immediately sold the inventory for $150, B and C would each recognize $25 of ordinary income ($150 fair market value less $100 total basis of retained and purchased inventory). Since B and C each recognized $15 of capital gain in the deemed exchange, their share of the partnership's ordinary income and capital gain is also recognized or preserved.

Example (20): Immediately before distributing inventory worth $180 to A in complete liquidation of her partnership interest, the ABC partnership has the following balance sheet:

	Basis	Value		Basis	Value
Assets			Capital		
Cash	$120	$120	A	$120	$180
Inventory	60	180	B	120	180
Land #1	30	60	C	120	180
Land #2	150	180	Total	$360	$540
Total	$360	$540			

A is treated as exchanging her interest in non–§ 751 property worth $120 for inventory of equal value, as shown by the following exchange table:

	(1) Value of Distributed Assets	− (2) Value of Pre-distribution Interest (⅓)	= (3) Increase (Decrease)
§ 751 Assets:			
Inventory	$180	$60	$120
Non-§ 751 Assets:			
Cash	$ 0	$ 40	($40)
Land #1	0	20	(20)
Land #2	0	60	(60)
Total Non-§ 751 Assets	$ 0	$120	($120)

In the constructive distribution, A is treated as receiving non–§ 751 assets specified by the partners (or a proportionate share of each non–§ 751 asset in the absence of an agreement identifying specific assets). See Reg. § 1.751–1(g) (Ex. (3)(c), (4)(c) and (5)(c)). For simplicity, assume that the partners agree to treat A as receiving $120 of cash. The constructive cash distribution is tax free to A and reduces her outside basis to zero. In the deemed § 751(b) exchange, A is treated as purchasing inventory worth $120 from the partnership for $120 cash; she recognizes no gain or loss and takes a cost basis in the inventory deemed purchased. The partnership recognizes $80 of ordinary income ($120 fair market value of inventory deemed sold less $40 basis), which is allocated entirely to B and C. Finally, A is treated as receiving the remaining inventory worth $60 (with a basis of $20 in the partnership's hands) in a liquidating distribution. Under § 732, A's basis in the distributed portion of the inventory cannot exceed her remaining outside basis (zero). Although B and C are taxed on their shares of the partnership's pre-distribution ordinary income ($80), A would recognize $60 of ordinary income ($180 fair market value less $120 total basis) if she immediately sold the inventory. The $20 overstatement of A's ordinary income is attributable to the step-down in the basis of the distributed portion of the inventory in A's hands under § 732.

The partners could cure this problem by agreeing to treat the constructive distribution to A as consisting of $60 cash and Land #1 (with a fair market value of $60 and a basis in the partnership's hands of $30). The constructive distribution would reduce A's outside basis to $30 ($120 less $60 cash less $30 basis assigned to Land #1). On the deemed § 751(b) exchange, A would recognize $30 of capital gain attributable to Land #1 ($60 fair market value less $30 basis) and take a cost basis in the inventory deemed purchased. The partnership would still recognize $80 of ordinary income (allocated to B and C) on the deemed sale of the inventory. Finally, A would recognize a capital loss of $10 on the liquidating distribution ($30 remaining outside basis less $20 basis assigned to distributed inventory). §§ 731(a)(2), 732(c). Thus, A's pre-distribution share of the partnership's ordinary income and capital gain would be recognized or preserved as follows: net capital gain of $20 recognized on the liquidation and $40 of ordinary income to be realized on a sale of the inventory ($180 fair market value less $120 basis of the purchased portion and $20 basis of the distributed portion).

(c) Current Distributions. Section 751(b) applies to both current and liquidating distributions. In a current distribution, however, the distributee's post-distribution interest in retained partnership property must also be taken into account.

Example (21): A receives a current distribution of $20 cash (reducing her partnership interest from 1/3 to 1/5) when the ABC partnership has the following balance sheet:

	Basis	Value		Basis	Value
Assets			Capital		
Cash	$60	$ 60	A	$30	$ 40
Inventory	30	60	B	30	40
Total	$90	$120	C	30	40
			Total	$90	$120

A is treated as exchanging her interest in inventory worth $8 for $8 of cash, as shown by the following exchange table:

	§ 751 Assets (Inventory)	Non-§ 751 Assets (Cash)
Value of post-distribution interest (⅕)	$12 (⅕ of $60)	$ 8 (⅕ of $40)
Plus distribution	0	20
Less value of pre-distribution interest (⅓)	20 (⅓ of $60)	20 (⅓ of $60)
Increase (decrease)	$(8)	$ 8

Accordingly, A is treated as receiving a constructive distribution of inventory worth $8 (with a basis of $4 in A's hands). In the deemed § 751(b) exchange, the partnership is treated as purchasing inventory worth $8 from A; A recognizes $4 of ordinary income ($8 fair market value less $4 basis) and the partnership takes a cost basis in the inventory deemed purchased. The balance of the cash distribution to A ($12) is tax free and reduces A's outside basis to $14 ($30 less $4 basis assigned to inventory less $12 cash). After the distribution, the partnership has the following balance sheet:

	Basis	Value		Basis	Value
Assets			Capital		
Cash	$40	$ 40	A	$14	$ 20
Inventory			B	30	40
Retained	26	52	C	30	40
Purchased	8	8	Total	$74	$100
Total	$74	$100			

If the partnership property is revalued in connection with the distribution and the inventory is later sold for $60, there will be no book gain or loss. Under § 704(c) principles, the partnership's tax gain of $26 ($60 amount realized less $34 tax basis) should be allocated $6 to A and $10 to each of B and C. In effect, A receives the entire benefit of the $4 increase in the basis of the inventory (equal to her ordinary income of $4 recognized on the § 751(b) deemed exchange), while B and C each recognize their full $10 share of pre-distribution ordinary income. By contrast, if the partnership recognizes gain or loss as a result of a deemed § 751(b) exchange, any such gain or loss (and the corresponding basis increase or decrease) must be allocated entirely to the non-distributee partners. See Reg. § 1.751–1(b)(2)(ii), (b)(3)(ii).

(d) Section 752(b) Deemed Distributions. Section 751(b) may also be triggered by a § 752(b) deemed distribution of cash attributable to a decrease in a partner's share of partnership liabilities. In Revenue Ruling 84–102, the admission of a new partner, D, to the equal ABC partnership reduced the original partners' shares of $100 of partnership liabilities from 1/3 ($33) to 1/4 ($25). Since the ABC partnership had unrealized receivables, the original partners were treated as receiving $8 of cash in exchange for a portion of their interest in the receivables, and accordingly recognized ordinary income under § 751(b). If the partnership revalues the original partners' capital accounts in connection with admission of a new partner (or specially allocates the built-in gain under § 704(c) principles), however, it may be possible to avoid triggering § 751. Thus, if the built-in gain attributable to the receivables in Rev. Rul. 84–102 were specially allocated entirely to A, B and C, the allocation might prevent immediate recognition of gain under § 751(b).

(e) Proportionate Distributions. If a distributee receives his proportionate share of the gross value of § 751 property, § 751(b) is inapplicable. Reg. § 1.751–1(b)(1)(ii). For example, assume that the equal ABC partnership owns cash plus two items of inventory: Inventory #1 with a basis of $30 and a fair market value of $60, and Inventory #2 with a basis of zero and a fair market value of $30. If A receives a liquidating distribution of his share of the cash and Inventory #2, § 751(b) is inapplicable because A has received his proportionate share of § 751 property. Because Inventory #2 has a disproportionately high level of appreciation compared to Inventory #1, however, the distribution leaves A with more than his proportionate share of potential ordinary income. The operation of § 751(b) is flawed because it measures disproportionate shifts in terms of gross value rather than potential ordinary income. Moreover, § 751(b) does not apply to a distribution to a partner of property which he contributed to the partnership. Reg. § 1.751–1(b)(4).

CHAPTER 10

DEATH OR RETIREMENT
OF A PARTNER

§ 1. Overview

Section 736 governs the treatment of payments made in liquidation of the partnership interest of a retiring or deceased partner. Essentially, § 736 defines two categories of liquidating payments: (i) payments in exchange for a withdrawing partner's interest in partnership property and (ii) all other payments. Payments in the first category ("§ 736(b) payments") are treated as distributions subject to the normal distribution rules. Payments in the second category ("§ 736(a) payments") are taxed either as § 702 distributive shares (if the amount depends on partnership income) or as § 707(c) guaranteed payments (if the amount is fixed). Thus, § 736 serves primarily to classify the components of a liquidating payment; the tax consequences are determined under other substantive provisions.

Section 736 was originally intended to enhance flexibility and reduce uncertainty in the tax treatment of liquidating payments. Prior to the Omnibus Budget Reconciliation Act (the "1993 Act"),

§ 736(a) allowed a partnership to deduct liquidating payments for a withdrawing partner's share of unrealized receivables and goodwill, at the cost of ordinary income treatment to the recipient. The 1993 Act eliminated such flexibility except for payments to general partners of partnerships in which "capital is not a material income-producing factor" ("service" partnerships). After the 1993 amendments, § 736(b) is the general rule for liquidating distributions to limited partners and to all partners in partnerships in which capital is a material income-producing factor ("capital-intensive" partnerships); in such cases, § 736(a) applies only if a partner receives payments in excess of his share of the partnership's property (including goodwill and unrealized receivables). In 1993, Congress also eliminated § 736(a) treatment for payments for a withdrawing partner's share of "nontraditional" unrealized receivables (e.g., depreciation recapture); regardless of the nature of the partnership, such payments are treated as § 736(b) payments.

Despite these changes, § 736 provides considerable flexibility and important timing advantages in connection with liquidation of a partner's interest. The partners may continue to choose between liquidation and sale treatment depending on the form of the transaction. Finally, the death of a partner raises special problems relating to the decedent's pre-death distributive share and his successor's outside basis.

§ 2. Section 736(b) Payments

(a) General. Under the general rule of § 736(b), liquidating payments in exchange for a withdrawing partner's interest in partnership property are treated as distributions. The normal distribution rules of §§ 731–737 apply, except that payments may be deferred. Generally, a withdrawing partner reports no gain from § 736(b) payments until he has fully recovered his outside basis; any recognized loss is deferred until he has received all § 736(b) payments. See Reg. § 1.736–1(b)(6) (election to recover basis ratably). Section 751(b) overrides this open-transaction approach, however, to the extent that the withdrawing partner receives § 736(b) payments attributable to his share of unrealized receivables and substantially appreciated inventory; ordinary income arising from the deemed § 751(b) exchange is recognized immediately.

For purposes of § 736(b), a partner's interest in partnership property is valued at its gross fair market value (i.e., without reduction for partnership liabilities). This approach is consistent with § 752(b), which treats the withdrawing partner as receiving a deemed cash distribution equal to his pre-liquidation share of the partnership's liabilities. The deemed § 752(b) cash distribution is included in the total amount of liquidating payments received by the withdrawing partner. Under the § 752 rules, the withdrawing partner may be entitled to include a share of partnership liabilities in outside basis until his interest is entirely liquidated.

Example (1): A, whose outside basis is $800, is a general partner in a capital-intensive partnership which has no § 751 assets. Upon liquidation of the partnership, A would be entitled to receive a cash distribution of $1,000 (the fair market value of A's interest). A agrees to retire from the partnership in exchange for five annual payments of $200 ($1,000 total) and will remain liable for her share of the partnership's recourse liabilities ($250) until receipt of the final payment. A is treated as receiving total § 736(b) payments of $1,250 ($1,000 plus $250 relief of liabilities). Under the general open-transaction approach, A will report no gain on the first four installments; in the final year, she will report capital gain of $450 ($200 installment payment plus $250 deemed distribution under § 752).

Section 736 permits considerable flexibility in timing the tax consequences of deferred liquidating payments. A liquidation of a partner's interest may have more favorable basis-recovery consequences for the withdrawing partner than an installment sale of his interest governed by § 453(a). Moreover, deferred § 736 payments are not subject to installment-sale interest charges under § 453A; the imputed interest rules of §§ 483 and 1272 are also inapplicable. Section 736 treatment may also be advantageous if the partnership owns assets that would be ineligible for installment-sale treatment. A deferral of income or gain to the withdrawing partner, however, is generally matched by a deferral of the corresponding tax benefit to the continuing partners.

(b) Excess Payments. Section 736(b) does not apply to payments in excess of a withdrawing partner's share of the fair market value of partnership property. Regardless of whether the partnership is a service or capital-intensive partnership, "excess" payments are treated as § 736(a) payments. Excess payments may be in the nature of mutual insurance or compensation for deferral of payments. For example, if a partner receives total liquidating payments of $75,000 when the fair market value of his interest in partnership property is only $60,000, $15,000 is an excess § 736(a) payment. Payments to compensate a partner for past services may also fall outside § 736(b). Nevertheless, it may be difficult to distinguish such "compensation" from goodwill payments.

(c) Basis Adjustments to Partnership Assets. Since § 736(b) payments are treated as normal distributions, the partnership is generally not entitled to adjust the basis of its remaining property. If a § 754 election is in effect, however, the partnership may be entitled to a special basis adjustment under § 734(b), subject to the allocation rules of § 755. The § 734(b) adjustment may benefit the continuing partners by preventing "double taxation" of built-in appreciation in the partnership's property with no adverse consequences to the withdrawing partner. The § 734(b) adjustment is deferred until the withdrawing partner recognizes gain or loss. See Rev. Rul. 93–13. Even if no § 754 election is in effect, the partnership takes a cost basis in any hot assets deemed purchased under § 751(b).

§ 3.   Section 736(a) Payments

(a) General. As amended in 1993, § 736(a) applies only to certain liquidating payments to general partners in service partnerships and to excess payments to any partner. Under § 736(b)(2), payments for a withdrawing partner's share of unrealized receivables (as defined in § 751(c)) and unstated goodwill are treated as § 736(a) payments. In turn, § 736(b)(3) provides that § 736(a) treatment applies to such payments only when made to a withdrawing general partner of a service partnership. In 1993, Congress also amended the definition of unrealized receivables, for purposes of § 736, to exclude nontraditional receivables such as a partner's share of depreciation recapture. § 751(c) (flush language). Nevertheless, these items remain unrealized receivables for purposes of §§ 731, 732, 741 and 751.

If a § 736(a) payment depends on the partnership's income, it is classified under § 736(a)(1) as a distributive share and reduces the income reportable by the continuing partners. Section 736(a)(1) payments retain the same character in the withdrawing partner's hands as the items included in the distributive share (e.g., tax-exempt income, ordinary income or capital gain). If the amount of the § 736(a) payment is determined without regard to the partnership's income, it is classified under § 736(a)(2) as a guaranteed payment (as described in § 707(c)). Such payments are deductible by the partnership under § 162(a) and taxed as ordinary income to the withdrawing partner under the normal timing rules for § 707(c) guaranteed payments. § 707(c); Reg. § 1.736–1(a)(4). Although § 707(c) guaranteed payments are generally either deducted under § 162 or capitalized under § 263, § 736(a)(2) guaranteed payments are apparently not subject to the capitalization requirement of § 263. Reg. § 1.707–1(c).

(b) Payments to Service Partnerships. Since the scope of § 736(a) is quite narrow, the definition of a service partnership is crucial. The legislative history indicates that whether capital is a "material income-producing factor" is to be determined by reference to criteria developed under analogous statutory provisions. For this purpose, capital will not be considered a material income-producing factor if substantially all of the partnership's income is derived from compensation for services performed by an individual (e.g., fees and commissions). Thus, most professional partnerships will be treated as service partnerships, as long as any significant capital investment is related to the performance of services. The 1993 amendments also make it important to determine when, for purposes of § 736, active participants in LLCs and similar entities will be treated as general partners.

In the case of a general partner who withdraws from a service partnership, any payments in excess of the partner's share of the fair market value of the partnership's property are classified as § 736(a) payments. In addition, § 736(a) applies to payments by the partnership for the withdrawing partner's share of traditional unrealized receivables (e.g., accounts receivable) and unstated goodwill. Section 736(a) treatment applies, however, only to the extent that the fair market value of these items exceeds their bases. Reg. § 1.736–1(b)(2), (3). This treatment is appropriate because otherwise the amount of § 736(a) payments taxable to the withdrawing partner would be overstated by his share of the partnership's basis in unrealized receivables and unstated goodwill. The total amount of § 736(b) payments is determined by excluding the total amount of § 736(a) payments.

Example (2): A, a general partner in an accrual-method service partnership, is entitled to liquidating payments of $45 for her share of the partnership's accounts receivable (basis $15, value $15) and unstated goodwill (basis $0, value $30). The portion of the payment ($30) attributable to A's share of zero-basis unstated goodwill is a § 736(a) payment; the remainder ($15) is a § 736(b) payment because it does not exceed A's share of the partnership's basis in the accounts receivable. Thus, A reports $30 of ordinary income as a § 736(a)(2) guaranteed payment; the § 736(b) distribution of $15 reduces her outside basis before triggering any gain.

(c) Traditional Unrealized Receivables. The 1993 Act left intact § 736(a) treatment for payments representing a withdrawing general partner's share of a service partnership's traditional unrealized receivables. Congress evidently considered that such treatment was nonabusive since the tax deferral resulting from an immediate deduction for payments for traditional unrealized receivables is likely to be short-lived. On the other hand, all payments by a capital-intensive partnership for unrealized receivables are treated as § 736(b) payments. Depending on the nature of the partnership, payments for traditional unrealized receivables are thus subject to either § 736(a) or § 751(b). Both §§ 736(a) and 751(b) reflect similar policy concerns but adopt different approaches.

Example (3): The only assets of the equal ABC general partnership are $30 cash and $30 of zero-basis receivables; when each partner has an outside basis of $10, A receives a cash payment of $20 in liquidation of her partnership interest. If ABC is a service partnership, A will be treated as receiving a § 736(a) payment of $10. Because the payment for A's share of receivables is classified as a § 736(a)(2) guaranteed payment, the disproportionate distribution rules of § 751(b) do not apply. § 751(b)(2)(B). Accordingly, A reports $10 of ordinary income and the partnership has a $10 deduction. The balance of the amount received by A is treated as a § 736(b) payment for her share of the partnership's remaining § 736(b) property (i.e., cash), triggering no gain or loss to A ($10 § 736(b) payment less $10 basis).

Example (4): The facts are the same as in Example (3), above, except that ABC is a capital-intensive partnership. The cash payment of $20 is classified entirely as a § 736(b) payment. Because A has received "excess" cash in exchange for her interest in the partnership's receivables, she will recognize

$10 of ordinary income under § 751(b). The partnership will also increase its basis in the unrealized receivables to reflect the $10 of ordinary income recognized by A. A recognizes no gain or loss on the remaining distribution ($10 § 736(b) payment less $10 basis).

Both §§ 736(a) and 751(b) thus produce the same net result to A, i.e., $10 of ordinary income attributable to her share of the receivables. Under § 736(a), the partnership is permitted to deduct (rather than capitalize) the cost of A's share of the receivables. Because the basis of the receivables is not stepped up in the partnership's hands, however, the continuing partners will eventually be taxed on an additional $10 of ordinary income (attributable to A's ⅓ share) when the receivables are collected. By contrast, if § 736(b) applies, the continuing partners receive additional basis of $10 in the receivables, resulting in $10 less ordinary income upon collection of the receivables. Apart from timing differences, the net effect on the continuing partners is a wash, regardless of whether § 736(a) or § 751(b) applies.

Only service partnerships are allowed to deduct payments for traditional unrealized receivables. In some cases, it may be difficult to distinguish between a service partner's interest in such items as unbilled fees and his share of the partnership's goodwill. Congress sought to minimize potential valuation disputes by treating both types of payments to service partners as deductible § 736(a) payments. By contrast, Congress adopted the oppo-

site approach in the case of capital-intensive partnerships and eliminated § 736(a) treatment for
both types of payments (i.e., goodwill as well as
unrealized receivables).

(d) Goodwill. Prior to 1993, the parties had
complete flexibility to determine whether goodwill
payments would be governed by § 736(a) or
§ 736(b). If the parties agreed on § 736(a) treatment for goodwill, the advantage of an immediate
deduction to the partnership was at least partially
offset by the disadvantage of ordinary income treatment to the withdrawing partner. Nevertheless, the
parties could generally reduce their overall tax burden by increasing the amount of liquidating payments allocable to unstated goodwill. Even with the
restoration of a significant capital gain rate preference, § 736(a) treatment for goodwill payments is
nearly always advantageous. If the exception for
service partnerships applies, the continuing partners in effect can deduct purchased goodwill.

Concerned that § 736(a) treatment might allow a
deduction for the cost of acquiring goodwill of a
going business, Congress required capital-intensive
partnerships to treat such payments as § 736(b)
payments. In 1993, however, Congress also enacted
§ 197, allowing "purchased" goodwill to be amortized over a 15–year period. Thus, the burden of
§ 736(b) treatment is reduced to the extent that the
purchased portion of the partnership's goodwill is
amortizable under § 197. This treatment also provides an additional incentive for the partnership to
make a § 754 election, since amortization is gener-

ally allowed only to the extent of any increase in the basis of the partnership's goodwill. See Chapter 8.

If partnership property is revalued (e.g., upon admission of a new partner), the partnership's goodwill may have a book value in excess of zero. It is unclear whether § 736(a) should apply to payments for a withdrawing service partner's share of the booked-up value of goodwill. Such payments might not be considered payments for "unstated" goodwill. To mitigate this problem, service partners who desire § 736(a) treatment should be careful to expressly state in their agreement that no portion of the payment is intended as a § 736(b) payment for goodwill.

Example (5): A, a general partner in the ABC service partnership, receives $30 cash in liquidation of her partnership interest when the partnership has the following balance sheet:

	Basis	Value		Basis	Value
Assets			Capital		
Cash	$30	$30	A	$10	$30
Accounts			B	10	30
Receivable	0	30	C	10	30
Goodwill	0	30	Total	$30	$90
Total	$30	$90			

The partnership agreement expressly provides that no portion of the payment is intended as a § 736(b) payment for goodwill. Because of § 736(b)(2), $20 is treated as a § 736(a) payment for A's share of the partnership's accounts receivable and goodwill. The remaining payment of $10 is treated as a § 736(b) payment ($30 payment less $20 § 736(a) payment).

Since the payment for A's share of the accounts receivable falls under § 736(a), § 751(b) does not apply. The $10 distribution reduces A's outside basis from $10 to zero, resulting in no gain or loss to A under § 731. In addition, A reports $20 of ordinary income, i.e., the § 736(a)(2) guaranteed payment for A's share of the accounts receivable and goodwill. B and C each reduce their outside bases by $10 as a result of the deductible § 736(a)(2) guaranteed payment.

Example (6): The facts are the same as in Example (5), above, except that ABC is a capital-intensive partnership. Because § 736(a) is inapplicable, the entire payment of $30 is treated as a § 736(b) payment. Under § 751(b), A recognizes $10 of ordinary income attributable to her relinquished share of accounts receivable, and the partnership obtains a $10 increase in the basis of the accounts receivable. Under the normal distribution rules, A also recognizes $10 of capital gain ($20 remaining § 736(b) payment less $10 basis). Assuming a § 754 election is in effect, the partnership receives a $10 upward basis adjustment, allocated entirely to goodwill. See §§ 734(b), 755. Subject to the limitations under § 197, the continuing partners may be entitled to amortize the additional $10 of basis in the partnership's goodwill.

With respect to A, the results are identical except for the treatment of the payment for A's share of the partnership's goodwill. If § 736(a) applies, A has $10 of ordinary income attributable to her share of the partnership's goodwill and no gain or loss under § 731(a)(1). If instead § 736(b) applies to the entire payment, A has $10 less ordinary income but recognizes $10 of capital gain under § 731(a)(1). Regardless of whether § 736(a) or § 751(b) applies, A is taxed on $10 of ordinary income with respect to her relinquished share of accounts receivable. The continuing partners receive either an immediate deduction of $20 or additional basis of $20 (allocated $10 to accounts receivable and $10 to goodwill).

(e) Allocating Payments Between §§ 736(a) and 736(b). Unless the parties agree otherwise, the regulations treat liquidating payments first as § 736(b) payments up to the value of the withdrawing partner's share of § 736(b) property and then as § 736(a) payments. With respect to payments which are fixed in amount and payable over a fixed number of years, each annual payment is treated as a § 736(b) payment up to the total fixed agreed payment for the year multiplied by the ratio of the total fixed § 736(b) payments to the total fixed payments. Reg. § 1.736–1(b)(5)(i). Contingent payments are treated as § 736(b) payments until the withdrawing partner has received the full value of his share of § 736(b) property; thereafter, all payments are treated as § 736(a) payments. Reg. § 1.736–1(b)(5)(ii); see also Reg. § 1.736–1(b)(5)(i) (payments fixed in part and contingent in part).

Example (7): A, a general partner in a service partnership, is to receive three annual installments of $10,000 in liquidation of his partnership interest; of the $30,000 total, $18,000 is a § 736(a)(2) guaranteed payment and $12,000 is a § 736(b) payment (none of which is attributable to depreciation recapture or substantially appreciated inventory). The regulations treat $4,000 of each installment as a § 736(b) payment ($10,000 agreed annual payment multiplied by $12,000 total § 736(b) payments divided by $30,000 total fixed payments); the $6,000 balance of each installment is a § 736(a)(2) guaranteed payment. If A receives less than $4,000 in any year, the actual amount paid will be treated as a § 736(b) payment, and payments in subsequent years will be applied first to make up any deficiency in § 736(b) payments from prior years. See Reg. § 1.736–1(b)(5)(i), (b)(7) (Ex. 1).

§ 4. Relationship Between §§ 736 and 751(b)

Section 751(b) comes into play once the amount of any § 736(b) payments has been determined. In the case of service partnerships, § 751(b) generally applies only to amounts received in exchange for substantially appreciated inventory and depreciation recapture; § 736(a) payments for traditional unrealized receivables are disregarded. By contrast, liquidating distributions from capital-intensive partnerships trigger § 751(b) to the extent that § 736(b) payments include payments for traditional unrealized receivables, depreciation recapture or substantially appreciated inventory. Section 751(b) does not apply if a partner receives a liquidating distribution consisting only of his proportionate share of the partnership's hot assets.

Example (8): A receives $90 cash in liquidation of her partnership interest when the ABC capital-intensive partnership has the following balance sheet:

	Basis	Value		Basis	Value
Assets			Liabilities		
Cash	$ 90	$ 90	Capital	$ 75	$ 75
Inventory	60	90	A	50	90
Equipment*	15	45	B	50	90
Land	60	90	C	50	90
Goodwill	0	30	Total	$225	$345
Total	$225	$345			

* Includes $30 of § 1245 recapture.

A's total amount received of $115 ($90 cash plus $25 relief of liabilities) is equal to her share of the fair market value of the partnership property. None of the liquidating payments are treated as § 736(a) payments. Under § 751(b), A is treated as surrendering her 1/3 interest in the depreciation recapture (basis $0, value $10) and inventory (basis $20, value $30) in exchange for $40 cash, triggering $20 of ordinary income to A. The partnership receives a $10 increase in the basis of each asset (equipment and inventory) deemed purchased from A, and A's outside basis is reduced to $55 ($75 less $20 basis assigned to inventory). In addition, A is treated as receiving a $75 distribution ($115 less $40 cash received in exchange for § 751(b) property) attributable to her share of other § 736(b) property, which triggers $20 of capital gain under § 731 ($75 less $55 remaining basis).

If a § 754 election is in effect, the partnership receives a $20 upward § 734(b) adjustment (allocated $10 to land and $10 to goodwill). After the liquidation of A's interest, the partnership has the following balance sheet:

	Basis	Value		Basis	Value
Assets			Liabilities		
Inventory	$ 70	$ 90	Capital	$ 75	$ 75
Equipment	25	45	B	50	90
Land	70	90	C	50	90
Goodwill	10	30	Total	$175	$255
Total	$175	$255			

If the partnership sells all of its assets for their fair market value, B and C will recognize their former 2/3 share of the partnership's ordinary income ($40) and capital gain ($40). In effect, B and C receive the benefit of a cost basis in A's former 1/3 share of the partnership's assets.

§ 5. Sale Versus Liquidation

(a) General. Although Subchapter K has traditionally permitted the parties to choose between sale and liquidation treatment, such flexibility is not unlimited. See, e.g., Foxman (1964). Because of the lack of substantial economic differences, courts have generally held that the form of the transaction governs. The parties should be careful, however, to observe formalities by ensuring that payments are actually made by the appropriate parties, i.e., the partnership in the case of a liquidation or the existing partners in the case of a sale. The disguised-sale rules of § 707(a)(2)(B) may also limit the parties' ability to choose between sale and liquidation treatment. See Chapter 7.

The economic consequences of liquidating a partnership interest may be indistinguishable from those of selling the interest to the continuing partners in proportion to their respective interests. The transactions may have different tax consequences, however, since sales are governed by §§ 741 and 751(a), while liquidations are governed by §§ 736 and 751(b). If a non-service partnership has a § 754 election in effect, the consequences of sale or liquidation treatment may be quite similar. One minor difference is that, under § 751(a), a sale of a partnership interest triggers ordinary income to the seller whether or not inventory is substantially appreciated; by contrast, § 751(b) applies only if the inventory is substantially appreciated. In general, the continuing partners will prefer to treat the transaction as a liquidation rather than a sale if § 736(a) treatment is available or if the partnership does not have a § 754 election in effect. In the absence of a § 754 election, the selling partner's share of ordinary income may be taxed twice, once to the selling partner and again to the continuing partners.

Example (9): The facts are the same as in Example (8), above, except that A sells her partnership interest ratably to B and C for $115 ($90 cash plus $25 relief of liabilities). A recognizes $20 of ordinary income under § 751(a) (determined as if the partnership sold all of its § 751 assets for their fair market value) and $20 of capital gain under § 741 (overall gain of $40 less $20 ordinary income). See Chapter 8. To reflect their purchase of A's interest,

B and C receive an upward § 743(b) adjustment of $40 ($115 cost less A's $75 pre-distribution share of the partnership's common basis) allocated equally between capital assets and ordinary income assets ($10 to each appreciated asset). See § 755. If the partnership immediately sells all of its assets, B and C will recognize their former 2/3 share of the partnership's ordinary income ($40) and capital gain ($40). Both the withdrawing partner and the continuing partners should be indifferent whether the transaction is structured as a sale or liquidation.

(b) Step–Transaction Doctrine. If a partner receives a distribution of partnership property and transfers the property to a third party who recontributes it to the partnership in exchange for a partnership interest, the Service may seek to recast the entire transaction as a sale of a partnership interest. See, e.g., Crenshaw (1971). If the distributed property does not end up in the partnership's hands, however, courts have respected the form of the transaction. In *Harris*, for example, the taxpayer received a liquidating distribution of § 1231 property with a value less than his outside basis. Harris (1974). On a subsequent sale of the property, the taxpayer recognized an ordinary loss under § 1231, even though a sale of his partnership interest would have generated a capital loss under § 741.

(c) Two–Person Partnerships. A two-person partnership does not automatically terminate merely because one partner dies or retires. The partnership is treated as continuing as long as a deceased partner's estate or other successor in interest continues to share in profits and losses. Reg. § 1.708–1(b)(1)(i)(a). If the deceased or retiring partner's interest is liquidated, the partnership would normally terminate even if the surviving partner continued to carry on the partnership's business as a sole proprietorship. The regulations provide, however, that the partnership remains in existence until a retiring partner or a deceased partner's successor in interest receives all liquidating payments. Reg. § 1.736–1(a)(6). Thus, two-person partnerships are allowed the same flexibility as other partnerships under § 736 with respect to the death or retirement of a partner. Of course, subsequent liquidation of the remaining partner's interest is not governed by § 736 because the partnership ceases to exist. Section 751(b) treatment may also apply to a non-prorata distribution in complete liquidation of a two-person partnership. See Rev. Rul. 77–412; see also Yourman (1967).

The difference between sale and liquidation treatment may affect the surviving partner's holding period in the partnership's assets. In *McCauslen*, the surviving partner in a two-person partnership purchased the deceased partner's 50% partnership interest, triggering a termination of the partnership under § 708. McCauslen (1966). Shortly afterwards, the surviving partner sold some of the former partnership assets and reported a long-term capital gain, claiming a tacked holding period under § 735(b). The court, however, viewed the transaction as if the surviving partner had acquired the decedent's share of the partnership assets by purchase (rather than by distribution). Since the survivor's holding period in the purchased half of the assets commenced on the date of the purchase, the portion of the gain attributable to such assets was short-term capital gain. This approach may produce particularly harsh results for two-person partnerships.

§ 6. Death of a Partner

(a) Closing of Partnership's Taxable Year. Unless a deceased partner's partnership interest is sold at death, his estate (or other successor in interest) is generally substituted as a partner. The partnership's taxable year automatically closes on the date of death with respect to the deceased partner's interest, although it remains open with respect to the other partners' interests. § 706(c)(2)(A). This treatment allows better matching of income and deductions on the decedent's final return (or a joint return filed by the decedent's surviving spouse). Since most partnerships and individual partners report on a calendar-year basis, the problem of income-bunching is unlikely to arise.

(b) Estate Tax Inclusion and Basis. Generally, a deceased partner's gross estate includes the fair market value of his partnership interest (net of liabilities), determined as of the date of death (or alternate valuation date). § 2031; Reg. § 20.2031–3. The decedent's successor takes his partnership interest with an outside basis equal to the estate-tax value increased by the successor's share of partnership liabilities and reduced by the value of any items constituting "income in respect of a decedent." Reg. §§ 1.742–1, 1.1014–1(a).

(c) Income in Respect of a Decedent. The term "income in respect of a decedent" (IRD) generally refers to amounts to which the decedent was entitled at death but which were not properly includible in his final year (or any prior year) under his method of accounting. Reg. § 1.691(a)–1(b). For example, IRD includes (i) rights to deferred payments for services performed by the decedent and (ii) unrealized gain from a sale of property completed before death. Reg. § 1.691(a)–2(b) (Ex. 1, 5). IRD items are includible in the decedent's gross estate and, under § 691(a), are reported for income-tax purposes by the decedent's estate or other successor in the year of receipt. Such items retain the same character in the hands of the recipient as they would have had if received by the decedent. Reg. § 1.691(a)–3.

To offset the burden of "double" inclusion (in the decedent's gross estate and in the recipient's gross income), § 691(c) allows an income tax deduction to the recipient. Reg. § 1.691(c)–1. Had the decedent lived long enough to include the IRD items in gross income, his gross estate would have been reduced by the amount of income tax attributable to those items. Section 691(c) is intended to approximate the same result by allowing an income tax deduction for the amount of estate tax attributable to net IRD items. Finally, the denial of a basis step-up for IRD items ensures that those items will not altogether escape income tax in the recipient's hands. See Reg. § 1.742–1; § 1014(c).

(d) IRD Attributable to Partnership Interests. Two categories of IRD items are of special concern in the partnership context: (i) § 736(a) payments in liquidation of the deceased partner's interest, and (ii) certain partnership items that would be IRD if held directly by the deceased partner. The first category is specifically identified in the statute and regulations, while the second is derived from case law.

Section 753 provides that "[t]he amount includible in the gross income of a successor in interest of a deceased partner under section 736(a) shall be considered income in respect of a decedent." The § 753 definition of IRD includes items that would not be treated as IRD outside the partnership context, e.g., payments for a general partner's share of unstated goodwill in a service partnership. Read literally, § 753 apparently treats all § 736(a) payments to a deceased partner's successor as IRD even if no binding obligation exists at the time of death. See Rev. Rul. 66–325. This expansive view suggests that IRD items are not necessarily limited to items to which a decedent was "entitled" at death. Given the narrow scope of § 736(a), the treatment of such items as IRD is unlikely to present problems outside the context of service partnerships.

The courts have created a second category of IRD in situations in which a successor receives a decedent's partnership interest itself rather than a right to liquidating payments. See Quick Trust (1970); Woodhall (1972). In *Quick Trust*, the court rejected the notion that § 753, which refers only to § 736(a) payments, might preclude IRD treatment of other partnership items; it disallowed a § 1014(a) basis step-up for a deceased partner's share of the partnership's zero-basis accounts receivable. Otherwise, the decedent's successor might have obtained a special basis adjustment under § 743(b) and avoided recognizing the decedent's share of ordinary income when the receivables were collected. Although the scope of this judicially-created category is unclear, it may include other items (e.g., installment obligations) that would constitute IRD if held directly by the deceased partner.

Example (10): The ABC service partnership is obligated, under a buy-sell agreement, to make liquidating payments to D (the successor to deceased general partner A) equal to the fair market value of A's interest in partnership property. At the time of A's death, her share of the partnership property consisted of cash ($600), accounts receivable (basis $0, value $900), unstated goodwill (basis $0, value $1,200), and machinery (basis $0, value $300). Under §§ 753 and 1014, D's basis in A's interest is $900 ($3,000 death-time value less § 736(a) payments of $2,100). Even though the depreciation recapture inherent in the machinery is an unrealized receivable for purposes of § 751, it is not an item of IRD (and is excluded from the definition of unrealized receivables for purposes of § 736(a)). If the partnership agreement provided for a goodwill payment, only the amount received for the accounts receivable would constitute a § 736(a) payment, and A's outside basis would be $2,100 ($3,000 less $900 § 736(a)). Thus, D recognizes $1,200 additional ordinary income if the goodwill payment is treated as § 736(a) payment rather than a § 736(b) payment. In the absence of a buy-sell agreement, the accounts receivable would nevertheless be IRD under the judicially-created exception.

(e) Optional Basis Adjustments. If a § 754 election is in effect, the deceased partner's successor is entitled to a special basis adjustment under § 743(b). The amount of the § 743(b) adjustment is equal to the difference between the successor's outside basis and his proportionate share of the partnership's common inside basis. See Chapter 8. Presumably, no portion of the § 743(b) adjustment may be allocated to partnership assets constituting IRD items. See Rev. Rul. 66–325. If a § 754 election is not in effect at the decedent's death, the successor's outside basis will be stepped up (except for IRD items) but he will not receive a corresponding step-up in his share of the partnership's inside basis. If the partnership holds substantially appreciated inventory and the successor later sells his partnership interest, he may recognize artificial ordinary income under § 751(a) and artificial capital loss under § 741.

If the partnership does not have a § 754 election in effect, a partner's share of inside basis will often be less than his outside basis as determined under

§ 1014. In this situation, it may be advantageous for the partnership to distribute low-basis property in liquidation of the high-basis partner's interest. Under § 732(b), the distributee generally takes a basis in the distributed property equal to his outside basis. In the absence of a § 754 election, however, the partnership is not required to adjust downward the basis of its remaining assets to reflect the increased basis of the distributed property in the distributee's hands. Thus, a liquidating distribution of low-basis property may benefit the continuing partners without any corresponding detriment to the high-basis distributee. Mandatory § 734(b) adjustments would preserve the continuing partners' share of unrealized appreciation inside the partnership.

INDEX

References are to Pages

349